Come and

Jesus I'

Robert (Bob) F   **Rob Jackson**

© Copyright 2014
By Robert (Bob) H. Jackson and Rob Jackson
All Rights Reserved

Published by Rainer Publishing
www.rainerpublishing.com

ISBN 978-0692209592

Printed in the United States of America

Contents

Acknowledgments

I am thankful to God for providing numerous people who helped make this book a reality. I am thankful for my godly dad. He lived his life in the reality of the living Lord. Through these words, I pray that many people will come to see that Jesus Christ is alive! Also, this work would not have been possible without my mom, Gail Jackson. Dad's victories were her victories. Mom was always supportive, always behind the scenes in loving prayer and support. Likewise I thank God for my wife, Tonya, and my daughter, Abigail, who were influential in finishing this book. Their love, prayers, and encouragement helped this project come to completion. Furthermore, my sister Jeannece Luhrs was helpful giving feedback, advice, and promoting this work.

I thank the board members and friends of Romanian-American Missions. They are tirelessly challenging a lost and dying world to *Come and See Jesus Christ is Alive*! Moreover, I would like to extend my thanks to the various churches that partnered along side Dad and me in the Gospel ministry. Specifically, I thank First Baptist, Flomaton, AL; Clio Baptist, Clio, AL; Beechridge Baptist, Bagdad, KY; First Baptist, Monroeville, AL; First Baptist Brandon, MS; Antioch Baptist, Double Springs, AL; Buck Run Baptist, Frankfort, KY; Brandon Baptist, Brandon, MS; and Central Baptist, Decatur, AL. These stories are your stories, and we rejoice together in our God who is alive!

A special thanks is also in order for Dr. Tim Beougher whose words of encouragement and proof reading were instrumental in Dad's first draft. Additionally, I am deeply grateful for Dr. Martin Bates Sharp who was extremely helpful in proofing and completing this project. Her personal interest in seeing this book to completion cannot be understated. I would like to thank the many people (the list is too long to include everyone) who allowed us to use their stories.

I would also like to thank Myra Phillips and April Baker for typing much of the early manuscript. Moreover, I thank Sam, Art, and Jess Rainer from Rainer Publishing for their help and passion to see this message in print. Thank you, God, for reminding us all to *Come and See, Jesus Christ is Alive*!

Foreword

Come and See, Jesus Christ is Alive! was the final project that my dad, Robert (Bob) H. Jackson, completed on this earth. The last year of his life he tirelessly worked hour upon hour praying and writing this book. Dad was convinced God desired him to journal some of the miraculous things he witnessed in his over fifty-five years of ministry. He believed many professing Christians live on the wrong side of Easter, totally missing the expectant power available to those who believe.

Instead of seeing the Church of Jesus Christ operating in resurrected power, he believed North American Christianity was far too often dependent upon, and therefore limited by, frail human abilities. What is missing in North American Christianity? According to Dad, the power of the Holy Spirit coupled with expectant faith is sadly missing! Dad longed for the Church of Jesus Christ to storm the gates of Hell in the power of the Holy Spirit. Therefore, Dad's invitation to you today is *Come and See, Jesus Christ is Alive!*

I will never forget the day Dad and I discussed George Mueller's *Autobiography*. Dad's amazement was not the miraculous answers to prayer Mueller recorded in his diary. Instead, his surprise was that so few professing Christians experience daily miracles like Mueller. After all, he exclaimed, "this should be *normal* Christianity." He was grieved that much of contemporary Christianity holds to "a form of godliness, although they have denied its power" (2Ti 3:5 NAS).

Come and See, Jesus Christ Is Alive! was written to encourage you to "taste and see that the Lord is good" (Ps 34:8). Not only is God good, but He is alive and moves on behalf of weak humans! This book is full of stories that Dad witnessed. Interestingly, Dad never sought to pastor a megachurch, never aspired to hold a denominational office or title, and had no goal of being in the limelight (although I am confident with his talents he could have accomplished all these things had he wished). Instead, Dad saw himself as "just a Carpenter's helper." What a helper he was! He impacted people all over this nation and world!

As you read, much of what Dad witnessed happened *after* a debilitating heart attack when he was only 44! To recap some of Dad's physical struggles: a third of his heart muscle was dead; his hearing continued to deteriorate; he had prostate cancer; arthritis pain all in his body; a deterioration of his calf muscle in one leg because of a statin drug; incontinence; bowel problems; bone on bone pain in his knees (knee replacement was out of the question because of his heart); and an inability to sleep without medication. This list is only a few of the "major" ailments in which he suffered. Additionally, this doesn't count the several years he went through a deep depression that he calls the dark night of the soul.

I will never forget the physician's prognosis of Dad (who was only in his late 40s), "You will live on disability the rest of your life. You need to be realistic and face it; your days in the pastorate are over." In other words, Dad was "washed up." What did he do?

He was "washed up" and in chronic pain, so at 49 he pastored Gullette's Bluff Baptist Church, Camden, Alabama and helped the congregation build a new church plant after their old facilities burned.

He was "washed up" and in chronic pain, so at 50 he became director of missions of the Bethlehem Baptist Association, Frisco City, Alabama, where he encouraged and promoted missions both locally and globally.

He was "washed up" and in chronic pain, so at 53 he went to a small, dying church and watched the hand of God fall upon her so that Buck Run became one of the fastest growing churches in Kentucky, and was soon the largest church in the capital city. This small rural church went from a $170,000 budget to over $1,000,000 and grew to over 1,200 members. Newspapers recounted the story of Buck Run, articles were written about this growth, and even a book, *Eating the Elephant* by Thom S. Rainer, chronicled some of the early growth at Buck Run.

He was "washed up" and in chronic pain, so at 58 he began planting churches and supporting pastors in Romania, spearheading mission work in Romania and Eastern Europe.
He was "washed up" and in chronic pain, so at 60 he founded Romanian American Mission (RAM) an indigenous church planting/mission sending organization that has its headquarter today at Central Baptist Church, Decatur, Alabama. RAM has now branched out to all of Europe, seeking to share the gospel of Jesus Christ and has a goal of planting 100 new churches in the next few years.

He was "washed up" and in chronic pain, so at 66 he helped start a new church, the Brandon Baptist Church, that became a rapidly growing church in a suburb of Jackson, Mississippi. After the first four years, they already had about 1,000 members. They reached people. They built buildings. They supported missionaries. They gave money. As I write this summary, Brandon Baptist Church is celebrating her 10th anniversary. I am convinced their greatest days are yet to be seen!

He was "washed up" and in chronic pain, so at 71 he came to Central Baptist Church to assist us in our relocation effort . . . coming on only a three-year assignment from the church. Once again, we witnessed the power of God as He has almost doubled our average attendance in the first four years.

He was "washed up" and in chronic pain, so at 74 he wrote the book that you hold in your hand, *Come and See, Jesus Christ is Alive!*"

With each assignment God gave Dad, there was a struggle. For example, even with this project he struggled with penning the things he had seen God do in his life. Dad began to pray, enumerating reasons he couldn't possibly be the man for this job. "Father," he began, "If I write this, who would ever publish it? I'm not a published author. Nobody knows who I am except the folks in the three communities you have blessed me to serve in following seminary."

Dad's name was not a household word, not even in his own town! He had never done anything of any great significance that would cause his name to be recognizable by many people. He had never been on anyone's preaching circuit. In fact, he only recalled having been invited to preach four revivals in the more than one-half century of preaching!

And so Dad prayed: "That should tell you something, Father. I have never held office in my denomination at any level. Never aspired to. I haven't even served as a moderator of a local Baptist (County) Association! All I ever wanted to do, Father, was to please you and tend the flock you placed under my care. I'm the least likely to write anything for you, Lord, and have people read it. I doubt there are many people other than my children who would read it. And, they would probably only scan it!"

The Father responded, "Few people have seen what I have chosen you to see me do. Many more need to, and to experience these things so that my Living Presence will become a reality before a watching world in their lives and in their churches." He said in conclusion, "You write what I've asked you to write, let me guide you in it, and trust me to take care of the particulars."

All Dad could say was, "Yes, Lord, yes – to your will and to your way!"

Shortly after finishing this manuscript, Dad headed to Brandon to share a new vision to reach Europe with the Gospel of Jesus Christ through RAM. I was to be the keynote speaker that night for the RAM banquet. Mom and I were in the car driving from Decatur to Brandon. In transit we received the call from Tommie Lou Ball, a dear friend of the family, with the news that Dad had died.

Dad had a massive heart attack walking into one of the classrooms of Brandon Baptist Church, a church that he pastored when the building was built. We had been told of his heart attack and the ambulance rushing him to the hospital thirty minutes earlier, but we thought he would be okay. After all, he had numerous close calls with heart issues over the years. A physical healing was not to be the case this time. Instead, God lovingly called him into His presence. We are sad;

we miss him greatly. We are not, however, sad for him. Today he is not dead, but alive! Right now my earthly father is in the presence of his risen Savior.

God did so much through Dad, an "ordinary man," to remind a watching world that it is not about you or me but about Him! If God can use an ordinary man like Bob Jackson, then he can use you and He can use me. It was Dad's prayer that in reading this book your eyes will be opened to the *"the immeasurable greatness of his power toward us who believe . . ."* (Eph 1:19 ESV).

The message of this book is very simple . . . Jesus Christ is alive and He seeks to use ordinary men, women, boys and girls to do extraordinary things for His glory. Will you be such a person? Will you come and see? Will you bring others to come and see? To God alone receive all glory, honor and praise!

Rob Jackson
Pastor, Central Baptist Church, Decatur, Alabama
President, Romanian American Mission

Introduction

Come and See, Jesus Christ is Alive!

Come and See, Jesus Christ Is Alive! is a glimpse into the reality that Jesus Christ is the same yesterday, today and forever. The destination of this journey is the empty tomb, where those of us and our churches who dare walk the way of the cross will meet the resurrected Christ in the splendor of His glory. The invitation that the women heard on that first resurrection morning is an invitation that every person in America – indeed, in all the world – needs to hear and respond to, *Come and See, Jesus Christ is Alive!*

Come and see for yourself that Jesus is no longer in the tomb, but has risen. Come and see that He is no longer dead, but is very much alive. Come and see that He is not powerless to save Himself as those who mocked him charged. To the contrary, witness the fact that He possesses the power, not only to save Himself but to save and liberate those of us who have been trapped in a tomb of despair and helplessness. Indeed, take note in the lives of persons who have met Him that He has the power to radically transform a fragmented human personality into a person of incredible wholeness and wonder. Come, and see!

This book is being put together by my son, Rob, and me. Rob is pastor of the Central Baptist Church in Decatur, Alabama under whom I had the joy of serving as associate astor for three recent years. It was "turn around, fair play" in that Rob served under me for eight years as Associate Pastor of the Buck Run Baptist Church in Frankfort, Kentucky. Together in Frankfort and in Decatur, indeed in Monroeville, Alabama and Brandon, Mississippi, Rob and I have seen the resurrected Lord come alive in His Church.

As we have witnessed Him being "lifted up" by His people who chose to embrace His cross, we have seen Him draw large numbers of persons unto Himself and give them His abundant life. This phenomena came not by slick promotion or human manipulation. It came simply through the response of radical faith – trusting belief and obedience – to the divine disclosure of the Father as set forth in His Son, Jesus Christ.

Such faith unlocked the door for an invasion by the Holy Spirit into the life and activity of each body of Christ where we have been privileged to be members. Each has been characterized by incredible, miraculous activity that made the congregation a magnet of outreach to the community.

This book is built around the things we have personally seen Him do. As such, it is a proposal to embrace the cross-life of Jesus and allow the Holy Spirit to do what only He can do – draw persons of all ages to the Lord.

It is our prayer that, whatever Christian tradition you or your church may represent, you will come together with us – each in his or her own church and sphere of influence – and reach into every village, town, and city where there are those who need to experience the reality of the living Lord.

If we are to find favor with our Lord, we must of necessity allow a watching world to see a united ody of Christ, in each individual congregation as well as among all of the congregations in a given community, who would choose to band together for this primary task of taking the Gospel to the world in both word and deed. Jesus prayed in John 17:20-21, in His High Priestly Prayer, for those of us who would believe as a result of the Apostles' witness, that we would be one even as He and the Father are One, *so that the world might believe that He is the Christ sent from God.* The reason is obviously clear. How can the Church convince those who have never embraced the claims of Christ that He has come into the world to be the Unifying Center of all that exists, in Heaven and on earth, if His Church is not united? At every level!

Let us not get bogged down in meaningless debate over what constitutes unity in the church that is like unto the divine unity, in order to defend our separateness. Surely, all of us must agree that it is no less than a spiritual oneness, expressing itself in love, fellowship, and purpose. That purpose was seen in the coming of Jesus Christ to redeem, that is, to set free those who are enslaved to the forces of sin and evil in this dark world. Jesus implied that we will never be successful in continuing and in fulfilling His mission on earth until we join our hearts and our efforts in pursuing means to accomplish the overriding purpose for which He came.

It is a matter of historical record that every great spiritual move of God in America, as well as around the world, came about only after the various expressions of Christ's Church came together in prayer and single-mindedness of soul, fervently seeking the Lord to do a mighty work of renewal and revival in their church, in their community, and throughout the land.

The local congregation, again, must be united in the effort to reach its community and its world for Christ. This proposal cannot be accomplished by mere human effort. *Come and See, Jesus Christ is Alive!* calls for radical faith that enables the Christ-follower to put self to death and walk the way of the cross. When this takes place, we are told in Scripture and know from experience, the risen Lord of the Church always comes alive in the life of His disciples and in His congregation, revealing Himself in miraculous ways! Such prepares the way for an expectant Church to "storm the gates of hell" with the reality of our Lord's living Presence. This is what a watching, unchurched world will respond to. In curiosity perhaps at first. But then in trusting belief and trusting obedience, after coming under the influence of the loving, powerful, Spirit of the Christ, found within His Body and the members thereof.

It is such a crucial time for the Church to mobilize in the power of the Holy Spirit. Many will die – physically, emotionally, and spiritually – unless we go quickly and share the good news of our Risen Lord. The Scripture screams with such urgency, "Now is the acceptable time; behold, today is the day of salvation." Tomorrow will be too late for hundreds of thousands of persons who are perishing all around us.

There is yet this other fact that begs for a greater sense of urgency among us in living our lives in expectant faith. The Church is standing at a crossroad. It is a crossroad that presents the body of Christ, especially in America, with more danger and possible pain and suffering than we have ever encountered, should we take the wrong road.

Churches in America are at a crossroad. It is well-known that the mainline denominations have been in a state of decline for decades. Southern Baptists, who have over this period enjoyed a measure of growth, though in reality it has been miniscule, for the first time are seeing statistical decline in most areas of its denominational life, including a diminishing church membership and a reduction in the number of baptisms. Even more alarming is the result of a 2011 Gallup Poll, revealing that seven in ten Americans feel that religion is losing its effectiveness in this country.

Churches, which throughout U.S. history has enjoyed a powerful role in shaping the religious, moral, social consensus in this country, predicated upon the Judeo-Christian ethic and value system, are quickly losing their position of leadership in the shaping of the American mind. With shrinking numbers of adherents we find a situation in which more than 100 million persons are found to be unchurched in our country. This means that America is now one of the largest mission fields in the world! Amazingly, China is now thought to have more active Christians than are to be found in the United States.

Missionaries from other countries, representing a myriad of religions, are streaming into the U.S., seeking to fill the spiritual vacuum that we in American churches have allowed to be created in the soul of this nation.

Islam doubtless poses the most serious religious threat to churches in America. It is well known that the radical expression of this religion not only has the eventual takeover of this country on their global agenda but that they also are committed to the eradication of Christianity over the world! Recently, a large contingent of Muslims congregated at the nation's capitol and staged a prayer meeting. This was ostensibly to convince the people of America that Muslim citizens love this country and desire to be loyal citizens. Nevertheless, one of the organizers of the event announced to our nation that his intention is "to invite your children to the worship of the one true God." You and I know to whom he was referring! And, what this declaration meant.

Who will reach out and extend an invitation to the unchurched in America first? Islam, some other religious group, or the Church of Jesus Christ? Will we Christians, of whatever tradition, express our devotion to our Lord Christ above all other sectarian considerations and join together in reaching out to our communities? Will we return to the main mission our resurrected Lord gave to His Church? Will we repent and turn away from our own personal self-absorption, the jealousies within our own congregations, our local church pride, our denominational arrogance, all of which is but an expression of our narcissistic navel-gazing, to look up and out to a "field white unto harvest?" A field filled with the teaming masses for whom Christ died? Will we commit ourselves to be the laborers into these fields Christ so agonizingly seeks?

Our churches are at a crossroad. We are being pressed at every hand for a decision! Time is running out on us. Which way, church? Do we keep traveling down the same easy, broad path that we've been on far too long and lose this great opportunity, not to mention our beloved land? Or, do we take another road? The road on which our Lord is traveling? The road that He now beckons us to take in following Him into a world of fearful, suffering, sin-sick humanity, to embrace with love and grace those who are wandering aimlessly in this life like sheep without a shepherd?

We in the churches are at a crossroad. What we need to understand, above all else, is that a cross stands at this crossroad. It is the cross of Christ! Do we embrace it for God's sake? For the sake of His Kingdom? And for the sake of those who have never experienced the victory of His resurrection? Are we willing to take that rugged tree of Calvary, put it on our shoulders, and walk the way of the cross? What does such a choice entail?

Chapter One

The Way of the Cross

Then he said to them all: "if anyone would come after me, he must deny himself and take up his cross daily and follow me. For whoever wants to save his life will lose it, but whoever loses his life for me will save it." Luke 9:23-24

The way of the cross is not a road to be negotiated only by a select group of super Christians who desire to take their discipleship to a higher plane than ordinary followers of Jesus.

Our Lord taught that this way – His way – is the only road down which those who truly follow Him will walk.

It is the road He walked on Earth. It is the road He continues to walk, a pathway revealed by His Holy Spirit to all who would join Him in fulfilling the Father's purpose in this world.

The way of the cross is the road down which those of us must walk if we would experience the power that raised Jesus from the dead in our lives and in our churches.

We when embrace the way of the cross we experience incredible wonder and glory!

What is the nature of this Calvary road that leads to an empty tomb and a risen, living Savior? Jesus suggested several things in Luke 9:23-24.

It is the Way of Death

Bonhoeffer was right when he said, "When Christ calls a man, He bids him come and die"! These words seem totally incomprehensible to most of us in the churches of America. Because of our obsession with, and possession by, the spirit of materialism, we are most uncomfortable with the thought of denying self for anything, much less costly causes. Let's face it, most of us have never truly sacrificed our wants, desires, or personal agendas for anyone or anything outside our family circles, not even for the Lord! But there it is, in black and white in sacred writ. Jesus said that we must deny self, take up a cross every single day of our lives if we would be His disciples! Wow!

Putting self to death through personal sacrifice has not been often entertained by most of us because, until recently, there have been few, if any, costly consequences for identification with Christ in this country. Outside the Western world, however, this is not true for Christ-followers. In those countries, especially Third World countries, where suffering and martyrdom for allegiance to the Lord Jesus are commonplace, the costs are great. Not so in America. At least, thus far! Why talk of the renewal of the churches today, of the resurrection of the body of Christ in America, when we have not yet embraced His cross?

In America, by and large, we have closed our eyes to what the Bible teaches about true discipleship and what that entails. Unless we wake up soon and discover the way Jesus outlined for us to walk, and walk in it, it is not difficult to foresee a time coming when there will be dire consequences for those of us who confess "Jesus is Lord!" In increasing frequency, we are

15

already seeing subtle, at times not so subtle, persecution being experienced by persons who dare take the witness stand for Jesus in the public arena, right here in the U.S.!

Might we in the churches, at this crucial moment, be willing to make significant voluntary sacrifices to reach the ever-widening sea of unreached persons in our land? These are they who hold the key to the shape and future of Christ's Church in our beloved country. Indeed, these are those who comprise the vast multitudes of persons who will be factors in the determinations that will decide how the unfolding American drama will play out on the stage of history!

The deal at the crossroad is either we choose to voluntarily embrace Christ's cross and follow Him down the demanding road He chooses for us to walk, or simply continue to travel the easy road most of us are now on. Please let us be aware, brothers and sisters, that if we continue to travel the road we are on at this time, perhaps sooner than we care to imagine, we will find ourselves impaled upon a cross of someone else's choosing!

A first, and major, step in what must be a forever-after journey of the churches in America, is following the Lord into our communities, and beyond, extending His gracious love, and liberating new life.

The success of this first step depends upon whether you and I and our churches, joining hands with other Christian congregations, are willing to move out of our comfort zone, and make the sacrifices required to extend a simple but profound, Spirit-led, invitation to come and see what Christ can do.

As you read this book, you may be moved to put self to death, making meaningful sacrifices during this time, so that each Christian might move around in, and get better acquainted with, the life of the Spirit of God. Getting in touch with God's precious Spirit, while allowing Him to take the lead in the simple invitation process, will be a key to victory as we seek to impact this world for Christ.

The individual church congregation also must be willing to put self to death and pay whatever price is necessary for the Father to be glorified, His Son exalted, and Christ's Great Commission fulfilled in its local community. Sacrifices of time, schedule rearrangement, and leadership commitment are not only in order, but necessary. Moreover, the financial resources needed – which may not greatly exceed the budget for the yearly revival, or renewal conference – must be committed. Corners must not be cut in implementing the suggested strategy. This strategy should be followed inasmuch as possible. The potential results are worth whatever the cost. The stakes in America at this moment are extremely high!

It is the Way of Commitment

When Jesus called His first disciples to follow Him and become fishers of men, the records indicate that they left all to begin the sojourn, then gave their all to the demands that their new life in following Him required. If you and I would embrace Christ's mission into our communities and our world we too must be willing to make significant commitment to the task of living our lives in expectant power of the Holy Spirit and reaching persons for Christ, as led by God.

Will you be willing to make an unquestioned commitment of the best each one has – the best of his or her time, energy, influence, and resources – to the tremendous opportunity at hand? This will be quite a challenge because, let's face it, commitment is often in short supply in many churches. Even, at times, among the leadership! Leaders of the congregation, in particular, must step up to the plate, giving more than just lip service to the Spirit-filled life if Christ is to be honored and His Church blessed. Congregations, and groups within the congregations, follow their leaders – at whatever their level of leadership. They emulate the attitudes and the actions of their leaders, for better or for worse. The seriousness of a leader's responsibility cannot be overstated in the church.

But those of us in areas of leadership in our churches at this present moment must realize that we are there by divine appointment, however we may have gotten there. You and I must not abnegate our responsibility to lead. If your church chooses to pursue this outreach venture, leaders must take the lead in the praying, planning, and implementation of the plans, as well as in the faith-talking, inside and outside the church. Believing God and telling others about the exciting thing the resurrected Jesus is going to do.

Churches in America, in general, have not lived up to the vision Jesus had for His special called-out people. There at Caesarea-Philippi our Lord saw a church, like a mighty army, storming the gates of hell, setting the captives free. This was a picture of a group of the truly committed. It modeled the kind of commitment He later received from his first band of rag-tag disciples who, when the Holy Spirit was added to the mix, went out to turn a world upside down! This still remains His vision for His Church in the world!

If we dare walk the way of the cross, total commitment will be required of all of us! All we are, all we have, surrendered to the task Christ called us to.

It is the Way of Victorious Life

It has become a well known axiom of Christian discipleship that without a cross there can be no crown! The understanding that the Christ-follower's necessary embrace of a cross to experience a crown of glory, at the same time, reminds us that, once we embrace a cross for His sake and the doing of His will, there can always be an expectation of glorious, new life up ahead. This is the unmistakable good news message Jesus taught.

Our Lord's own sojourn through this world mirrored the philosophy He espoused. When He surrendered to the will of the Father, He embraced the lifestyle of personal sacrifice and self-denial. When death became the inevitable result, He discovered that the cross He was impaled upon was not the end of His life; it was only the beginning of a dimension of life far more wonderful and triumphant than could ever be humanly imagined or experienced.

The lesson for you and me and churches today is clear. When we embrace the Father's purpose, His will on earth, as set forth in Jesus Christ, and surrender to its demands, we will, like our Lord, discover a new life of unimaginable wonder, joy, and victory opening to us as the amazing consequence.

What does the way of the cross look like in the life of a church and its leadership that dares to obediently follow the leadership of Her Lord? How does it impact the invitation that it issues to its community? Consider the following story of one church that experienced an incredible turnaround, from loss to gain, from death to life. While its issues and challenges may be quite different from those of other congregations, and yours, the biblical principle that was embraced by this church holds true for all congregations that truly desire that the Lord of the Church be alive and active in its midst, leading the church to fulfill its reason for being in its community.

Dying to Live: A Case in Point

When Rob came as pastor of Central Baptist Church in Decatur, Alabama, the old downtown congregation was in a state of decline. In particular, over several years it had continued to lose significant numbers of its young adults. Consequently, the disheartening sight of fewer and fewer children in the life of the congregation became a discouraging, constant, visible reminder of where the church was heading. There was no united vision at Central. The lack of unity of vision had the church attempting to move in several different directions, resulting in frustration among the people and an undercurrent of mistrust of the leadership. The church lacked a sense of commitment to any one plan that might unite, excite, and motivate the congregation toward some meaningful goal. While it was the repository of multiple master plans for various building projects, for one reason or another, the church's several efforts to get any one of them off the ground met with abysmal failure.

The coming of the new, young pastor filled the hearts of many within the church with renewed hope. Nevertheless, while he poured out his heart and soul in loving pastoral ministry, and in preaching and teaching the Word of God faithfully, Central continued to lose membership. He soon recognized that something more was needed if there were any hope of seeing the trend reversed. He was well aware of what was needed because of an earlier experience in his ministry when an old dormant congregation came to life and exploded in growth and ministry for the Lord.

During his seminary days, and immediately following, while Rob was associate pastor of the Buck Run Baptist Church in Frankfort, Kentucky, he experienced first-hand the miracle-working power of God when a congregation chooses to make prayer a priority, allows Christ to be head of His church, and follows Him through the Spirit's leading in walking the way of the cross. Reflecting back on the unbelievable witness of that church's subsequent victories in Jesus, Rob knew that he must take the first step to lead the congregation under his charge to walk that victorious road. To begin the journey his heavenly Father desired that he and the congregation walk, he must devote himself to a protracted time of intense prayer and fasting.

The heavenly Father, in time, responded to Rob's earnestness, even his desperation in prayer, and made His will for Central Baptist and her pastor known to him. God told His servant that he, the pastor, must lead the congregation to move from downtown to a more strategic location for reaching Decatur for Christ! Talk about a bombshell. This was it! It was a mandate from God that Rob had feared; one he didn't want to hear. He had been warned by friends in the ministry, including denominational colleagues that, whatever else he might do in Decatur, for the sake of his ministry, he must not attempt to relocate the church!

He was apprised that more than one of the former pastors had suggested a move like this as a possible solution to Central's challenging situation, suggestions that were not received well by the congregation. Indeed, Rob was warned that pursuing such a project could mean professional suicide! But God spoke and Rob had no choice but to obey, even if it meant a cross, death to self and his promising future.

Wishing to corroborate this audacious challenge that had come to him through prayer, Rob sought confirmation from the Lord. In so doing, he asked two of the most respected, saintly men in the congregation, two retired ministers of the gospel, to implore the Lord through prayer and fasting as to His will for Central Baptist. After a time, they returned to give this message: "Pastor, God told us what He told you. We must relocate!" Assured in his heart by this confirmation, Pastor Rob began to move forward as the Spirit would lead, to face whatever obstacle, to pay whatever price to be obedient. He knew that the waters up ahead would, at times, be turbulent but he also knew that His Father would calm every storm that would threaten to destroy him and this church if he and they were obedient.

The pastor took the vision first to the staff. They were cautious at best about this proposal. Some felt it might not be the best thing to do. But, after they too began to engage in prayer and fasting, the Holy Spirit brought them together in uniformity of Spirit, a unity that helped maintain a calming, harmonious spirit among the members of the congregation during what became a tumultuous time.

Next, the matter was taken to the deacon body that, surprisingly, showed an openness to entertain the idea. After three months of prayer and fasting, they also came aboard in a secret ballot vote with one person in opposition and two abstentions.

The initial response from the congregation seemed encouraging. Few negative remarks were voiced publicly whenever the church gathered.This was amazing since there was understandably much sentiment attached to the old building site where generations had met to worship, fellowship, and study God's Word.

Little did those who came to support the move realize what was taking place behind the scenes. A group of angry, determined people were marshaling forces to defeat the move, as well as to get rid of the pastor and staff! Everything came to light on the night of November 14, 2004 when the congregation convened to discuss relocation. The sanctuary was packed! Those in opposition were prepared.

One by one, persons stood and inveighed against moving the church while the congregation, including the leadership, sat stunned and silent. More than this, the meeting turned into a personal, ugly, vicious attack on the character and integrity of the pastor and staff of the church. Rob caught the brunt of the hostility. He recalls how all alone he felt on that night, more than at any other time in his life. One deacon finally came to his rescue. Standing, he said, "I don't know about the rest of you, but I'm following the leadership of my pastor!" The meeting adjourned with much confusion because of the heated opposition that had literally taken control of the congregational meeting and, apparently, the will of the body. The pastor was asked about what percentage of a vote to relocate he thought he would feel comfortable with in moving the church. He replied, "80%."

Over the next few weeks, letters, messages, phone calls, and emails suggested that the pastor "Leave our church, the sooner the better!" Some even wanted the entire staff to leave. A steady stream of hostile members continued daily with their attacks on the pastor. There were those human moments when he wished he could step down. After all, he was a pharmacist when God called him to preach the gospel and he knew that he could move at any time into a financially attractive situation given the shortage of pharmacists that existed.

Then, there was this other turn of events that provided a tempting way out for God's appointed shepherd at Central. The senior pastor of a huge church in a neighboring state approached Rob and invited him to come on his church's staff and be mentored by him, stating that he had Rob picked out as his successor, once he retired. What an opportunity!

But Rob could not turn his back on the Lord's will that had been revealed to him so vividly through days and nights of intense prayer and fasting. Nor could he turn his back on the majority of the congregation that, by this time, had come to the same conclusion in their prayers about the move, who began rallying to their pastor's support.

A congregational meeting was called for Sunday morning, December 5, to vote on continuing discussion toward relocating. The vote carried on an almost 80% (79.2) majority. The date of May 22, 2005 was then set for a binding vote on the move.

There were some people who developed cold feet on the project following the December meeting, because of the vocal opposition and of the fact that, in actuality, the vote garnered less than 80%, though the difference was infinitesimal. A turning point came at the annual deacon's retreat in January when, during the time for fun and fellowship following dinner, the men came under such heavy conviction of the Spirit of God that they began to be drawn into small groups of twos, threes, and more, on their knees, where they agonized and prayed, some all night long!

When the sun came up, a new day dawned on this band of servant leaders who, emboldened by the Spirit of their Lord Christ, returned to Decatur to call for the church to support the vision of relocating that had been cast by the pastor. And to proceed with the plans for a final and binding vote on May 22, 2005. The meeting was held and a vote taken at both morning worship services and carried by about the same percentage as before. The congregation was ready to move on!

The opposition didn't go down without a fight. Before that final vote, they took out a large ad in the local newspaper against the move and against the leadership that, of course, included the pastor. It called on all members of Central Baptist Church to come and vote against relocation. Some spread malicious rumors throughout the community against the church leadership. Especially, the attacks were ruthless and vicious against Rob! Added to this was the prediction that, if Central did move, the church would lose so many members that the congregation would not survive and would end up in humiliating financial bankruptcy.

The church, steadfast in its faith, voted to follow the leading of the Lord. Did they dry up and blow away? Of course not! Did they bite off more than they could chew? Well, yes, humanly speaking. But there was a certain Someone who chewed it for them. And it turned out to be the most delectable appetizer the church had ever been served. A feast then awaited them and what a spread of God's rich morsels it was and continues to be! If you would like to take a first-hand look at a miracle of God in our day, the congregation would invite you to come and see the great things He did and is now doing. "We serve a risen Savior!"

But there is a great deal more to the Central story that must be told before you understand the miracle that has taken place. The steps of faith and commitment to the obvious leading of God's Spirit, borne out of fervent prayer, fills volumes. Central adopted as its theme "Mission Possible," with its scriptural underpinning found in Mark 10:27. Jesus said, "With man this is impossible, but not with God; all things are possible with God." These powerful words permeated every action taken by the congregation and decision made by individual members.

Consequently, before Satan could pull the plug on a declining congregation, God chose to work through the heroic efforts of His people to save this particular body of Christ in Decatur. They were simply faithful! They had sought the will of the Father above all else, had committed to embrace His will and to take up a cross whatever it might mean for each individual and the church corporately, and to sacrifice whatever it would take to do the bidding of the Father. They then trusted completely in the belief that, whatever the Lord asked them to do, He would make it possible. He did! He still does!

Understand what the vote to relocate forced the church to consider. First, they had no place to move to, no money to fund such an ambitious proposal, and no interest from anyone or group to purchase its considerable downtown property on and around 4th and Grant Street.

"Okay, Father, here we are, empty handed. Do with us, in and through us, whatever you will. We're ready to be obedient, even if it somehow means death!" That was the turning point that came for the deacons that the church bought into.

Before the final vote was taken a church consultant from Nashville was called in to evaluate matters pertaining to relocation. The congregation advised him of their desire to be true to Central's original founding vision: to be located in the center of the population growth, to be in the most advantageous position to reach as many unreached persons as possible. His study revealed that such a place would be close to the intersection of US 31 South and the Decatur Beltline. He also advised that the church would need 25 acres if it truly desired to reach the metropolitan area for Christ.

Such a location presented two major problems. First, property in this commercial area is some of the most expensive property in Morgan County. Hardly within the financial reach of this congregation, especially when considering purchasing as many as 25 acres. Only three parcels of land that seemed to meet the established criteria were discovered. Each one possessed negatives that called into question their suitability as a home place for Central.

As the church continued to seek directions about their future, my wife and I came over from Mississippi for a brief family visit. At that time Rob drove me around to see the properties that appeared available. None seemed to me to be adequate. However as we passed the beautiful Mutual Savings Life Insurance campus, with its huge, imposing, roman-arched portico on its building, its gorgeously manicured landscape, and its million dollar fountain that spewed water 30 feet upward toward heaven, the setting leaped out to me. I said, "Rob, this is it! The property you need to reach this city for Christ." "Yeah, Dad," he said, "There's only catch to it. It's not for sale. And, if it were, we couldn't afford it."

After the church took its final vote on May 22, the local paper featured a story on the front page of the following Sunday paper about Central's decision to relocate, pointing out that the church did not know where it was going nor how it would get there. That very week, an officer of the Board of Mutual Savings called Rob and, would you believe, informed him that the company was interested in selling its property to Central? And for a price that was absolutely unbelievable in its favor of the congregation.

A 140,000 square foot building, covering 29 acres, almost square dab in the population growth epicenter, with softball field, lighted tennis court, fishing lake and many other amenities for community life. Were the people of Central surprised? Not really. They had come to expect anything and everything from God. Miracles just seem to be, and still are, commonplace.

How amazing our God is, when His people choose to walk the way of the cross; when they become willing to die to self so that Christ can be glorified in the church and in the community!

But there was the matter of funding this exciting adventure of faith. Where would the finances come from? It was decided that, rather than engage a professional fund-raising organization to lead a drive to raise sufficient capital for the purchase and renovation of the property, the church would undertake to do it itself, following God's leadership. The congregation engaged Ken Miller, a friend of Rob's in the Alabama Baptists State Mission Board, to give guidance to this effort.

The first thing that the consultant did was to ascertain what the giving potential of the congregation might be. This, of course, takes into consideration such factors as the size of the congregation, the places of membership employment, approximate levels of income, etc. The significant number of defections in the membership, due to the decision to relocate, had also to be factored prominently in the equation. The analysis of the situation placed the optimum figure that could be raised-over-and-above budget giving for a three-year commitment to be two million dollars. Rob understood, as did the church leadership that at a very minimum, four million dollars was needed.

The campaign began. The results were phenomenal because the sacrifices and faith conduct of the church members were unbelievable. Nevertheless, initial indications of what the results might be gave cause for real concern. The church staff and lay leadership (deacons, Sunday School teachers, general church officers, etc.) were first to make their pledges. This group in a normal financial campaign accounts for one-half the money that will usually be committed. Central's leadership commitment came in at approximately one million dollars. This was not a good sign! It was then that Rob challenged the church members to pray fervently and to bring their five loaves and two fish as God leads and place them on the altar for His glory in His Church. The Spirit began to move again in people.

Individuals and family units began to make incredible, Spirit-directed, faith-based sacrifices. Some ladies came to the altar with treasured sentimental pieces of jewelry, one with her precious engagement ring, and placed them there. Some two-car families sold their best auto and gave the proceeds to the church. Some guys sold their boats and other possessions to give to the building fund. One elderly lady gave her house and land to become the church's at her death. One middle-aged man cashed in a retirement account and gave it to the Lord. Many who had little gave more than they could actually afford. Macedonian giving all over again! God honored such sacrifice. When the final count was tallied, the church had pledged almost six million dollars!

There were so many miracles that took place during this campaign. Among them was a young couple who informed Rob that the Lord had told them to pledge two million dollars. hey told the pastor that they did not have that kind of money and didn't know where it would come from, but that this was an unmistakable leading of God in their lives. The husband shared with Rob that before he had come as pastor of Central Baptist, the wife had had a most vivid dream that Central Baptist would relocate. In that dream, God told her that she and her husband would be used by God to make a decided financial difference in a campaign to launch the project. God did it again! At some point during the second year of the campaign, two million dollars was placed in the church bank account by an anonymous young family whom the Lord touched with yet another miracle.

Even with such remarkable monetary provisions from God, the church needed to cover other necessary financial bases in order to get the building ready for occupancy, such as hire an architect, and secure the services of a construction company to gut the three-story edifice, then build it back so that Central could do church in and through it.

God again blessed by leading the congregation to a Christian construction company in Birmingham whose desire was to please God above all else in their business dealings as well as through their work. This company offered a remarkable deal to allow the church to help defray expenses on the project by doing as much work themselves as possible.

Again, it was amazing to see the commitment of God's people, sacrificing time and effort to help in this area. Young and old, especially senior adults – men and women – worked tirelessly around the clock to pull this project off. Such loving service saved the church perhaps as much as between one and one and one-half million dollars. "They had a mind to work."

But what about the downtown buildings the church was up and leaving behind? Oh, yeah. How could one forget? That was the church property many were saying would be as sellable as an ice maker in the North Pole. Who wants to buy an old empty downtown church building? The church prayed and God again responded. A wonderful African-American congregation purchased it to house their fast-growing church. What a double blessing this turned out to be!

Now, you may ask, what does the above Central Story say to you and me today? *It's the principle not the principals that matters the most.*

The Central story finds its being in the central message of the cross. When an individual, a family or an entire Christian congregation chooses to follow Christ in walking the way of the cross, His victory is always assured.

When victory comes as a result of the activity of His Spirit, it inescapably brings glory and honor to Jesus Christ. When Christ is lifted up, Scripture tells us, the Holy Spirit begins to draw persons to Him and, with those who are drawn, our Lord begins to build His church.

Consider this: in Central's first year on her new campus, from October 2008 to October 2009, the church experienced remarkable growth. There were some 200, mostly young adult, additions to the church, with an army of kids coming with their parents, overflowing the children's wing of the new church after only the first two months! Of the 200 additions, there were 88 baptisms, 52 of them being adults.

Besides this, morning worship attendance jumped from an average of approximately 502 to over 900. Additionally, Central saw an increase of 16% in budget giving over the previous year. It also led all churches in the association and was one of the top churches in Alabama in gifts for Southern Baptist mission endeavors! All this during the worst year economically in our nation since the Great Depression. Central believes that we serve a great God, greater than the Great Recession!

Keep in mind that it's the principle that determines the blessings of the Lord, not the principals. People are vitally important, of course, to kingdom advance. But only those who embrace the principle of the cross ever truly discover the blessings of an empty tomb, new life, and unbelievable growth. Central is a church of ordinary people upon whom the Father has poured out his extraordinary blessings because the congregation dared to attempt the extraordinary thing. They sought God's will above all else and became willing to pay the price for it to be fulfilled. Remember, the way of the cross, whatever that means to you and your particular situation, is always the way of victory!

This isn't to suggest that you and your church must be precipitous in your undertakings and attempt something far-fetched to prove your faith or test the Father's power or to prove His magnificent promises. It is to suggest, instead, that through prayer and fasting you ascertain the Father's will for you and your church, however great or small it may be, and then make the determination to pay the price, to pursue it in radical commitment, self-denial, and cross-bearing for Jesus.

Your great challenge may be as simple, and yet as profound, as your involvement in seeking the face of God and His power so that you might be a more effective witness to the unreached in your community! It may be as simple, and yet as profound, as your commitment to seek the Lord's guidance through prayer to a person of His choosing to whom He may wish you to share the love of His Son. It may be as simple, and yet as tough, as getting out of your comfort zone and reaching out in friendly embrace of that person or persons God brings across your path.

Your invitation is to join with other Christians and churches in discovering afresh the power that raised Jesus from the dead. It is a power so explosive that lives thought incorrigible can be radically transformed into persons becoming–like–Jesus; so dynamic that even the flow of history for individuals, congregations, or nations, thought to be cascading into certain death, can be dramatically rechanneled toward a new day and a thrilling, better tomorrow. Oh brothers and sisters, come and see!

The Central story is one that God is writing in and through his faithful people in Decatur. Please understand that He has a story to write through you and your congregation just as eternally important. The story He would write through you, if you permit, will be unique to your situation and the unique role He has designed for you to play in His unfolding plan for the Ages. It is that plan that was finalized on Calvary and set in motion on the first Lord's Day morning. A plan to reach a world with the love, grace and forgiveness of Jesus Christ.

Will you choose to be major players in God's plan for the world, beginning with where he has planted you in your appointed sphere of influence? Will you join those who are committing to this endeavor of reaching people unreached by the gospel, for the sake of His passion and purpose? As we walk by faith and not by sight, we often see God do some things in and through our lives and churches so miraculous that even the most hardened skeptic will marvel. And, prayerfully, come to believe!

Where must you begin? Right where you are just now. At a crossroad. At one of the most important intersections you will ever come upon in your journey here on earth. Which road to take? Take the one marked by that cross standing there. Yes, that's the one. The one with that commanding-looking figure standing, embracing the cross. Listen! He is lovingly calling out to you. Listen carefully to Him. He is issuing you an invitation.

Come and see! Come and see what?

Come and see the miracles that he will do in and through you and your church, for His glory. Listen! He continues to speak to you: "Follow me and I will make you fishers of men."

Chapter Two

Respond to the Divine Initiative

"By faith we understand that the worlds were framed by the Word of God, so that the things which are seen were not made of things which are visible." Hebrews 11:3

The Divine Initiative

In the very act of creation, God took the initiative to frame a kind of world in which the man He would create to be His caretaker would be especially fashioned with facility to respond trustingly to his Maker, in a shared life of togetherness and fellowship. Within this creative framework, as seen in Scripture, one may find the means that God would utilize to make Himself and His longing for fellowship with humankind known.

The Divine Initiative in Creation

Throughout the Bible we are told that, in the beauty, the wonder, and the orderliness of His Creation, God makes Himself known to those He places within the garden. In Romans chapter one, the Apostle asserts that God's revelation of Himself in the natural order is so adequate that no one may excuse his disobedience to God because of limitations to the divine disclosure. There is more than enough evidence for His existence to hold women and men responsible for their failure to respond trustingly to their Creator.

Man's responsibility to God for his response to the divine Initiative may be better understood once we consider that, in His initiative to establish a love relationship with those He creates, He implants within each individual's being a need for his Maker, a "God-hunger" if you will.

This seems to be what the Preacher is talking about in Ecclesiastes 3:11 when he writes: "He has set eternity in the hearts of men; yet they cannot fathom what God has done from beginning to end."

God sets within each of our souls an awareness of that invisible world beyond our senses, along with a desire to experience it and the Someone who governs it. And submit to His authority and expectations.

The Preacher was right. God reaches out in love to those coming into the world so as to establish an intimate, purposeful relationship with them. But, alas, he admitted "they cannot fathom what (He) has done from beginning to end."

Something happened after the original blueprint was laid out. Men and women in their natural state became no longer able to picture who God is and what He is about. And what that understanding should mean to them. The *"Light that lights every person coming into the world"* was darkened. Man's perception of God was noticeably blurred. His desire to trustingly respond to God became perverted and changed into a hunger for gods other than the One and Only God who made heaven and earth. These were false gods that falsely claimed to bring fulfillment to a person's life. They still make this outrageous claim. What happened? Sin entered the world and man fell from his original state and lost the garden and, in that, lost his life of fellowship with God. It then became virtually impossible to get back into that paradise without "enlightened" help.

This discussion right now may seem to be rather pedantic and unnecessary in a presentation of expectant faith. However, if we will accept it, it posits an important while often overlooked aspect of the present danger you and I and our churches face in America. Indeed, throughout the Western world.

Unless we wake up and grasp the significance of people all around us – and all over the earth – who are literally "starving to death" because of a deep unmet hunger placed within them by their Creator, we in the church will doubtless never embrace the urgency to reach out to them in the name of Christ, to offer them that which can truly satisfy their hunger. Our failure will be catastrophic to them, as well as to us!

Those of us who stand by and allow others to die an eternal death – a death that is experienced both here and now as well as in the hereafter – will be held accountable by God for several serious sins. First, we will be guilty of *robbery*. Robbing God of His right to establish Lordship over, and a loving relationship with, the men and women He has placed in our world for His Name's sake and pleasure. Second, we will be guilty of *murder*.

When we stand by and allow persons within our circles of influence or persons whom God sends across our pathway to die eternally we become guilty of murder. At the very least, of gross criminal neglect. I am fearful that far too many of us and our churches are on trial at this present moment for such criminal activity!

And what about our country? Are we so arrogant and oblivious to the spiritual as well as natural law of sowing and reaping that we can honestly continue to live as if God will, like a coddling parent to a small child's antics, forever sit by passively and smile at our rebellious behavior as if saying, "O, how cute!" What do *you* think? The time of our innocence has long since passed when the Father would wink at our sins!

We can be certain that we will be held accountable to God for allowing persons within the reach of our influence to "starve to death" spiritually as well as materially. The Bible says that we will give an accounting not only over "there" but right "here" in our life of self-absorption and apathy. *"We can be sure our sins will find us out!"*

For those with eyes to see, divine consequences are already being suffered by us in America. If we were living in biblical times what do you think an Isaiah or a Jeremiah or a John the Baptist would be saying about America with its moral and spiritual implosion? About the calamities we are facing? Might they not be speaking out and asserting that the judgment of God was being poured out on our beloved country? Might they be issuing a clarion call, "Wake up! Before it is too late!"?

Does such a call resonate with you? The question then is: what do you and I plan to do with this urgent warning? With our responsibility?

The Divine Initiative in Christ

When our heavenly Father sent His one and only Son, Jesus Christ, into the world, it was His response to man's need of love, grace, forgiveness, and meaning in life. And of man's need to see God's perfect revelation of Himself. A revelation in creation that had been blurred and made difficult to perceive because of sin. This revelation in Christ – the One who perfectly mirrored the nature and life of God and His purposes in this world – was culminated by His death on the cross and in His resurrection from the dead.

This special revelation displayed with unmistakable clarity what God is like and what He desires man on this earth to embrace and embody. What do we see in Jesus Christ about the God who made us and, following our fall, yearns to restore His divine image in our lives? This is the revelation: God is love! Sacrificial, suffering, self-giving love! A love that thinks and acts to meet the needs of others rather than self. A love that brings heaven down into every man's hell for the glory of God the Father. What a mandate for you and me! And, for our churches!

It was, and is, a revelation to rectify the gone-wrongness in man's life and in his world by turning the true light on to dispel the chaotic darkness that after the Fall began impinging on life on this planet again, threatening to destroy it altogether. A darkness that seeks to snuff out the light of the knowledge of God on earth! God acted decisively when He sent His only Son to turn the light on again to dispel this darkness in our world.

The beautiful poem about the Logos, the living Word of God, as found in the Prologue to John's Gospel, tells us that Jesus Christ is the Eternal Word who in the beginning was and of course remains the creative agent of the Godhead. He is the divine Initiative who implants the God-hunger in every life that He creates. Thus, we understand the Authorized Version's rendering of those verses dealing with the Word of God who became flesh, as He exists and acts in his eternal state. Note John 1:3-4 and 9 in the NKJV: "All things were made through Him, and without Him nothing was made that was made. In Him was life, and the life was the light of man . . . (He) was the true light which gives light to every man coming into the world."

However, this inborn light that the Word of God implants in every person entering the world, that occasions a hunger for a Higher Being and to the experience of His life, finds itself nevertheless encompassed about by the deep darkness of our fallen humanity. This darkness, in turn, blinds every person to the meaning and purpose of the light. And how to respond appropriately to it. Each member of the human race therefore finds himself or herself incapable of clearly understanding this revelation from God that is built into the fabric of human life and helpless to please Him adequately in faithful response. So God sent the eternal Word down to earth and dressed Him up in the garb of humanity so that those coming into the world might see the Father clearly and come to respond to Him in faith and obedience. Thus, "The Word became flesh and dwelt among us, and we beheld His glory, even the glory of the one and only Son of the Father, full of grace and truth."

The Incarnated Christ, Jesus of Nazareth, became God's final divine Initiative reaching out to fallen humankind, seeking an appropriate response of faith from each and every person on earth. It was and is His last attempt to elicit trusting belief in, and trusting obedience to, God the Creator and Lord of all that exists.

God's divine Initiative in Jesus Christ was passed onto His Church, His body, which exists to continue His revelation within this world order. Each day we individuals, and our churches, present the divine initiative to a hurting, hungering world. The light of Christ we now share in our darkened world through the preaching of the gospel and in the witness of the cross and resurrection that has been actualized in our lives. Thus we understand what the depth of the call of Christ to each of us really is and requires when we surrender to Him in discipleship. Dare we say it again? We must *"Deny ourselves, take up our cross daily, and follow Him!"* Follow Him in making known the Father's love, grace, and power. And engage the task of rescuing men, women, and children from the turbulent waters of this chaotic world.

How must you and I respond to God's great revelation of Himself and His purposes to you and me in the Lord Jesus Christ?

Come and see, we have a responsibility!

All of us surely agree that the only truly appropriate response to the divine Initiative in Christ is the response of faith. Scripture is clear that faith is the channel through which the Father pours His great love, grace, and power into our lives. The importance of faith in this outreach journey cannot be overestimated. For, as the Hebrew writer puts it in 11:6: "Without faith it is impossible to please God."

This being true, a companion fact is also true and vital to our proper response to God and His divine initiative in Christ. Without *genuine* faith it is impossible to please Him!

It is necessary to point this out because so much that goes under the guise of "faith" in contemporary Christianity is not faith at all! The Imposter among us is misleading multitudes of persons in our communities – and many within our congregations – as to that which constitutes the faith that initiates a genuine saving, liberating, and victorious relationship with God in Jesus Christ!

Such deception has been a problem within the church from its earliest years. We must never forget nor ignore the words of James, our Lord's brother, who excoriated those who claimed to have faith because they "believed" in God but whose lives evidenced no trusting response to Him and none of the characteristics of a love relationship with Him. Said he bluntly, "Faith without works is dead!" Belief that is lifeless cannot woo the heart of the heavenly Father nor engage Him in an intimate, fruitful relationship.

Martin Luther often said that it is by faith alone that we are saved, but not by a faith that is alone. Let us therefore boldly proclaim from our pulpits and teach from our lecterns that those who claim a right relationship with God, based on nothing more than an intellectual embrace of certain religious ideas and dogmas, are living in spiritual deception, with no basis for the surety of kingdom citizenship! And without hope of experiencing the power of the resurrection here or hereafter.

The problem of bogus faith is a major factor in the decline of churches in America. It explains the loss of passion to understand and undertake God's will as revealed in the light of Christ and the loss of power to do it. A "faithless" church made up of "faithless" congregants is for all practical purposes dead. The sad state of affairs may be seen in the fact that those of us within are often not even aware of it. Consequently, we continue to dress up and gather each week, paying our respects to a cosmetologized body, oohing and aahing over how wonderful she looks but, at the same time, speaking wistfully about the way she used to be and the good times we all *used* to have together. How often we mourn her lifeless state and our seeming helplessness to resuscitate her like we imagine she used to be!

At the core of the problem we are encountering is the loss of God's Spirit in our midst. Such is the predictable results of superficial faith. When genuine faith is exercised by an individual or a congregation an invasion of the Spirit takes place within that person or his church as miraculous, transformational dynamics go to work. These spiritual forces issue in unashamed witness from the Christian and his church and the awe-struck readiness to listen to the claims of Christ by a watching world!

Let's face it. The Holy Spirit is the missing factor today in the church growth equation. n most instances, He is absent at every level of church life up to, and even in, the life – or lifelessness – of our denominations. Mainline denominations – I include Baptists in America in this group because of cultural affinitives – have been successful in at least one thing recently: we have buried the Holy Spirit in the respectable coffins of Ancient Creeds, and in matter-of-fact categories of orthodox confessions of faith. Because of the Spirit's absence, far too many of us are doing not much more each Sunday than attending services of last rites for a church, especially in America.

What a tragedy! Because the Church was and is the Lord's special chosen people to continue His presence on earth, existing to continue His purposes in human history. The Church is His body, but we must recognize the fact that His body is dependent upon – and cannot succeed in Her mission without – the wind of the Spirit to give her life and breath to boldly speak His good news!

There is a great deal of discussion today in Christian circles, among them is my own denomination, about restructuring our organizations to be more efficient and to accomplish greater things for our Lord. Most of us surely understand that from time to time we must adapt what we are doing to the realities of what we are dealing with in our society so as to give us the greatest advantage for reaching more people for Christ.I have become more thoroughly convinced than ever before in my long ministry that what we in churches need now is not new wineskins. What we need is new wine! We need the Holy Spirit!

We need revival in America! In your church and mine. In your heart and mine. An outpouring of the Holy Spirit that, like a fast-spreading conflagration, burns away our great sin while sweeping hundreds – if not thousands – in your community and mine, and millions in our country, into the kingdom of our Lord Christ. A revival that changes the direction of the spiritual and moral flow in our Land and in the world. Would you pray that there might be a spark that sets Christians ablaze to get under a burden for God's intervention in our increasingly godless society? A burden of such magnitude that this certain congregation and its people might become willing to pay the price in putting self to death so that the power that raised Jesus from the dead might be let loose in that church and community? But, much more than this, that the mighty wind of God's Spirit might blow across our land?

Without faith, genuine biblical faith, this will not be possible. For *"without faith it is impossible to please Him."* Now, what is this faith that unlocks the chamber room of power in God's eternal habitation and allows His Spirit to flow into a human life? Or in a church? It is again the response of one's very being to the divine initiative as set forth in Christ, that is characterized by both trusting belief and trusting obedience.

Faith as the Response of Trusting Belief

The writer of Hebrews 11 reminds us in verse 6 that, "Anyone that comes to God must believe that He exists."

The belief in the factual existence of God is obviously foundational for the Christian religion. Remove this doctrine and the entire house of cards tumbles. I presume that all of us who read these words will assert that we most assuredly believe that God exists. But, do we *really* believe?
The treatment of faith in this book has sought to make the distinction between belief that is nothing more than intellectual assent to thoughts *about* God, and belief that engages the mind, heart, and will in a trusting, life-changing relationship *with* God.

We have pointed to the dangers of this so-called faith that is nothing more than mere intellectual entertainment of certain ideas about God. We have talked about how misleading this erroneous idea is to multitudes of persons – even in our churches – who have concluded that, because they "believe" that there is a God, they have a valid claim on His life and favor. The Apostle James again has a word about such worthless, barren faith. *"Even the demons in Hell believe and they tremble!"*

True, life-changing faith is to be seen as not just belief *about* God but belief *in* God. It is belief that is driven by trust, the essential element of faith. When I, as an act of will and heart, entrust my life *in toto* to the Reality that stands behind and gives substance to the idea of God, I then discover the faith that unlocks the door into God's eternal presence! Without trust there is no true belief. When we keep this fact before us, we can then see more clearly why a mere intellectual embrace of the idea of a supreme being falls short of what the Bible indicates genuine belief really is. And of what God desires and expects of us.

The difference between belief in the existence of God as a mental concept and belief as a commitment of one's will may be rather easily drawn.Superficial belief entertains the existence of God only within the realm of ideas. Genuine belief, on the other hand, moves through the realm of ideas into another realm, the invisible spiritual world, to grasp the reality of God beyond and behind the mental in a total trust and surrender of life to Him.

Hebrews 11:1 elucidates this understanding when it declares that, "Faith is being sure of what we hope for and certain of what we do not see."

Because of God's divine initiative there emerges the hope of eternal life with an Eternal Being within the breast of all who come into the world. Faith is the response of those who move beyond the mental formulation of the concept this hope conjures up to embrace, without doubting or reservation, the One to whom this image points as reality.

When we accept the reality behind the idea of God in our innermost being and surrender all we are and have trustingly to His lordship we are told - and we know from experience – that the Father does a remarkable thing. He grants us the inner assurance and unimpeachable knowledge that the Invisible God we have trusted is indeed the Truth behind and beyond our best thoughts and ideas of His existence. And that we are accepted in Him! Thus, the Apostle Paul could write in Romans 8:16: *"The Spirit Himself bears witness with our spirit that we are the children of God."* Proof-positive assurance!

It is in this light that we understand Paul's emphatic statements about the assurance God grants us concerning certain aspects of our hope in Christ when we truly believe. Among many are these:

> "For I *know* whom I have believed, and am persuaded that He is able to keep what I have committed unto Him against that day." 2 Timothy 1:12

> "And we *know* that in all things God works for the good of those who love Him, who have been called according to His purpose." Romans 8:28 (NIV)

> "For we *know* that if our earthly house, this tent is destroyed, we have a building from God, a house not made with hands, eternal in the heavens." 2 Corinthians 5:1

The Apostle John pipes in with these two verses among a number of his that speak directly to the truth before us: "This is the *confidence* we have in approaching God: That if we ask anything according to his will, he hears us, and if we *know* that he hears us – whatever we ask – we *know* that we have what we asked of him." (1 John 5:14-15)

What do you know for certain about the God who exists and the reality behind the hope He has implanted within you? Do you have the blessed assurance, the unchallengeable evidence within your spirit that guarantees you all your best hopes of things eternal? And that the results of God's initiative in creation and in Christ, informed by the Spirit and the Word, are absolutely true?

Such assurance is the critical by-product of genuine biblical faith. If your life is devoid of this assurance, this certainty, it may signal your need to pause in your journey long enough to consider where you actually stand with God. If yours is not a personal, know-so, trusting relationship with Him, one that has changed your life and purpose in this world, then you may wish to consult someone who can help you with this matter. I would recommend that you turn to a person in whose walk there is no doubt that God exists. One in whom the fruit of His presence is very much in evidence.

The response to God's initiative to us in Christ Jesus is crucial. Faith is the trusting belief that accepts Jesus as the very image of the God who exists. Paul declared, in Colossians 2:9, "For in Him (Christ) all the fullness of the Godhead dwells bodily." Jesus said, "If you have seen me, you have seen the Father also!" He is the light that illumines all our thinking about God and His eternal life. He sets our misguided thinking straight about God and His will for each of us. It was on the cross that He showed us perfectly who God is and what He is about. God is love! Self-giving, unconditional love. Therefore, we Christ-followers are called to give profound testimony to this love that has come as a result of His grace, through faith, and was revealed to us at Calvary.

> At the cross, at the cross, where I first saw the light,
> And the burden of my heart rolled away,
> It was there by faith I received my sight,
> And now I am happy all the day.

Some ask why we in the church today must put so much emphasis on making the trusting acceptance of Christ as Savior and Lord the normative experience for all who would worship God and seek to discover why they are here in this world. Indeed, they ask, why is it important that we reach out in our communities, as well as across the globe, seeking to engage persons of different cultures, backgrounds, and religions with the gospel of Jesus Christ? Some sincerely ask how a God of love could hold people responsible for failing to accept Christ as the light of the world, when these people live up to the light that they have had opportunity to see. Surely, they say, such people will go to heaven.

As well meaning as this sentiment is, it misses altogether the point of why we are here on earth. God does not send people into the world so that He then can get them to heaven, although heaven is the wonderful outcome of the life of trusting belief! No, God sends us here so that we can bring heaven into the hell we encounter, wherever it may be found, dispelling the darkness in the lives of persons, institutions, and nations. He sends us here to carry out the mission of Christ in this world, to the glory of the Father!

Jesus Christ came into human history as the Light of the world and, among other things, to rescue the failed vision the Father had given to Israel to be a "light to the nations." He built His Church – and continues to build it – on the trusting belief of those who would accept Him as the Father's Chosen One, those who would choose to carry His light to everyone, everywhere.

The plan He laid out for us was simple: start right where you are at this moment in time, in your own Jerusalem as Luke would say, and wherever your life's journey takes you, understand that you are there for Him and His glory! You are there to take the witness stand wherever and whenever Christ is placed on trial, to testify in His behalf everything you know for certain to be true about Him. In other words, you and I are to be lights that bear witness to *the* light that alone can enable women and men to see God and His glory clearly.

Of course, each of those to whom we go will have had some light – it was given in creation. But, alas, because of their sins, the light of those who know not Christ will be a flicker at best, if not snuffed out altogether. These we reach out to are consequently unable to comprehend just "who" they are and "why" they are here in this world. And "what" they must do in order to discover their place in God's mysterious scheme of things. Herein is our mission as Christians and as churches. To share Christ, God's revelation of His holy will, so that no one will misunderstand.

One remembers the words attributed to Immanuel Kant, the philosopher who, allegedly, was sitting pensively one day along a dusty road, *incognito*. The oxcarts passing by covered this apparent peasant with dust and dirt. Finally, a concerned man stopped to see if he could help the poor fellow. He asked the disguised philosopher, "Who are you, sir? And, what are you doing here?" To which Immanuel Kant is reported to have said, "I wish to God I knew!"

Dear reader, there are multitudes all around us in our communities, and some even in our churches, who do not know who they are and what they are doing here. They have no idea that they are persons created in the image of God, their Creator, to have loving fellowship with Him and to please Him above all else in this life! Nor, do they know about the journey they're on in the world – its mission, its purpose, *their* purpose. So they drift through life and, without the perfect revelation of Christ, fail to discover their reason for being on this journey. How sad.

It is imperative that we in the church reach out to all people, regardless of their state of religiosity or irreligiosity. Because, they can never fulfill their purpose in life of truly worshipping, fellowshipping, and pleasing God with their obedience to Him unless the blinders are removed and they are enabled to see and know God as He truly is. Neither can they fulfill their purpose in Christ to be engaged in sharing His perfect light and therefore in dispelling the darkness of this world, wherever it is encountered. Dag Hammarskjold, the first and some believe the greatest Secretary General of the United Nations, an unashamed Christian and philosopher, once said, "To fail to become what I may have become is what it means to be lost eternally." Powerful words for those outside the church! For those of us inside the church!

What do we understand to be the church's approach today to those outside the church? It is to be the same as it was when Christ commissioned His Church. We see it in the missionary journeys of the early Apostles, called forth by the Spirit of Christ at work in His Church. Their forays into the world reveal to us that the Church's task, our task, is to share the good news of the gospel with all persons everywhere.

The Apostle Paul's encounter with the Stoic and Epicurean philosophers in ancient Athens informs for us the Church's starting point in its outreach to persons who do not have a Christological orientation to their belief system.

In Acts 17:22-23, the church's first missionary began the presentation of his faith to the curious intellectuals. He said, "Men of Athens! I see that in every way you are very religions. For as I walked around and looked carefully at your objects of worship, I even found an altar with the inscription: TO AN UNKNOWN GOD. Now what you worship as something unknown I am going to proclaim to you."

We go to the unchurched today because of their incomplete, distorted knowledge of God, His will for their lives, and their total helplessness to discover their need for the Christ of Calvary. We go to bear witness to the light He alone possesses to dispel the darkness of their souls. That alone serves as a beacon to the meaningless drift of their lostness in the turbulent sea of life. We go because Christ tells us to go that they, like we, might experience the wonderful process of being made like Him, to the glory of God the Father.

What is faith? It is a response to the divine Initiative in one's life that is characterized both by trusting belief and trusting obedience. It is the response of a trusting belief in the God who exists. It is, at the same time, the response of trusting obedience to the one God who desires that all persons, everywhere, come to know Him, enjoy Him, and join Him in dispelling the darkness on this earth.

Faith as the Response of Trusting Obedience

It must not be lost on us that the root word for faith in the original language, *pistis,* is sometimes translated "faith" in the New Testament, and at other times, "faithfulness." As much as any other evidence that has been presented, this fact underscores the validity of our thesis: that genuine biblical faith is characterized by two movements within the one act of a person's surrendered will to God. There is the movement of *belief* and the movement of *obedience,* operating together. Thus, we are told, that the transformational experience of conversion entails both repentance and belief. Obviously repentance is the activity of belief in which a person changes his mind about his life and the direction it is headed to do a radical about-face and move obediently in the direction of God and that which pleases him. Belief and obedience cannot be separated in a person's faith response to Jesus Christ.

This truth is clearly seen in the miracle-working, healing ministry of Jesus Christ. While He exerted His remarkable powers at times by *fiat*, in most instances faith was required and was engaged in as an act of obedience. So, the man with the lame hand was told to "stretch forth" his hand.

It was healed *when he stretched it forth*. Or, the lepers were told to go show themselves to the priests and, *as they were going*, were healed. Or, the nobleman who was told to go back home and find his son well. He went and found as he had been told. Trusting obedience was most often the vehicle in which trusting belief was moved along.

There were times, to be sure, when the trusting belief of one person, or several persons, affected the healing of still another who did not yet believe. One recalls the incident when the four men brought the invalid to Jesus on a pallet to be healed. Jesus said that "their" faith had made their friend well. It is to be remembered that their faith was occasioned by their faithfulness. They "brought" him to Jesus, hoisted him up on the roof of the house, tore through the ceiling, and let him down in the Lord's presence.

In view of this revelation, seen in Jesus' ministry, let us examine more closely the role of obedience in the faith that pleases God and engages His pleasurable response. Hebrews 11:6 reads in its entirety: "Without faith it is impossible to please God, because anyone who comes to him must believe that He exists and that He rewards those who earnestly seek Him." (NIV)

A.T. Robertson notes that the most accurate translation of the concluding words in this verse is not "seek Him," but "seek Him out." In this light we may come to see even more plainly how belief and obedience are inseparable manifestations of a person's one act of will, as he "seeks out" the God who truly exists in a never-ending continuum of faith-faithfulness surrender to Jesus Christ.
God rewards those who "seek Him out." What does "seeking Him out" in the life of faith have to do with obedience?

The writer of Hebrews 11 follows verse 6 with two illustrations of the point he is making. In verse 7 he gives a synopsis of Noah's remarkable faith in building the ark in, of all places, the desert. In verse 8 he gives a succinct statement of Abraham's equally remarkable faith when he left the security and prosperity of home to move out with his family into dangerous, uncharted waters, not knowing where he was going. It is noteworthy that both men obviously enjoyed personal conversations with God.

They were men who sought out the God who had taken the initiative to seek them out for His holy purposes. When He made known His will to them, both men responded with a faith-act that was both an experience of trusting belief and trusting obedience.

Without Noah and Abraham's obedience, there would have been no evidence of genuine faith. Without "seeking Him out," there would have been no obedience. Let us be candid. Both men could have given the Lord the best offerings that could have been afforded in hopes of satisfying God and meriting his favor. But these would not have "worked."

There is a world – no, an eternity – of difference between a work of merit that seeks to earn the favor of God and an act of obedience issuing from trusting belief that seeks to please Him above all else! God was pleased with them because they "sought Him out" and once His will gripped their wills, they trustingly believed and obeyed.

The prophet Samuel once asked a rhetorical question concerning whether God was as pleased with burnt offerings and sacrifices as He was with obedience to the voice of the living God. His answer was brief: "To obey is better than sacrifice!"

God rewards those who earnestly "seek Him out" in obedient faith. What does that mean to you and me as we seek to be men and women who walk by faith and not by sight? What does this mean as you consider the great invitation, "Come and See, Jesus Christ is Alive"? In what areas of life does "seeking Him out" result in the manifestation of the miracle-working power of our resurrected Christ that is at work in and through us and in His Church?

Come and see.

Chapter Three

Seek Him Out in Prayer and Fasting

Significant Prayer

Doubtless few would disagree that prayer is fundamental to the empowerment of the church for a victorious walk in the world, and that it is the key that unlocks the storehouse of God's limitless provisions for His people for whatever the need or task. That it somehow mysteriously uses the Spirit of the resurrected Christ to move in and through the congregation of faith to accomplish immeasurably more than any could ever hope for or believe to be possible.

No one argues with the testimony of history that declares that prayer has always been a vital and precipitating factor in every great season of true revival and spiritual renewal, beginning with Pentecost. You will nod your head in the affirmative as I assert to you that this marvelous opportunity to change our communities and world is useless unless the first step we take is in significant prayer. But will you and yours, and me and mine, truly pray? That is the question that begs for an immediate answer.

The sad reality in the church in the Western world is that we simply do not pray! When it is generally accepted that the average American churchman prays not much more than two minutes a day, and that includes the blessing at meals and the brief night-time thoughts lifted to heaven as one dozes off to sleep, you and I begin to realize the reason for the sad spiritual state of affairs in our own lives and in our churches. And in our communities. And in our country. In other parts of the world where hours of prayer are a significant part of the daily regimen of discipline for the Christian and his church, we see the gospel of the Lord sweeping multitudes of unbelievers into the kingdom. We see little of this in our country because, let's face it, we simply do not pray. Not significantly!

May this reiteration of the well-known facts of the matter not be lost on you, as you contemplate taking this journey to spiritual revival. If you and I and our congregations are not willing to commit to serious, significant prayer, we will not radically impact our communities and world for Christ. God, the progenitor of all things good, must be placed in the driver's seat in our journey, making all the decisions along the way, or else those of us who travel will end up on a thoroughfare going nowhere of any real spiritual significance.

What may we understand about this significant prayer that God desires to honor and bless with His living presence and power?

The Prayer that Fits Us with Clothing for the Journey

> "I am going to send what my father has promised; but stay in the city until you have been clothed with power from on high." "You will receive power when the Holy Spirit comes upon you and you will be my witnesses..." "Then they returned to Jerusalem... (and) all joined together constantly in prayer, along with the women and Mary the Mother of Jesus and his brother." Luke 24:49; Acts 1:8, 12, 14 (NIV)

Jesus indicated that you and I need a special dress for the journey we take with Him and for Him. It is the powerful presence of the Holy Spirit to guide us, equip us, encourage us, and empower us with the same power that raised Jesus from the dead! And we are told that it is prayer – significant prayer – that moves the hands of the Father to dress us up in this Christ-like apparel!

What kind of prayer is it that wraps us and our churches in this supernatural garb? Notice several things from Luke's accounts of some of the last words our Lord uttered on earth.

It is a Waiting Prayer

"Stay in the city until..." Jesus told His disciples. Stay put! Don't make a move! Cease what you are doing! Wait for the traffic light to turn green! *"Be still and know that I am God."* The most critical problems most of us Christians and our churches face emerge because we run ahead of, and without, the Lord in daily assignments and important undertakings. We move out without having first been moved within and from above! Significant prayer demands that we cease from our plans and activities. Wait until the Lord gives us direction and then dresses us up in proper attire for the journey ahead.

Victory in Jesus doesn't work the way too often we seek to make it work. Living in the power of the resurrection can't be experienced until we stop striving to do our best and allow what God did best for us to become a reality in our lives. Thus, the great invitation for the world to *"come and see, Jesus Christ is alive!"* will not be embraced by the unreached in our communities and will not result in appreciable gain for our churches if we reach out to do His work, however sincere, without first experiencing the dynamic that alone can make us effective witnesses for the resurrected Christ.

When I was a boy we were taught that, when approaching a road to be crossed, we should first do three things:

> Stop, look and listen,
> Before you cross the street,
> Use your eyes, use your ears
> And then use your feet.

Marvelous advice for the negotiation of any decision-making crossing in life. Essential advice for a church at the crossroad, struggling to maintain its life in the community while seeking meaningful connection in an increasingly alien, sometimes, hostile culture. Necessary for those who choose to commit to seeking the face of God. The first step we must take is this: Stop! Then while stopped, it is important that we look and listen until God makes Himself known to us.

Stop what you're doing and devote yourself to prayer. Stay where you are until you are ready for God to do something out of the ordinary in your life and in your church. Stop at this very first way-station in your journey until you get to know your Guide personally. Then ask him to get you and your church ready for the trip of a lifetime, whatever that may mean for you and yours.

At the same time, please look! Look inwardly and outwardly and consider the many ways that Satan will come against you, to turn you away from God's will for you and your congregation. Look back on opportunities you have missed in the past to involve yourself in the exceptional thing for the

Lord and recall the obstacles the Enemy placed in your pathway to block your walk of victory. He'll do it again if you are not careful! Look for him to create in your mind a thousand and one reasons why you can't and shouldn't pay the price to experience the powerful, living Presence of our Lord in your life and in the life of the church you attend. Jesus said, "Watch and pray that you do not enter into temptation."

Listen to Him! Listen to your Guide as He speaks to reassure you of His presence with you at all times, and His provisions for everything you will need for the journey ahead. Listen to His promises to protect you from the Enemy. Listen to His voice as He instructs you on how to negotiate each step ahead. Listen as He begins to guide you to those special people He has picked out for you to invite to come and see Jesus is alive!

It is a Reconciling Prayer

"And, they all continued with one accord in prayer and supplication . . ." (Acts 1:14). Those words in some translations that follow the Authorized Version of the Bible have spoken volumes to us for many years. (Note in Acts 2:1 that when the Day of Pentecost came – and the Holy Spirit was poured out on the church – the disciples were "*all in one accord!*"). What a different picture this is of the Apostles than is found throughout the Gospels. Heretofore, they were a contentious group. Power-seeking. Jockeying for position. Jealous of one another. Even Peter, after he was restored and commissioned as a shepherd of Christ's sheep, displayed his jealousy of, and hostility toward, John the beloved disciple!

Our Lord knew that His disciples would not be ready to move out on mission immediately following His ascension. Issues had to be resolved between them. They had to come to grips with their estrangement from each other before they could accomplish His purposes of bringing together a fragmented world. The fact was, the Holy Spirit would not come upon them nor flow in and through them, if the channels of their hearts and souls were clogged with pride, selfish ambition, envy, suspicion, deceitfulness, and whatever other sin might hold sway in their lives.

So, Jesus told them to cease all their plans and activities and their attempts to rush out to change the world without first stopping and staying in Jerusalem *"until you are clothed with power from on high."* And, they did. And, He did! What happened that changed their hearts toward each other during those ten days of prayer, before the Spirit of God was poured out on them?

We can only guess at the apologies sought, the forgiveness given, the embraces that warmed, and the tears that flowed freely down their cheeks. What we do know for certain is that they prayed constantly, significantly. hey prayed until their broken relationships were mended and they became one with each other and, as a result, became one with the Triune God! And, their hearts became broken for a world that needed a Savior!

We have already alluded to what is well known by students of Church history, that every revival in which there has been a tremendous visitation by the Holy Spirit, resulting in large numbers of conversions to faith in Jesus Christ, and remarkable changes for the better being made in the social fabric of communities, even nations, were all an out-cropping of Christians devoting themselves to significant prayer. What is often overlooked, however, is the fact that these times of spiritual revival and renewal always were characterized by individual brokenness over sin, the seeking of forgiveness among brothers and sisters, with loving reconciliation taking place!

It was true of the Asbury Revival in 1970, one of the last of the great outpourings of the Holy Spirit of God that moved across large portions of the United States and into several countries around the globe, resulting in untold multitudes of persons who either became radically converted to Jesus Christ or, had life-changing spiritual renewal experiences.

It began on February 3, in a chapel service at Asbury College, a small independent Christian school of the Wesleyan tradition. The service was led that Tuesday morning by Custer Reynolds, Academic Dean, and Methodist layman. Reynolds did not preach.Instead, he gave a brief testimony, and invited any student who wished to share about his or her spiritual experiences to do so. This was not an unusual thing to do in this evangelical school that required chapel three times a week. But, this day was different.

One student responded. Followed by another. Then by another. They then started pouring to the altar. The revival broke out. Gradually, and inexplicably, students and faculty members found themselves quietly praying, singing, and weeping. They began to seek out persons to whom they had done wrong and ask forgiveness. And the chapel service went on and on and on. For days it went on – day and night. The 1,500 seat auditorium stayed packed as not only students came and went, but people from communities close by and far away came to be touched by the presence of God. His glorious presence was not only *felt* in that place, but could be *seen* in something of a divine hue that permeated what truly became a house into which Jesus had literally walked!

President Dennis Kinlaw, who was away in a conference in western Canada when the revival broke out, shared with me several years later that, when he heard the news, he was frightened to death. He was afraid that what was going on might turn into some kind of emotional type of expression that could easily get out of hand. It was two days before Dr. Kinlaw could get back to Wilmore, Kentucky where Asbury is located. He arrived at 2:00 am in the morning and went directly to the chapel. His fears were disarmed when he not only felt the presence of God, unlike any other time in his life and ministry, but saw the Holy Spirit at work in total orderliness. The unusual event was marked by no loud talking or speaking out of turn, nor any demonstration of unbridled emotionalism. Just a quiet time when hearts touched the heart of God, after touching the hearts of each other with love, forgiveness, and grace.

The revival spread to at least 130 college and seminary campuses and scores of churches from New York to California and into South America. It is believed that the wake of this tremendous flood of the Holy Spirit was felt even into the summer months. Asbury was bombarded with requests during this time from churches large and small, of many denominations, for students who had participated in the revival to come and share their testimonies. Wherever they went, the Spirit of God went with them and brought true revival. It was if they were "clothed" in the Spirit of God. One church in Anderson, Indiana was so touched by the Spirit that services continued for 50 nights and had to be moved into a

2,500 seat city auditorium to handle the crowds of people who longed to experience the living, risen Christ.

The Buck Run Church in Frankfort, Kentucky experienced a fresh touch from God during this time as students at nearby Georgetown College led a weekend revival that saw numerous conversions and renewed commitments from church members. My son, Rob, tells that it was during this meeting that his heart and life were touched and changed forever by the Lord Jesus Christ.

Tim Philpot, a judge today in Lexington, was one of the several students who were sent out to churches to share their story. He recalls that, at times, even before Asbury students finished sharing their testimonies, the congregations would be kneeling at the altar, weeping softly, quietly confessing their sins to God, repenting, and making things right with fellow church members.

Philpot, son of the late Ford Philpot, well-known Methodist evangelist of his day, told me that this revival was the turning point in his life. Indeed, he said, he was not truly saved until his experience in the 1970 visitation of the Holy Spirit on his college campus. He now speaks for Christ in churches of various denominations all across America and into the country of India where his organization, Fishhook International, has a significant evangelistic-discipleship ministry as well as ministries of Christian compassion.

Now, keep in mind that there had been a small group of faithful warriors who had been praying for some time for God to send true revival to Asbury. But, it was not until the dimension of spiritual restoration of students and reconciliation among students was added that God answered the prayers of His faithful children. Philpot emphatically states that the primary evidence of revival was confession of sin and reconciliation of relationships.

Prayer is the first step we must take in order to see the resurrected power of Jesus in our lives and in our churches. It is of great necessity, however, that it be a prayer of reconciliation. A prayer that is punctuated by confession of sin, asking for forgiveness, and seeking more of the thrilling presence of the Father than is ordinarily experienced in the so-called "nominal" Christian life.

Does your church need to pray this kind of prayer? Do you? Are you willing to do it? There are doubtless individuals in your congregation and mine with whom you and I need to address estrangement because of something that has come between us – real or imagined! There are some deacons, possibly some elders, Sunday school or Bible teachers, church officers, or members who need to apologize for a wrong comment or a hurtful attitude toward another brother or sister.

There could even be someone who always seems negative about most everything going on in the church, with a critical spirit toward the pastor, a staff member, or some other leader, that is causing division in the fellowship, who needs to make things right. There may be husbands and wives who have allowed a root of bitterness to sink deep into their relationship that is causing not only great damage to their marriage and to their children, but is creating division among friends who are quick to take sides, who need to come back home to love, through forgiveness and grace. Probably, more than a few of us need to confess sin because of a flirtation with Satan, the world, and the flesh.

Let us not forget that the sweet communion of love and the fellowship of His Holy Spirit cannot flow freely in and through our lives and congregations when there are these spiritual hindrances blocking the channels through which flow the Father's grace, power, and blessings to you and me! Jesus Christ simply refuses to be entertained in the hearts and lives of those of us who at the same time entertain sin, selfishness, pride, hard feelings, hostility, anger, and estrangement. These things must be removed so that the resurrected, life-giving Christ can move in.

I have come to believe increasingly that personal and unashamed confession of sin, repentance, the asking for and the giving of forgiveness, may well be the highest form of cross-bearing a Christ-follower can embrace in our Western society where execution for faith in Christ is not yet a threat. It is the willingness to swallow pride, be honest with one's self and be transparent to the Lord and to other persons that allows the process of crucifixion to begin to happen in one's life.

It is putting self to death, or perhaps more aptly stated, it is asking the Lord to put one's self to death as he or she becomes willing to pay the price for Him to do so. As we proceed in our walk with Christ, let us be aware that walking the way of the cross is the shortest route a disciple can take into the arena of his Lord's resurrected life and power! Those of us who dare die daily in walking this way will find the Father dressing us up, as He promised, for the most wonderful occasions and victorious encounters this journey has to offer. I pray that you and I will not miss out on them!

It is an Expectant Prayer

The Apostles were told to stay in Jerusalem until they were clothed for the journey with the promise of the Father. It was something of an open-ended kind of promise in that they were not given any time or specific date that this special event would take place. In spite of this, they went into the Upper Room and there gave themselves constantly to prayer. They stayed with this prayer until the Father fulfilled His promise. Why such commitment? After God raised Jesus from the dead the complexion of their faith changed radically and the measure of their faith had increased exponentially. They had come to believe that God would be true to His Word. So they waited – in prayer! But it was now a different kind of faith than they had known before. It was a belief filled with excited expectancy.

Excited expectancy is a key and necessary component to embrace the resurrected Christ in our lives. In our doing business with God, we usually receive what we expect! Who could ever forget the slogan of the early English missionary, William Carey. He lived and labored by the dictum: "Expect great things from God, attempt great things for God!" He did both and the so-called modern mission movement was swept into being.

What do you expect God to do daily in your life? Do you expect Him to be faithful to His promise of dressing you up in new spiritual clothes, suitable for the task, if you ask? Do you expect He will "direct your path" and lead you, through prayer, to one person He has prepared for you to invite to *come and see, Jesus Christ is alive!*? Do you likewise expect God to do miraculous things in your church as, corporately, you walk together the way of the cross? Do you expect God to do remarkable, unbelievable things in your community, and beyond, as your church joins together with other Christian congregations to reach this world for Jesus Christ?

Expectancy is bound up in the phenomenon of faith. Might we not define expectancy as the "faith-life lived on tiptoe?" The writer of Hebrews captured this unique aspect of faith when, for example, reflecting on the life of Moses and the sacrifices he made for the coming Messiah, he reported that the great deliverer of Israel "Regarded disgrace for the sake of Christ as of greater value than the treasures of Egypt, because he was looking ahead to his reward." (11:26).

Here is that principle again: embrace the cross for the sake of the Lord and His purposes and expect God to do something wonderfully new up ahead!

We will deal with other important aspects of faith in greater detail later. But, it cannot be overstated that the aspect of faith we call expectancy is a significant, necessary part of the prayer that results in God decking us out in suitable attire for the exciting journey to an empty tomb, and beyond, to a living, risen Savior!

It was my honor and blessed privilege to serve as pastor of the Buck Run Baptist Church on two occasions, totaling over 21 years. Buck Run is located on the Georgetown Road outside of Frankfort, Kentucky, in a historic little village called Forks of Elkhorn. Over the years I watched with great delight a congregation that knew what it was to deny self and make unbelievable sacrifices for our Lord and His Church. What a privilege it was to share their journey with them and to witness the Lord always following their periods of cross-bearing with His thrilling victories.

It seemed on this one particular occasion, however, that He had forgotten His congregation of believers. It was 1997, following seven years of unimaginable congregational growth, that a devastating flood inundated the community, bringing together the North Fork of the picturesque Elkhorn Creek with the South Fork, turning these creeks into one powerful river that looked to the residents like the mighty Mississippi! Buck Run Church, which had buildings built on the banks of both creeks, separated by U.S. Highway 460, had waters flowing through them that were clocked at 60 miles an hour, demolishing walls, tossing pews around like matchsticks, leaving the old church building looking like a war zone. And with approximately $1.25 million uninsured damages!

The members of the congregation labored to clean up the buildings, including the floors that had mud on them in places three to four inches thick. It took the better part of six months for the people to get things back as they had been before the flood. It was a demoralizing time, made worse by the fact that not one church in the city or county extended a brotherly hand to help, except a tiny little Baptist church in the county that took up a love offering of around $112 and gave it to the devastated congregation. What a beautiful act of love and sacrifice this handful of people made!

The church found itself at a crossroad. What direction would the members go? Would they stay in the Forks and risk another flood – which all agreed the church might not survive emotionally as well as physically? Or would they make plans to relocate?

The congregation chose to pursue the path of relocation. Actually, this had been under consideration for a couple of years because the church buildings were at maximum capacity and parking was so critical that for several Sundays following the opening of the new sanctuary across the road from the old historic one, cars were turned away. Not conditions conducive to continued growth.

But, where would they go? The congregation took the step to appoint two laymen, Buddy Costigan and Lester Smoot, along with the pastor, as a committee, giving them the authority to find suitable land with enough acreage for growth for years to come.They were also empowered to work out financing from a lending agency and come back to the church with a package deal.

There was only one hitch to the deal. There appeared to be no available land in a prominent location within or outside the city limits that fit the church's specifications. Things rocked on for almost three years and no breakthrough whatever. The committee's update at every monthly business meeting was the same: "No report!" The people of faith over time became leg weary and, by now, were attempting to negotiate the journey flat-footed.

Then it happened. In April of 2000 Bruce Wilkinson published a book that shot up to the number one bestseller on the *New York Times* bestselling book list. By December, it was marketed as an ideal Christmas gift by practically every bookseller in the country.

A friend in the Buck Run congregation gave me a copy that I devoured one night during the holidays. *The Prayer of Jabez* was a little book promoting the potential power of a brief, largely unknown scripture prayer, by a biblical character most Christians had never heard of.

Today, of course, the Prayer of Jabez, found in I Chronicles 4:9-10, is a prayer that is rather well known by churchmen all across America. Indeed, all over the world! The words of this remarkable little prayer, as recorded in the NIV translation are as follows: "Jabez was more honorable than his brothers. His mother had named him Jabez, saying 'I gave birth to him in pain.' Jabez cried out to the God of Israel, 'Oh, that you would bless me and enlarge my territory! Let your hand be with me, and keep me from harm so that I will be free from pain.'"

Upon reading it I was immediately overwhelmed by the possibilities of this prayer for our church's situation. The next Sunday, the first Sunday in January, 2001, I felt led by the Holy Spirit to preach on this text and challenge the congregation to memorize it and join me in praying it three times a day throughout the month. I also announced that we would pray the prayer together in every service of public worship on Sundays and during the week.

Know what happened? The excitement came back into the lives of those who had become lethargic and despondent about where we were as a congregation and where we were going. The people began to walk on tiptoe again, expecting God to be God and to answer the cries of His people. And He did!

In the second week of our prayer commitment the announcement came. The Father had dropped 97 prime acres on a prominent thoroughfare from Frankfort to Lexington in the church's lap. At an unbelievably reasonable price. Can you imagine the incredible wonder and joy that clothed that congregation for some time to come? As they engaged an architect, finalized drawings, and negotiated a successful fund-raising effort to kick-off plans to begin to move their church campus for the glory of God?

Are you and your church ready to take the step in the thrilling journey to that first way-station called significant prayer? It's there that you'll meet and get intimately acquainted with your Guide, hear His instructions for the trip, and be fitted by Him with traveling clothes that will amaze a watching world.

Am I suggesting that you and your church pray the prayer of Jabez three times a day for a month? Of course not! I'm simply suggesting that you listen to the voice of the Father concerning your life, being obedient to his will whatever that may be for you in your unique situation, while standing on tiptoe in exciting expectancy of what He is going to do!

But there's something else. Your Guide will encourage you to involve yourself in fasting over those forty days. He knows that this discipline can make your time with Him even sweeter and your walk with Him ever more powerful!

Fasting: Taking off a Little Here and There so That God's Clothing Might Fit Us Better!

> "And when you pray . . . and when you fast."
> Matthew 5:16

While for some fasting stands by itself as a practice, I have concluded that it is most effective in the life of a Christian when seen as a co-laborer together with prayer. It is a discipline called upon during special times to strengthen and reinforce prayer, when exceptional spiritual purposes and goals are embraced by the Christian and his church. It is, again, the willingness of the followers of Christ to "Deny self, and take up a cross daily" so that the presence of the living, risen Christ, sought in prayer, may be more surely experienced by the believer and more powerfully actualized in the church.

Have you and your church discovered how effectively fasting augments prayer and enables it to be an incredible conduit for the Spirit of God to be poured out in your life and your congregation? If engaged for the right reasons, with seriousness of intent and faithful observance, fasting as a significant partner of prayer can turn an ordinary, perfunctory life and church into an extraordinarily explosive spiritual venture for our Lord. Fasting, along with prayer, can infuse an aura of such spiritual magnetism that persons will literally be drawn to the reality that, in you and in your congregation, Jesus Christ is indeed alive.

Might you be willing to allow fasting to be the traveling companion of your prayer commitment? What may we know about fasting? Let's look at several things.

It is Biblically Based

Jesus fasted. When, following his baptism, he was led into the wilderness to be tested by the devil, we are told that he fasted for forty days and nights (Matthew 4:1-2).

Jesus assumed his disciples would fast. Our Lord, in the Sermon on the Mount, addressed three prominent "acts of righteousness" his disciples would surely participate in during their journey of discipleship, stressing the need to guard against wrong motives that can render these religious exercises of absolutely no value to God or to others.

His teachings began with these introductory phrases, "And when you give to the needy;" "And when you pray;" "And when you fast" (Matthew 6:1-18). The implication is clear. He expected them to give to the needy. And to pray. And to fast.

Moreover, in answering his critics who took pot shots at Him for not stressing fasting to his disciples, Jesus suggested that so long as He was with them they had no reason to fast. Nevertheless, He insisted that when He was gone they would need to fast (Luke 5:33-34).

It was practiced in the early church. When important decisions were being made by the apostles or by the congregations in New Testament times, fasting became a prominent part of their prayer life. For example, it was practiced when ministers were being installed for positions in churches or missionaries sent out as heralds of the gospel (Acts 13:2; 14:23).

Its Value is Noteworthy for You and Me

Fasting is a discipline that has shown through the years to be of exceptional value to Christians. Among many noteworthy benefits, the following that speak to this outreach venture continue to be named by persons who have found liberating joy in this practice.

Fasting enables one to get more completely into the presence of God for significant prayer. The gate is narrow that we must enter to get into the eternal life and Presence of God (Matthew 7:13). Cutting away the fat of the flesh (worldly pleasures and sins of the spirit) while putting away the excess baggage of this life and its cares, enables one to get through that narrow gate into the fullness of the Lord's presence. Occasionally, we hear people say, "I just can't seem to get in touch with God in my prayers." The problem may be that they are carrying too much junk around with them and simply can't squeeze everything they wish to hold on to through the gate!

Fasting enables a person to cooperate with God in putting to death the desires that have taken control in his or her life. Is giving up sweets, tobacco, alcohol, for example, over a forty-day period of real value? Won't a guy or gal come right back to that desire or habit after the fast is over? Not necessarily. Especially if one combines self-denial with significant prayer during this time – and after! Those who take it seriously usually find that, when the process is completed, God's amazing grace and tremendous power – the power that raised Jesus from the dead – will have done a miraculous work in their life.

Consider this personal testimony. I have always been a sports enthusiast. I came into the world that way. played every sport that my little hometown school offered. Like many fellows of my generation, I could tell you the names of every major league baseball player, who he played for, what his batting average was, and what it had been! Likewise, I could tell you the roster of almost every college basketball team of note, scoring average of the players, etc. Football was and is my real love, however. I was – and still am to a degree – conversant with

77

particulars concerning teams and players from the Southeastern Conference, especially those on my favorite team. (Hint, my teams colors are crimson and white.)

My favorite football team is my hobby. I own no guns for hunting, no boats and motors, rods and reels for fishing, and no golf clubs for the links. (The last time I tried my hand in golf, the game literally teed me off!). But, until recent years, I attended as many football games as I could and still watch every game my favorite team plays on TV. Since acquiring a computer and getting on the Internet, I have subscribed to five services that bring me sports news around the clock (game analyses, recruiting, the whole nine yards). Of course, each of these I have selected focus most of their reporting on my favorite team. While hanging out with these guys about 1½ hours each evening before bed, I faced up to the fact that I might be hooked on all this stuff. So for the forty days leading to Easter 2010, I made a commitment to fast by not turning to any of my sports services on the Internet and to use this additional time to get even more seriously in the presence of my Lord in prayer!

An interesting thing happened. On the Monday following Easter Sunday, I went to my computer to check on my championship team. I discovered something amazing. All the spectacular news I wanted to catch up on had no more allure for me. It was gone, and, it is to this day! Yes, I flip to it occasionally and spend a few minutes scanning the headlines. Nothing more.

What happened? The spirit of the triumphant Christ powerfully put to death in my life what I willingly denied myself for His glory. What a Savior! Did you catch it again? An example of the cross and resurrection motif that fills the glorious story of God's salvation, found in His Holy Word?

Are there some things in your life that need to be put to death by the Spirit? Add fasting to your regimen of prayer. It will bring much excitement and a renewed sense of purpose to your prayer life if you replace the thing that is claiming control of your life with significant time with your Savior. If, with Him, you walk the faith-walk on tiptoe, victory will be yours!

Closely akin to the above, fasting enables one to more clearly hear the voice of the Father. It is during times of decision-making as well as during significant moments in the journey when an appropriate word from our Guide is desperately needed. As has been noted above, our Lord prayed and fasted when He selected the twelve to be apostles from a group of at least 72 disciples. He wanted the Father's guidance in such a crucial decision. The apostles and teachers in the early Church, when making important decisions, listened for the voice of the Lord.

When you and I fast and intentionally shut out certain voices and sounds from the world that clamor uniquely for our undivided attention, the Father's precious voice is heard with greater clarity! Might not this be the context our Lord had in mind for His disciples when He reassured them that they need not be concerned when pressed for an answer or words of reply in times of crisis? That the Holy Spirit would provide words to be fitly spoken?

Indeed, it is perhaps in this context that we at times may understand those instantaneous Spirit-promptings, I call them missional messages, that totally amaze us and fill others, inside and outside the church, with wonder and awe at the incredible ways of our God.

It happened just three weeks ago as I was writing this material. It was Wednesday, April 14, 2010, three days following a glorious Easter Sunday in Central Church. On this Wednesday night, our small discipleship groups were continuing to explore Max Lucado's marvelous ten-week Bible study, *Experiencing the Heart of Jesus.*

There were numerous groups meeting throughout the church. Our pastor, Rob, was leading a large group of perhaps 100 persons, mostly senior adults, in the Manna Hall. This particular night's study was on "Experiencing the Power of Jesus."

Rob brought this study session to a close by reminding the group that there was great power to be found in prayer. Indeed, as an example, he suggested that if they asked the Lord in faith, He could cause someone who needed Jesus, driving past the church at that time, to stop and be drawn inside the building to discover His salvation. Rob completed the session in prayer, prompted by the Spirit to ask God to do just that.

Know what? Before many of the crowd had dispersed, a crowd that had increased in number as the other groups disbanded, an Alabama State Security Officer walked in the front door. Said he was just passing by and felt the urge to stop and come in. He didn't understand why. Rob shared with him why, and after some time, led him to faith in Jesus, as Lord and Savior!

Obviously, Rob doesn't feel led everyday to take such a daring step in prayer, though he is without question a prayer warrior with whom God speaks on a daily basis. Could his intense forty-day fast, just concluded, have had something to do with his having heard the prompting voice of the Holy Spirit with so much greater clarity than at other times in his walk with the Lord?

What has been your experience in the employment of the practice of fasting as a necessary traveling companion to significant prayer? I encourage you to choose and use faithfully a fast from the following that will enable you to embrace a cross for Jesus sake and, ultimately, to more fully experience the power of His resurrection.

Types of Fasting Often Employed

There are numerous fasts and combinations of fasts employed at times by followers of Christ who desire to enhance their experience of His passion through sacrifice and His powerful Presence in prayer. Before you should ask someone to *come and see, Jesus Christ is alive!* perhaps you should select one of the fasts below, based on the need of each life, as directed by the Holy Spirit.

Food Fasts

The normal fast. Total abstinence from food while subsisting on water or fruit juices (Luke 4:2). Often done as a Sabbath fast (from sundown on Friday to sundown on Saturday); sometimes done over a weekend.

The partial fast. Also called the Daniel Fast (Daniel 1:1-21; 10:3), it is a vegetarian diet. No meat at all. Water and fruit juices are the acceptable drinks. Fruits may also be eaten.

The absolute fast. Abstinence from both food and water, usually one day in duration, no more than three days (Acts 9:9, Ezra 10:6, Esther 4:16). Imperative to have a physician's approval.

Pleasure Fasts

Addictive fasts. Abstinence from anything one may be addicted to, such as alcohol, drugs, caffeine (coffee, tea, or colas), tobacco, sweets, gambling, sex, etc., to give the control of the body back over to God.

Entertainment or recreational fasts. This involves denying self of those otherwise necessary outlets of relaxation and exercise that can get out of hand and claim an inordinate amount of one's daily or weekly schedule and crowd out time for spiritual and relational development. This fast can be absolute for a designated period (such as cutting out television, golf, etc. altogether) or partial (such as, for example, denying self of television during the evening) to allow for more time to be spent with the Lord and His Word, so as to hear his voice as He seeks to speak to us and guide us.

Once you have selected your fast and chosen your time and place to meet the Lord each day you have taken a magnificent step in seeking the face of God so that others might experience the reality of the risen Christ in and through your life.

Come and see, Jesus Christ is alive!

Chapter Four

Seek Him Out in Scripture

*"Ask, and it will be given to you; seek, and you will find; knock,
and it will be opened to you." Matthew 7:7*

God may not only be found in prayer, He may be found and
sought out in Scripture, His written Word. Martin Luther said
that the Bible cradles the Christ. The Old Testament points
toward the Christ event.The New Testament looks back on that
pivotal moment in human history when God revealed Himself
perfectly to humankind. When true faith is enjoined in the
engagement of Scripture, whether read or heard, Christ leaps
out of its pages with words that embrace us in grace,
forgiveness, and love. He then sends His Spirit to make
whatever changes are needed in our lives to enable us to grow
in Christ-likeness, as revealed in Scripture, and to indulge the
tasks God has sent us here to perform.

For this reason we in the church have always been encouraged
to spend quality time each day in God's Word. It is the reason
we in leadership positions understand how vitally important it
is for us to take time for this daily discipline as well. When we
believingly and obediently interact with His Holy Book, He
makes Himself known to us. He speaks to bless us with words
of comfort and encouragement, warning and conviction, grace
and forgiveness, peace and joy, as well as instruction and
guidance for the daily journey. Sometimes, even for the
unfolding of the future. Do you know the joy of having this
daily conversation with the living God of this universe?

But more than the messages we get from Him regularly, that you and I receive from our traditional daily Bible reading, I have discovered that at significant junctures of our journey with Christ, at crucial crossroads of decision-making, when we implore Him to specifically reveal Himself and His will to us in His Book, He does so. Clearly! Unmistakably! Perhaps you have discovered this as well. You then are aware that such timely, unique messages from the Father are occasioned by more than our routine readings of Scripture. They come rather as a result of earnest, diligent and, at times, prolonged and anguished prayer, seeking Him out in His Word, attended by radical, some would even say, foolish faith and obedience.

So it was in my first encounter with this remarkable experience. It was out of a sense of utter desperation that I sought Him out on that morning in mid-January of 1981. I had been given a deadline. My need of an answer had become urgent. What should I do?

I was pastor of the First Baptist Church of Monroeville, Alabama at the time. I had been there for 6½ wonderful years. I had come to Monroeville when I was 36 years old, the same age as my predecessor, the venerable Dr. L. Reid Polk, when he began his ministry in that lovely Southern town made famous by Harper Lee and Truman Capote. Many in the congregation, and this preacher as well, thought that I, like Dr. Polk, would be there the remainder of my ministry. When I made the decision to leave the Buck Run congregation in Frankfort this first time and come to Monroeville, I said as much.

At the same time, I shared with family and a few friends that the only positions I would be tempted to leave Monroeville for, in the unlikely event they should open up to me, would be the pastorate of the First Baptist Church of Frankfort, Kentucky, at that time a strong congregation in the heart of the capital city, or a position at Samford University in Birmingham. Nevertheless, the call to FBC Monroeville was an unbelievable one. I had a number of friends there. Guys I had grown up doing Boy Scouts together with in the Gulf Coast Council. Several fraternity brothers from my University of Alabama days. Some relatives. Indeed, Gail and I both had spent the first three years of childhood just north of there, in separate communities in Monroe County. It was almost like going home.

Joining the congregation in Monroeville was a wedding made in heaven. My life with that congregation was marked by an unusual relationship of deep love and camaraderie. Indeed, one of special felt kinship and heritage. More than this, we shared the same goal in the desire to please God with nothing less than excellence in all things. As the years rolled by, and the bonds that united us grew even stronger, to entertain any thought of leaving such an idyllic situation seemed equally as unthinkable as, well, the killing of a mockingbird!

But would you believe that the only two opportunities that I had ever thought I might consider leaving Monroeville for came calling? However, one day out of the blue I received a call from a member of the pastor search committee from FBC Frankfort. His opening sentence was in the form of a question: "Bob, how would you like to move back to Frankfort?"

Oh, my! What a great opportunity. As I stated earlier, First Baptist at this time was a strong congregation, with magnificent resources – human and financial. I fancied all that could be done there in missions and ministries. Tempting? No longer. We were extremely happy in Monroeville. Besides, we had just begun a building program at FBC Monroeville and, in my heart of hearts I didn't see how ethically I could consider a move.

It happened again. A phone call came, this time from Dr. W.T. "Dub" Edwards, in the Philosophy and Religion Department at Samford University. Dub was to the point. Said that they were looking to create a Chair of Pastoral Theology in his department and that one of Samford's benefactors said he would fund the chair, with one provision: that I would occupy that chair!

Think I didn't love hearing the things Dub was saying? Can switching to Geico save you up to 15% or more on your car insurance? (Or, *cost* you up to 15% or more?) Dub said, "Bobby, we have candidates that meet the academic criteria that have been established for the position, but you are the only one we know and feel comfortable with who knows how to "do it" in the local church. "Besides," he reiterated, "our donor said he would not fund the chair unless you take the position!"

Talk about hyper-inflation. It came to a head quickly. Mine. Obviously, it didn't help the problem I have struggled with through the years, the one that Lord has had to deal with, at times harshly, in attempting to get me to a place where He could use me more effectively for His glory. The problem of pride. Do you know anything about this problem?

I simply felt led to decline the once-in-a-lifetime opportunity that had opened at Samford for several reasons. At the top of the list was this simple fact: I didn't want to leave Monroeville. Ever. But there came a time that down deep in my heart I knew

I must. I had allowed my spiritual life to become victimized by the seductiveness of a life and lifestyle I enjoyed too much, not only in the church but also in that lovely community.I had faced up to the seriousness of my spiritual condition several weeks before being confronted by the *deadline*. The moment of truth came one night after I had come home extremely late, totally exhausted, with serious questions about the authenticity of my faith relationship with Jesus Christ. The encounter I had with Him later that night, and on subsequent nights and days, indeed over the years, and the commitment I chose to make was, and continues to be, the most glorious, life-changing happening that could ever be imagined. I pray that you have had your own authenticating experience. I was 43 years of age and had not!

But, early on that night, I came to the conclusion that I was spiritually dead. Or nearly so. I had grown up in a devoted Christian home. And in the most loving, nurturing church in the world, the First Baptist Church of Flomaton, Alabama. I had accepted Christ as my Savior and was baptized at age nine one cold November day in the Escambia Creek that runs through my hometown of Flomaton. I had surrendered to the gospel Ministry while at the University of Alabama and had graduated from Samford University (then Howard College), an excellent Baptist school in Birmingham. I had received a couple of theological degrees, including the Ph.D., from Southern Baptist Seminary in Louisville, Kentucky. I was considered to be a highly "successful" pastor. I had seen God do some of the most remarkable things. But something was missing in the depths of my soul.

Here I was in Monroeville, pastor of a remarkable church, continuing to watch the Father do incredible things. The church was growing rapidly. Reaching out in mission work among the Appalachian people in eastern Kentucky, as well as to the Mexican people across the border from Brownsville, Texas. Besides that, we were reaching internationals whom God was sending our way. In 1975, we baptized persons representing five different nationalities.

One of the highlights of those years was seeing First Baptist touched over the plight of the Vietnamese boat people. Constant pictures in the media of these helpless folks fleeing the overrun of South Vietnam by the Communists, packed into undersized boats with persons frequently falling overboard to their death, moved the heart of this special congregation. FBC Monroeville voted to invite several of these families into our community with the promise of housing and a job for them through the U.S. State Department. What a joy it was that every adult among them – without any coercion save the love of Christ – in time, came to faith in the Lord Jesus.

More than this, I was privileged by the Father to see Him develop an exceptional cadre of young, strong leaders in the church. From their number came an outstanding "lay witness team" that God blessed in reaching people for Jesus throughout the southland. Thirty years later, I had a staff member from the Alabama Baptist State Board of Missions tell me that FBC Monroeville may have the largest number of strong, male leadership than any other Baptist church in the state!

But, here I was, empty. I know not if it were in the temple or in the celebration taking place all around it, but somewhere along the way I discovered, like Mary and Joseph, that I had lost Jesus!

The thing that had been eating away at the core of my being for some time was the realization that the dynamic, living presence of the resurrected Christ of Easter seemed nowhere to be found in my life. The extraordinary power of the Holy Spirit that the New Testament simply assumes is at work in and through the lives of those who sojourn on this side of the empty tomb, who follow Christ in faith and faithfulness, was missing in my life.

I was – and to a certain extent, I suppose I still am – a workaholic. The difference is, at that particular time in my ministry, I was working as hard as I possibly could to maintain an outward appearance of "success" in the eyes of those I desired to impress, rather than experience the joy of simply pleasing the Lord in the thrilling walk of trusting belief and obedience. And I was going full throttle on an empty tank. I was traveling recklessly at breakneck speed, going nowhere of everlasting significance, with an engine on the brink of shut-down. The looming results were predictable.

On this night, I cried out to God in brokenness and despair. I confessed to Him what He, of course, knew. That, there was a major disconnect between what I preached in the pulpit and what was true in my personal Christian walk. That, for example, while I spoke often of the victorious, miraculous, life of prayer I was praying far too little and witnessing even less of the supernatural activity of the Holy Spirit, about whom the Bible teaches works increasingly in both the believer and the church. I owned up to the reality that I didn't *really* know the Holy Spirit. At least, at this moment, He didn't seem real. How grateful I am that I began to get acquainted with Him intimately on that night. Thankfully, this experience has been ongoing and growing ever since. But, needless to say, I still have a long way to go!

I asked the Father to forgive me of my hypocrisy and of other damaging sins that were keeping Him at bay in my life! In the bankruptcy of soul, I confessed that I needed much more of Him! I pled with Him for the ever-present reality of the Lord to become resident in my life. If I were to remain in the ministry I knew I must have this certitude, this evidence of that which the Bible taught and I proclaimed. I knew also that any church I may serve in my ministry needed their pastor to model this certitude if this presence of the resurrected Jesus, in all His glory, were to become a reality in its body life. I was aware of that which the Pentecostal event in Acts 2 revealed: That the flow of the Holy Spirit into and, then, throughout the church always flows from the top down. It must first pass through the leadership. If the leadership blocks the flow of the Spirit with pride, unrepented sin, jealousy, broken relationships, or disobedience, God's presence will not be manifested in power in and through the congregation.

Earnestine Hardin, Christian bookseller in our town, had just that week given me a book. A little book. Only 151 pages in length. I picked it up on this night of despair. When I needed a word that would address the desperation of my soul, it was here in my hand. I devoured its content in a couple of hours. I was hungry! And it was easy reading. It became to me a special *missional message* from God, a concept we will explore more fully just up ahead.

Ray Ortlund, Sr. was the book's author. The book's title was the author's plea, *Lord, Make My Life a Miracle*. It was the outgrowth of an experience this beloved Presbyterian minister had while pastor of the Lake Avenue Congregational Church in Pasadena, California. He had come to the place in his ministry where he no longer desired to be simply an ordinary pastor, nor the pastor of an ordinary church. Ortlund made a commitment of total surrender to God, to practice His presence as a way of life and, like his Savior, to lose his life for others, both those in Christ's church and those without for whom Christ died. He announced his decision to the flock God had placed under his care at Lake Avenue and, surprisingly, approximately 600 persons made the commitment to follow their shepherd. It revolutionized Ortlund's life and ministry. And his pastorate became a slow-burning revival for many years.

The little book, again, was God's special missional message to me. It represented what my heart ached for. I got down on my knees next to my yellow recliner and cried out, "Lord, make my life a miracle!" I then added, "Father, I'll pay any price, bear whatever cost, if you will make my life a miracle!" Dear reader, never make that promise unless you are truly willing for God to take you up on such a commitment. He did me. But more on this later.

Immediately, but at the same time slowly, the Father began to give affirmation to the commitment I had made. For starters, I had one of the more pleasant night's sleep that evening I had had in years. I awoke the next morning to some of the most rhapsodic music I had ever heard, playing in the chambers of my soul. An experience that lasted for several days. I knew that God was up to something. just didn't yet know what.

Perhaps the most tell-tale sign that something new was taking place was the discovery of new spiritual eyes and ears my Lord began to give me to see His truth and hear His voice more clearly in Holy Scripture. As the deadline approached and I cried out again in desperation to God, His Spirit graced the request with an incredible, some might call it an unbelievable, reply from His Holy Word! But, first, back to the deadline itself.

As I began to sift through the ramifications of this new dimension that the Father was forming within me, I received a call from another extraordinarily wonderful congregation. It was the First Baptist Church of Brandon, Mississippi. I knew I had to consider it.

Brandon, like Monroeville, was a wide-awake town with a heavy dose of Old South charm. Brandon was different however, in that not only was the church almost twice the size of the Monroeville congregation, the town had begun to explode in growth. A historic town, it nevertheless was rapidly becoming a bedroom community of the capital city of Jackson. With good schools and lower property taxes, it had become an ideal place for young couples to plant their families as they started careers in the city. It also was becoming a haven for wholesale numbers of persons taking flight from a city with increasing crime and declining home values. It was a young preacher's dream. It seemed that just to open the doors of the church folks would flock in. At least for an initial look-see. What an opportunity!

After the formalities of fellowship times, Q & A sessions, and a trial sermon on the weekend of January 2 to 4, 1981, followed by a week dedicated to prayer, the Brandon congregation officially issued an invitation to me to come as pastor. When the chairman of the pastor search committee contacted me, he had hoped for an answer. The decision seemed to be a no-brainer. Right? Wrong! It may have been the most difficult decision ever I have had to make in my life. I simply didn't want to leave Monroeville. I told the committee that I needed a couple of days to pray about it, just to make certain it was God's will that I come to Brandon First. Gail and I did indeed pray, though she prayed for her husband during what she knew was a most stressful time for him.

Brandon didn't hear from me in a couple of days. After one week had elapsed the committee chair called. I couldn't give him an answer. I was in agony over the decision. Over a several week period I lost about 15 pounds struggling with God's will. Or was it my will? He called again. Again I couldn't give him an answer. Finally he set the *deadline*. He needed to have an answer by Friday of that week, January 23, so he could announce it to the church on Sunday.

It was a hectic week of prayer – and sleeplessness! In seeking an answer, I plunged into the stream of divine instruction found in the Bible. Ordinarily the Father honors such earnest diligence in negotiating His will through prayer and in seeking Him out in the Bible. It didn't appear to be working this time for me. I simply could not seem to get peace about going or staying. Although in my heart I knew I needed to leave my beloved Monroeville I kept saying, "But, Lord, does it have to be now?" At the same time, I desired to please my Heavenly Father more than anything else in the world. I truly wanted to know His will – and to do it!

Early on that Thursday morning I met with a group of pastor friends in our church gym for our weekly prayer and recreation time. On my way home for breakfast, I called out to the Father as never before: "Please, Lord, give me an answer! One that will be so clear that there can be no misunderstanding."

God immediately fired back through His Spirit, "I have an answer for you in my Book." He said. "When you get home I want you to open your Bible and you'll discover these words, *'Arise, let us go from here.'*" He added, "What do you think the odds are that you find these exact words just as I have said?" I replied, "Lord, it must be about a trillion to one!" He said, "I'm more than a trillion to one God!"

I hurried in the house upon arrival, picked up a Bible and raced into a quiet room. I opened it just as His Spirit had instructed. A sense of temporary relief filled my soul. The fourteenth chapter of John stared me squarely in the face.

"Great!" I shouted out loud, "I know that chapter by heart*: 'Let not your heart be troubled*, etc. etc. etc.' in this passage is the phrase God said I would find there. This means I'll not have to leave!"

The Father said, "Keep reading!" And, there it was! In the last sentence, of the very last verse in John 14, in the NASB: "Arise, let us go from here."

The dam broke and tears of joy began to flow. I became overwhelmed by a sense of His presence and leadership in my life. The regret of leaving the people I loved so dearly immediately dissipated. I knew God had spoken. And, how! I felt a peace at once. I became instantly excited about the great church He was leading me to. With an overwhelming sense of awe and tears of joy I greeted Gail with the news. She was grateful the decision-making struggle was finally over. Also there to rejoice with us was Larry Baldridge, my dear friend and missionary to the Appalachian people of Kentucky who, along with his family, was visiting us in Monroeville.

It was a thrilling moment. hrilling when I called the search committee in Brandon to give them God's answer. Not my answer. It was thrilling as Gail and I prepared to leave old friends and make new ones in what became one of the most loving, caring congregations I have known anything about! The First Baptist Church of Brandon, Mississippi.

It was even more thrilling as I contemplated over and again what the Father had done. He had heard the desperate cry of His struggling servant and had spoken definitively by His Spirit to give him unquestioned direction from His Book. Miraculous! Praise His name!

In saying this I must hasten to point out that the Father does not normally choose to speak to you and me in such a dramatic, unbelievable fashion. I'm certainly not one of those "simply-close-your-eyes-now-open-the-Bible-place-your-index-finger-on-a-random-verse-and-receive-God's-answer" kind of a guy. Not one who thinks we can obligate God to give us answers and guidelines by a flippant approach to ascertaining His will. I'm surely not one that disregards the desire of the Father for intimate heart to heart intercourses, interactions, and exchanges with His sons and daughters so as to make Himself fully known to them. Hearing His voice is a much more serious venture of faith and obedience in exploring the depths of His Word.

Nevertheless, it must also be said that any attempt to disavow the right of the Father of all creation to speak to His children from within or through His Word in any manner whatsoever, however unthinkable it may seem on occasions, serves only to tie the hands of His Christ who seeks to make the Father's will known to those of us who are indwelt by His Spirit.

The little song some of us sang as children in Sunday school said it very well. Its words and the truthfulness of them were embedded down deep in my soul very early, and have never left me:

> God can do anything, anything, anything,
> God can do anything but fail!

I catch myself singing or humming this little chorus many times when faced with a seemingly impossible task or situation which appears on the surface to be far too difficult to negotiate or understand. I have to remind myself from time to time that the Lord doesn't need me to help Him do whatever He cares to do, nor tell Him how He must do it.

Having said all this, there is one thing you and I can always be absolutely certain of. When we through significant faith – trusting belief and obedience – earnestly seek the Father and His will out in Scripture we will find Him. He will speak to us there. And, in some instances, His divine disclosure to us will knock our socks off!

As an example of yet another of the incredible ways God speaks to us, I wish to share with you the experience of a friend of mine who, because of hearing the Spirit's voice in and through Scripture, made the decision to seek the Father out for his life. It resulted amazingly in the total conversion of his soul.

David Ruth was chief investigator for the police department in Brandon when I came back in 2003 to lead a new church start that had formed out of the First Baptist Church. The Brandon Baptist Church was yet another blessed gift of God to my life. One day in mid-September 2006, David called and made an appointment with me. I had never met David but a mutual friend had recommended that he see me. He came to tell me that his marriage was at a place of breakup, that it had reached the point of no return. He wondered if I could do anything to help him.

I soon discovered that he did not know Jesus in a personal, intimate relationship of significant faith and love. I spent quite some time sharing with him the difference that Christ could and would make in his life and in his marriage, if both parties would truly desire it and would allow the Lord to put things back together, *His* way!

I walked David through the steps of commitment to Christ as the Spirit gave leadership. I felt as if he might be close to taking that final step, one in which he would take his hands off the controls of his life in the surrender of absolutely everything to the Lord, letting Him take complete charge of all he was and had. I didn't push. Never do. I just let the Spirit do all the convincing and pushing when such is needed.

David said that he was not ready for such a step. Nevertheless, I felt so positive that he was not far from the kingdom that I gave him a membership application card to take home with him. I suggested that at his leisure he might want to fill out the card and bring it back to me or to a church service and have it ready for that moment when the Lord and he would seal the deal. I invited David to church on the Sunday upcoming. He didn't make it. He came, however, the following Sunday, October 1, with card in his pocket, still not filled out.

October 1 is my precious wife's birthday. I felt led on that Sunday to preach one of her all-time favorite sermons that I from time to time deliver, "Come Before Winter." For those of you conversant with that provocative biblical entreaty, you will recall it to be found in Paul's second letter to Timothy, chapter four, verses 9-13, 16, 21a. The Apostle, now in old age, all alone in a Roman jail facing execution at any time, cries out to the only person he knows who truly loves him. He pleads with young Timothy, his son in the ministry, to "do all diligence" to come to him before winter. Paul knew that for many reasons winter would be too late for him.

There are times, crucial times, in your life and mine when we irresponsibly put important matters off, thinking we have plenty of time up ahead to take care of what needs to be done. How foolish this is. Refusing to embrace the pressing needs of today, especially commitments we need to make to the revealed will of God, is extremely dangerous. Winter comes and it is too late. If we are to do the magnificent thing, engage the great undertaking, we must do it before winter.Winter comes with its icy blasts and blows away all the lovely leaves of good intentions from the tree of golden opportunity. Can you not hear at this very moment Paul's plaintive, pathetic plea, "Come, come before winter?"

The poignancy of this scriptural text was first brought to my attention by the sermon Clarence McCartney made famous while pastor of the First Presbyterian Church in Pittsburgh, Pennsylvania, preached first by him on October 18, 1915, then each successive year until 1952 when he retired. I first heard the sermon preached in chapel by a Birmingham pastor, Dr. Edgar Arendall, Jr., while I was in college. Never one to preach someone else's sermon as my own, I nevertheless took the basic idea that actually jumps out from the text when one reads it and fashioned my own version as the Spirit of God led. That haunting plea by the Apostle Paul became the refrain that I, like so many preachers since McCartney have repeated over and over again, "Come Before Winter."

David Ruth was present in the service on October 1 and heard that message. He went back to his lonely house – his wife had already left – and stuck the application for membership card in the edge of the mirror in his bedroom. There it remained unattended for three years.

I left the pastorate of the Brandon Baptist Church to come to Central Baptist Church in Decatur to work with my son, Rob, November 1, 2007, a little over a year after I had had the joyful privilege of meeting David. It was then on December 6, 2009, two years after my departure from Brandon that the remarkable thing happened.

David woke up on that Sunday morning and as he approached the dresser in his bedroom he happened to glance at the membership application card residing in the corner of the mirror. A verse of Scripture that had found unconscious lodging down deep in his soul three years before began to cry out. It was 2 Timothy 4:21. He seemed to hear it as a voice calling out to him. Was it Paul's voice? No. It was the voice of the Lord Jesus who through His Spirit kept saying to David,

"Come before winter!" "Come before winter!" "Come before winter!"

He said to himself quite acceptingly, "I must go!" So he dressed, filled out his membership application card and showed up for church unannounced at Brandon Baptist on December 6, 2009. After Dr. Clarence Cooper had preached he issued an altar call. David Ruth stepped out from where he was sitting and walked down the aisle to an awaiting, loving pastor.

More than this, he walked away from a life of sin, lostness, and meaningless wandering into the embrace of a loving Savior, from whom he found plenteous forgiveness, amazing grace, and the beginning of a new, exciting journey through life. It was and is a journey of thrilling purpose and clearly marked direction in the following of Jesus as his newly-found Lord.

After David had indicated to the pastor the decision he was making, he was seated on the front row as the hymn of invitation continued to be sung. A friendly deacon came to greet David and told him that he had a membership application card to give him. David responded, "I already have one. Filled out." The deacon seemed taken back and asked, "Well, where did you get *that*?" "Brother Bob gave it to me" was the reply, which appeared momentarily to confuse the deacon even more.

Following the service David asked a mutual friend, Tom Kennedy, if he would call and tell me what he and God had done. My joy was inexpressible in the hearing. I called David to congratulate him on taking that final step of commitment, which became but the first step of a lifelong journey of radical faith and obedience to our Lord. He was baptized on December

20 to the delight of his family and many friends, especially his mother who had prayed for years for her son to come before winter.

It was again my joy to speak with David on the first anniversary of his becoming a new man in Christ. We talked for perhaps an hour on the phone as he shared with me the details of his remarkable story. He gave me permission to share the following with you:

"Brother Bob, no one knows how troubled I really was. And had been, for many years. You see, I didn't have a childhood. When I was 16 I was involved in a horrible accident. One Sunday morning as I was going after something for my dad, I topped a hill and ran into a car, killing the lady driver who had just backed out of her driveway. I was charged and convicted of manslaughter. I was tried as a juvenile and received two-year probation.

"It was awful. While I was in the hospital a preacher came to see me and told me if I had been in church that day the accident wouldn't have happened and the lady would still be alive. I went to church soon afterwards and at the end of the service, with everybody's head supposedly bowed and eyes closed, the preacher asked that those who would like to be prayed for to raise their hands. I raised mine. All of a sudden I felt the preacher, pulling me to the altar. I was humiliated. In school I lived with the kids calling me 'murderer.' I came to a place where I didn't care if I lived or died."

"I chose a career in law enforcement. I sought to be the best officer I could be. I gained the respect of the community, which meant a lot to me. But, inside I was troubled. As an investigator

I was most often a plain clothesman. Which meant I had to walk around in the world of drugs, child molestation, prostitution, and all kinds of sordidness. It was easy to become callous and hardened. Over time, profanity became a large part of my vocabulary with which I mostly expressed myself. I was lost. I didn't really know who I was. And, of course, my family life was in shambles.

"On December 6, 2009 I saw the card you had given me three years before, and heard the Voice. And I went. I surrendered my life to Christ completely. I became a changed man, immediately! Overnight I began to look at life differently. God put a big smile on my face. He liberated me from the stress I was under. I found myself caring more for others than I cared for myself. It was a miracle.

"One day my daughters said, 'Dad, you don't even use a single curse word anymore!' I wasn't yet aware of that change. I then noticed that I didn't even have to try to clean up my talk. God was doing it for me. When someone asks me to explain the changes they see in me I just say, 'I have walked with the worst. Now I am walking with the Best.'

David Ruth is an active member of the Brandon Baptist Church. The respect that he once elicited from the community as an honest professional pales in comparison to the respect he now has. The impact his life is making for the cause of Christ is immeasurable. Today he is chief investigator for the DA's office in Mississippi's 20th Judicial District where he works with an outstanding young Christian district attorney, Michael Guest, a beloved brother in the Lord in the Brandon Baptist Church. "Praise God from whom all blessings flow!"

The facts are indisputable. Jesus Christ is the Resurrected Son of God. He is very much alive for those who acknowledge Him as Lord over all things. For those who continue to give the controls of life over to Him and, in and through His Word, listen to His Voice as He leads and guides them, for those who continue to follow Him in faith and obedience.

Is He alive for you? Is His living presence a reality in your life? Is He speaking to you personally in and through His Word? David Ruth, as a respected professional in the community, outwardly gave the appearance that all was well in his soul. But, the interior of his life – mind, heart, and spirit – was troubled. There are many all around us who, if the truth were known, are in a similar, tragic state of existence. They need the liberating power of Christ desperately! hat's the reason they need to come and see. But what about you?

You wonder, "Can He bring peace to *my* troubled soul?

Can He change *my* life radically? Can He fill *my* life with joy and give *me* meaningful purpose for the journey?"

Why not come and see?

However, please understand that you must come *now*. Winter will be too late!

Chapter Five

Seek Him Out in Missional Messages

"The Spirit told Philip, 'Go to that chariot and stay near it.'"
Acts 8:29 (NIV)

God's message that directed Philip to the Ethiopian eunuch riding in the chariot is a reminder that there are times when the Father speaks to us apart from Scripture. Such messages, delivered to us by the Holy Spirit, I call *missional messages*.

While these missional messages take many forms, I have found that they have this in common: they always have to do with divine purpose. God's purpose in Jesus Christ and in His Body, the Church. Thus, God's purpose for your life and mine. They are missional in that they are promptings by the Spirit that enable us to fulfill each his or her own unique mission in the world, in little momentary assignments as well as in greater, longer-term tasks.

It is through faith-full obedience to these remarkable spiritual messages that you and I are enabled to plumb the depths of the reality of God in Christ and therein discover His will for our lives. As a result of our faithfulness in seeking Him out in His wonder-full messages to us the Father rewards us with the incredible privilege of seeing and experiencing His majestic glory, a supernatural blessing ordinarily withheld from those who fail to respond to His personal communiqués in faith, that is, in trusting belief and obedience.

Daily Missional Messages

You and I receive missional messages from the Lord each day. He speaks to us in the form of inner impulses to do a specific good thing. At times, even a heroic thing. He nudges us, for example, to say an appropriate word: one of encouragement, of comfort, of thanks, of forgiveness. The Spirit impresses us on occasions to reach out to someone in need - a person we know who is doubtless hurting, and desperate - with a phone call, a note or letter, a visit, with a loving heart reaching out with a helping hand, extending a gracious invitation to that person to come into our lives and fellowship. His prompting is like a blaring horn seeking to awaken us from our indifference, our apathy to matters of extreme urgency and, if the whole truth be known, each one fraught with life and death significance.

On September 23, 2000, six graduating classes of Flomaton High School, my alma mater, held a joint reunion. I was a member of the 1954 class and was honored to be selected as the inspirational, after-dinner speaker for the event. Before dinner, as we mixed and mingled for an hour or so with *hors d'oeuvres*, someone asked me, "Has Richard found you, yet? He's been looking for you." My question in response was, "Richard who?" "You remember," this friend said, "Richard Ramer!" "Why, of course!" How could I ever forget Richard Ramer? "Crazy Legs," we called him because of the unorthodox way he ran with the football. He took this designation as the compliment it was because we borrowed it from the nickname of a great football player of our day, Elroy "Crazy Legs" Hirsch who played for the Los Angeles Rams.

Richard had been something of an enigma to us at Flomaton. He blew into town just before football season our senior year, recruited by one of our team's boosters, with whom he lived for that brief time. He played with us for the 1953 season. When the final gun sounded on our last game of the year he vanished as suddenly as he had appeared. No one knew where he had gone. Nor how to get in touch with him. We knew nothing about his family. He never mentioned them.

We spotted each other, now fifty years later. We embraced – warmly. Before we parted, after he had told me his story, we embraced again - in tears. I was humbled by his story. More than this I was left overwhelmed by the power possibilities of missional messages, even those that on the surface appear to be small and insignificant. And I was left troubled.

I have pondered the ramifications of the matter many times since. I have wondered how many opportunities I have fumbled away across the years to make a difference in a life and, consequently, in this world because I did not heed an inner impulse the Holy Spirit issued to me to reach out to another in the name and Spirit of Jesus. I wondered how many times I must have closed a deaf ear to a *missional message* from God that could have made a difference in someone's life.

Richard began, "Bobby, I know I'm crashing the party here tonight because I didn't graduate at Flomaton. For that reason we're not staying for the festivities. Have plans in Mobile. I'm leaving before dinner, as soon as I accomplish what I came here to do. I have driven down from Birmingham to see you and say, 'thank you.'"

I retorted, "Crazy Legs, what for heaven's sake are you thanking me for?"

He continued, "I came to Flomaton those many years ago and didn't know a soul. But you reached out to me. You were kind. Sometimes you made a point to sit by me on the team bus to and from a game. ou included me. On occasions when you didn't have a date you invited me to go with you and your friends to the movies. You had me in your home for a meal. You invited me to go to church with you. I didn't make it but a couple of times, but I remembered."

"And then," Richard's voice trailed off, "Then one day after football practice you said, 'Crazy Legs, how 'bout going to the Sweet Shop with me and having a burger and a shake?'" He teared up a bit and said, "Bobby, I wondered then. Still do. Did you know? Did you know?"

"Did I know what, Richard?" I replied. He went on, "Did you know that I had not eaten in two days?" I choked as I muttered through tears, "No, Richard, I didn't know. But God did!"

"Bobby," Richard continued, "I wasn't brought up in church. Didn't know much of anything about the Lord. But I saw in you something that I needed. Something I wanted very much to have. After our last football game I left Flomaton and joined the Marines. While there I made friends with the chaplain. He told me about Jesus and, in time, I gave my heart and life to Him. And I want you to know that from that moment on Christ has been my everything."

All I could say was, "Praise the Lord, Richard!" "Well," he said, "that's not all. I took the GED exam and passed with such a high grade that I was given an academic scholarship to Birmingham Southern College – a free ride."   "That's wonderful, Richard!" I responded. "But," he said, "That's not all. I did so well in college that I was admitted into dental school at UAB." "Tremendous, Richard!" I exclaimed. "But that's not all," he said. "I married a wonderful girl and we've got a great family." "How thrilling, Richard!" "That's not all," he said, "We are active members of the Shades Mountain Independent Church." "Richard, how I thank God!" "But that's not all, Bobby," he volunteered. "I set up a dental practice in Alabaster and I've made good money. I invested wisely and God has blessed me financially beyond anything I could ever have dreamed." "Wow!" was my reply, my favorite word of exclamation. "But that's not all. Bobby," Richard said. "I just wanted you to know I'm supporting missionaries all over the world!" I answered with a shout of praise, "Glory be to the Father!"

We hugged and parted. I never saw Dr. Richard Ramer again. He went home to be with his Lord not long after that, following a heart attack. Nevertheless, I think of him often. Richard's wife, Margaret, shared with me recently some things that will forever live with me and serve to inspire me to be a better witness for Jesus Christ in my remaining days on earth. She said that, after Christ captivated Richard's life, he never met anyone – in the grocery store, at the gas pump, or wherever – with whom he failed to share what the Lord had done for him. She said, moreover, that he never parted from the company of anyone, friend or stranger, that he did not conclude the conversation with the warm, tender words, "I love you."

Now that I know "the rest of the story," each time I remember this special guy the Father allowed me to know for no more than four months of my journey here, I catch myself saying: "Great game, 'Crazy Legs!'" Whenever I do, I thank the Father that He spoke to me in simple ways and gave me the privilege of offering a few cheers from along the sideline for a fellow football player who, unknown to me for many years, became a tremendous teammate in the raging contest for the hearts and minds of individuals, young and old alike. One who discovered in Jesus what becoming a true winner is all about!

The Father sends Richards and Bobs and Beths and Monicas across your path and mine constantly. Seldom are we aware of the crucial significance of those moments when we rub shoulders with that other person – known or unknown to us. Less seldom, perhaps, do we consider how eternally important those impulses of the Spirit we receive within us really are? Prompting us at strategic moments to smile, laugh, and cry with the other. Prompting us to care, share, and include her or him in our lives. It is faith that causes us to believe that God does not speak idle or meaningless words to us in regards to others – even strangers – that moves us in obedience to what the needs of the moment or the situation dictate.

What a provocative, awesome, thrilling, but also frightening thought to consider that you and I will doubtless be chosen by the Father to write a few, or perhaps more than a few, telling lines in "the rest of the story" for some person very special to God. Someone who will, in turn, become special to many others down the corridors of time and who will help rewrite the developing history of the Church in America.

And impact the whole world for Christ's sake! Most of us will not learn "the rest of the story" for that person or for other persons we may have touched positively or negatively along the way until it is revealed in heaven. Regrettably for some of us it will be everlastingly too late!

The living Lord of the Church through His Spirit speaks to you and me daily, through *missional messages*, calling us to do His bidding. Listen to Him. Do you hear Him? Someone desperately needs you to hear Him right now and respond in trusting belief and obedience in her moment of need. Listen to Him in the morning as you bump into the shopping cart of that dear little man who looks so forlorn at Wal-Mart.

Listen to Him today at lunchtime as you encounter the waitress at Cracker Barrel who looks as if she is completely overburdened with life. Perhaps her husband has left her and she is working two jobs to eke out a mere existence for herself and her two kids. Listen to Him tomorrow in the classroom as you observe again, but now in a different light, that girl no one invites to the party or the dance, or that boy that always seems to walk the trail alone. Life is tough. Often grossly unfair. But God is good. And He seeks to speak to you and me and challenge us to reach out to persons He brings across our path and, in each instance, as William Blake suggests, "To build a heaven in hell's despair."

It is important that we are aware not only of receiving missional messages but usually at the same time of encountering what I call *contramissional messages.* The Adversary also speaks to us, you know.

To counter God's words to us and undermine His mission in our lives. "You can't do *that!*" "That's none of your business!" "Touch that and you'll likely get burned, badly!" He's right, of course. Dare to lose your life lovingly in another person's predicament may just get you nailed to a cross. It's happened before! But what marvelous rewards are waiting up ahead when we, like our Savior, choose to take the risk of love and give ourselves away unselfishly to others, for His sake and His purposes in the world.

Missional Messages Through Music

There are many other ways the Spirit speaks to us missionally at certain moments in time, to direct our paths so that we might fulfill our purpose in Christ Jesus. Sometimes the voice calls to us through the arts. Especially through music. Would you believe even through secular music? It was through a popular hit song that played for weeks on jukeboxes and over the radio that God's Spirit called me to my present international mission involvement. Each time this particular song was played an unusual thing happened. I burst into tears! I could not control it. I was only 12 years of age. Amazingly, it was not until I was 57 years old that God made plain what He was saying to me as a boy.

From the very first I had, as a lad, made myself available to God for whatever He might be saying to me in the song. I even opened myself for the possibility of a life given in foreign missions, but the Father didn't make His will clear at that time. He did so forty-five years later! The lyrics of the song that stirred me to the depths of my being were written by Joan Whitney and Alex Kramer, and made popular by Bing Crosby, the crooner himself. As I listened to the song, my heart longed to carry the Gospel to those "far away places with strange-soundin' names, far away over the sea, those faraway places with strange-soundin' names are callin', callin' me."

In 1994 I heard and answered the call of God into Romania and into cities, towns, and villages with strange-sounding names. Across these seventeen years of mission endeavor, God has called me into strange-named places not only in Romania but Moldova, Serbia, Austria, and Spain. Many other countries are beckoning.

Be on the alert for God to speak to you in the music you listen to over the next little while, sacred or secular. As you commit to reaching out to others, keep in mind that He may not call you to faraway places, that is, faraway over the seas. Your call may be to go across town - which to many of us is a faraway place – to that neighborhood where an enclave of immigrants are domiciled. You'll doubtless find a people there with strange-sounding names waiting, consciously or unconsciously, for you to open your heart – and your church – and invite them to come in!

Missional Messages Through Good Books and Literature

The Spirit also speaks to us in good books. I have shared with you the turning point in my ministry when, searching for something more in my relationship with God, I picked up the little book by Ray Ortlund, Sr. entitled, *Lord, Make My Life a Miracle.* Ortlund's prayer and plea became my own that night as I poured out my impoverished soul to the Lord and promised Him that, if He would make my life a miracle, I would pay whatever price was necessary. Immediately, as I earlier recounted, I began to see noticeable changes in spiritual perception, culminating with the incredible confirmation the Father gave to my call to Brandon First Baptist from within His written Word.

There was another book besides Ortlund's, however, that the Father used to speak to me, that made the beginning step of a more meaningful walk with Jesus Christ a great deal surer. It was Norman Vincent Peale's *The Positive Power of Jesus Christ*. I read it not long after arriving in Brandon. Even though I don't agree with all of Peale's theology, the Spirit's word that I heard clearly in Dr. Peale's personal story was a message I desperately needed to hear. What a life-changing blessing it turned out to be. What precipitated the gift of this impactful book?

I preached my first sermon as pastor of FBC Brandon on Sunday morning February 15, 1981. It was a thrilling moment for me. I thought to myself, "We're off to the races toward a great future together as pastor and people." On Thursday night of that week something happened that caused the wheels to come off my dreamland express, at least for a significant time.

At a big family fish fry and game night welcoming the new pastor and his wife, I was playing volleyball when it hit. Like a bolt out of the blue. My throat began to tighten, pain began to run down my left arm and my chest began to cave in. I knew what it was. Everyone else did. I hoped that I could make it to the hospital in time. So did my friend, Dan Martin, deacon at FBC who got me in his old pickup truck and noticed as he raced to Rankin General Hospital that his gas gauge was below empty!

We did make it! Thank God! Waiting for me at the hospital was Dr. Curtis Roberts. Somehow Hayes Graves, goodwill ambassador for the hospital and close friend of its medical staff, and FBC deacon, managed to call ahead and alert ER of my soon arrival. I passed out when I sat down on the hospital bed and didn't wake up for a long while. It was touch and go for several days.

The dear members of First Baptist held a continuous prayer vigil in the waiting room for their pastor, beseeching the Father to spare his life and permit him to serve the congregation. The Father heard those prayers. But the road back was long and arduous fraught with much despair and, at times, utter hopelessness. It was a dreadful experience waking up in ICU, flat on my back, totally helpless. "Dear Father, I don't understand. I thought we had so much going on between us." We did. I just didn't realize what it was. And why and how God would choose to work it out.

The testing that followed the stabilization of my condition wasn't all that encouraging. Dr. William Bennett, well-known cardiologist from Jackson who, as a favor to Dr. Roberts, came to Rankin General to attend me while I was there, gave the verdict. I had had a major thrombosis, leaving me with approximately one-third of my heart dead. Nothing could be done surgically. (Today that might not have been the case.) He said that I would be like a one-arm, one-leg man the rest of my life. Moreover, the tests revealed that I had a severe case of atherosclerosis that could not be reversed. He did say, however, that I could enjoy a reasonably good life expectancy with proper diet, exercise and medication. But he couldn't promise that I would be able to handle the demands of a large pastorate again.

I went home to my darling wife, Gail, and our new house on 120 Gilder Drive. For more than two months I struggled emotionally, spiritually as well as physically. Doing not much more than walking in the neighborhood. I continued to be perplexed. "Father, why? Here I am in the prime of my life and ministry and I am absolutely worthless. What can I, what must

I do to experience the miracle of your healing power and restoration?"

"A matter is established by the testimony of two or three witnesses," we are told in Scripture. The Father answered the gnawing question concerning His healing on that beautiful spring day in April when, first, He gave me a message through a dream He had given Gail that was, then, interpreted by a Scriptural message given to me by the Holy Spirit. More on this phenomenon later.

God's answer was confirmed in the book by Norman Peale. My niece, Letha Stuckey of Montgomery, went to a local Christian book store and, after some time looking for just the right book that might be helpful for me at this time, put her hand on Peale's book and felt "this is the one."

Other than his classic work, *The Power of Positive Thinking* which I had read in college, I had not indulged much in Peale's popular offerings. I suppose I was dissuaded because, upon entering the ministry and following, I had often been told that his writings were shallow and the messages he preached contained little if any gospel.

All I can tell you is that God spoke powerfully to me through this book. Chapter two was all I needed to hear His message loud and clear. Dr. Peale tells about coming as a young pastor to the historic Marble Collegiate Church in New York City in the midst of the Great Depression and preaching to empty pews. He tells of doing everything he had been taught to do in the seminary to make a congregation come alive and grow. It simply didn't work. He rose early and retired late each day, working himself into a frenzy while putting himself on a collision course with a physical and emotional breakdown.

Marble Collegiate gave Peale a summer sabbatical. He and his wife, Ruth, went to England for much-needed R & R. The problem was, Norman couldn't rest or relax. He kept struggling with thoughts that he was a failure. One day they were seated on a park bench when Ruth said to her distraught husband: "Norman, you are my husband, but you are also my pastor. I sit in church and listen to you preach the gospel of Christ with love and enthusiasm. But to hear you talk now, I wonder if you actually have any faith at all. God never promised that you could have it easy, and it is out of struggle that victory comes."

She continued to talk plainly to her life's partner: "What you need to do is to surrender your church, your problems, your entire self to Christ. As you do this, I promise you will receive peace, joy, new energy, and a quality of enthusiasm that will never run down."

Dr. Peale followed his wife's counsel. He prayed: "Dear Lord Jesus, I cannot handle my life. I need help. I need you. I hereby with all my heart surrender my mind, my soul, my life to You. Use me as you will. Fill me with your Holy Spirit."

Then it happened. A peace the preacher never thought possible surged through his body and with it, a burst of joy – like light and the glory of God. Dr. Peale said that in that experience every dark and gloomy part of his soul was swept away as if with a huge broom.

He had time left on his summer vacation but when he arose he was so filled with new vision, enthusiasm, and power that he jumped up from the park bench ready to go home and back to work for the Lord Jesus in the New York church the Father had placed him over to pastor.

When he got back home the Holy Spirit immediately began to do the work of drawing people to Marble Collegiate and Jesus did His promised work of building His church. The growth was phenomenal. Norman Peale was always quick to disavow any part that he might have had in the incredible burgeoning of that congregation and its ministries among the people of New York City. His testimony never wavered. He said that the reason unbelievable things began to happen was because John 12:32 (KJV) became the Scripture for his congregation, "I, if I be lifted up from the earth, will draw all men unto me."

As I read this remarkable story of that event that changed Norman Vincent Peale's life and ministry, I heard the voice of God speak with extreme clarity: "This is what you need. What you need to do to experience my liberating, miraculous power in your life."

I knelt, again by the yellow recliner in our den, and put the finishing touch on a commitment I had made several months prior, before I left Monroeville to come to Brandon. Prompted by the dream Gail had a few nights before, and now confirmed by this timely story in this most provocative book, I placed all that I was and had wholly on the altar, repenting of sin and asking the Father for a fresh filling of His Holy Spirit. At once, as if warm oil were being poured from the top of my head to the bottom of my feet, the Father obliged with the most thrilling sense of cleansing, purging, and fulfillment I had ever encountered. I was immediately flooded with energy, filled with hope and faith, and anticipation.

I jumped to my feet and told Gail what had happened. She was elated. I then picked up the phone and called my secretary at the church and told her to call Dr. Earl Kelley, Executive-Secretary of the Mississippi Baptist Convention Board, who was filling the pulpit in my absence, and tell him that I would be preaching Sunday, just three days away!

Getting ready for that message was one of the great thrills in sermon preparation I had experienced to that point in my ministry. The Holy Spirit took control, leading me to the Church's Pentecostal Event as recorded in Acts 2. The sermon He gave me for the day was, "The Power That Equips Us for Service."

At last, the Lord enabled me to hit the ground running. Incredible healing had taken place: emotional, attitudinal, and spiritual. But not physical. The heart muscle was still impaired and my body continued to feel weak and incomplete. Nevertheless, the energizing power of God's Spirit kept me revved up and hitting on all cylinders most of the time. Like the Apostle Paul I prayed and asked God to remove my thorn in the flesh. The Lord answered me, as He did the man from Tarsus, in 2 Corinthians 12:9: "My grace is sufficient for you. For my strength is made perfect in weakness."

Ever since the experience of His filling, as my body has encountered a myriad illnesses and has grown even weaker in many respects, I have seen God do the most remarkable, miraculous things. Some of the miracles have come in the form of, and as a result of, astounding *missional messages* the Spirit has given me. At times, through good books and great literature.

Missional Messages and Vocational Calling

In most instances a person's vocational calling is initiated or confirmed through a missional message voiced in the depths of his soul. The Spirit at times issues His call through individuals. These messages may be borne in the form of an expressed recognition of that person's unusual giftedness in an area of his or her life.

Those of us who have been called to preach or to serve in some other vocational ministry in the church, remember that moment, or those moments, when the Father spoke through a godly saint, calling us out to our calling. How memorable are those couple of occasions when L.G. Curtis, my pastor during high school years, reached out and pulled me close to his side with a big bear hug and stated simply, "Bobby, God has His hand on your life!" He never pushed the matter further. He didn't have to. I couldn't shake the message that sank deep into my innermost being.

At times, missional messages are delivered by strangers. Angels in the best biblical sense of the word. While I was a pastor of the First Baptist Church in Brandon, Rob was a pharmacy student at Samford University in Birmingham. Plagued by recurring acute tonsillitis, Rob came home on a particular holiday to have his tonsils removed by Dr. Ted Blanton, outstanding ENT man in the Jackson area, and a member of our congregation.

In those days a person checked into the hospital the afternoon before the procedure to get prepped for the next morning's surgery. Rob's surgery was scheduled for 8 am. Gail and I chose to get there early, about 7 am. Coincidentally, we arrived at Rob's room at the same time the chaplain on duty did. Indeed, as we walked in the room together with the chaplain, a gentleman wearing a white jacket over his shirt and tie was leaving. Each of us greeted the other with a polite, "Good morning." Looking back, we have come to understand how radically "good" it really was!

After the chaplain exchanged pleasantries with Rob, he asked for and was of course granted permission to say a prayer. Before the prayer Rob said to him something to the effect, "Sir, you and your staff are really on the ball this morning. The other chaplain who just left and I had a wonderful conversation and he offered a prayer for me as well."

The chaplain was puzzled and replied, "I am the only chaplain here at this time. I have never seen the man who just left the room before in my life!"

What had the stranger said to Rob? With a clipboard in his hand he at first seemed to seek routine information. He asked, "You're Robbie Jackson?" "Yes, sir." "You're a student at Samford?" "Yes." "Tell me, Robbie," he continued, "What are your career goals?" Rob replied, "Well, first, I'm going to finish my degree in pharmacy." "Yes," the man nodded, "and then what?"

Rob then shared that after graduation his goal was to either become a pharmaceutical rep or to own his own drug store. The stranger replied, before saying a prayer and leaving, "Robbie, it's true that you will graduate from pharmacy school but, son, you will never be a drug salesman nor will you ever own your own drug store. God has different plans for your life up ahead!"

Missional Messages in the Preaching – Witnessing Task

The above notwithstanding most special missional words from the Father come to us as the Spirit speaks within the confines of our own spirit. We who preach the gospel of our Lord Jesus from time to time experience the wonder of a missional message. One that at a strategic moment before a prepared sermon is delivered completely changes the direction of the sermon. We have learned that the rewards of God are unbelievable when we are willing to take the risk of receiving such a timely message of the Spirit in faith, that is, in trusting obedience.

It was in the summer of 1995 that the Buck Run Church of Frankfort sent its second mission team to Romania. The team of 37 were mostly members of Buck Run but included several friends from other churches and from other states who also felt the leadership of the Lord to go and make a difference for Jesus' sake in that impoverished country.

Buck Run had received an unmistakably clear and miraculous call of God to go to Romania in August, 1994 and plant seven churches. On the 1995 journey we were, among other things, seeking confirmation from the Lord that our calling there was sure. The bulk of the team was headquartered in Onesti, a city in the Southeastern part of the country where a Buck Run construction team engaged in building a chapel for a new congregation that our '94 team had planted.

Several smaller teams ministered in towns within driving distance of Onesti. One of our teams, however, served in Pascani, a large town to the northeast and were stationed there the entire tour of duty.

There were three preaching assignments made for our first Sunday. Wayne Ball, deacon and lay preacher from FBC, Brandon, Mississippi was selected to preach in Onesti. Rob Jackson, Buck Run's Associate Pastor at the time, was the preacher in Pascani. Since I was the pastor of the group – and Romanians follow protocol to the letter – I was invited to preach in the city of Bacau, in the strongest Baptist church in that area of the country.

A funny thing happened on the way to the pulpit that Sunday. A few minutes before leaving Hotel Trotus, the Lord told me in my spirit to change the sermon I had prepared for the day. I don't remember now what the sermon was I had planned on preaching. All I remember was that the Lord said clearly, "I want you to preach from I Kings 18." It was the story of Elijah's confrontation with the prophets of Baal on Mt. Carmel. He said to me, "I want you to talk about watching the fire fall!" So I changed the sermon, preparing it as the Spirit led on the way to the preaching engagement.

Upon my return to the hotel in Onesti later in the afternoon I sought out my friend, Wayne, to inquire about the service held in the courtyard back of the hotel. Excitedly he told me that things had gone great. That he had preached to a large crowd of people who stood in the rain to hear the gospel, a significant number of whom came to confess faith in Jesus Christ. Wayne then told me about his strange experience. "Before the message I felt strongly that I needed to change my sermon. God told me to preach from I Kings 18. I did, and preached on 'Watching the fire fall!'" Wow!

I was anxious to get a report from Rob and his day at Pascani. Now, at this time, few people in that part of Romania had phone service. Almost none of the believers did. Not even the pastors! Sometime later that night the telephone rang in Cristi Chivu's hotel room. I heard him run down the hall. "Brother Bob," he exclaimed as I came to my door, "I just heard from Rob. He and his team had a wonderful day in the Lord." "And, guess what he said? He had an unusual experience. Just before preaching God told him to change his sermon. He turned in the Bible to I Kings 18 and preached on 'Watching the fire fall!'"

The fire did fall on our ministry in Romania that Summer and has continued to do so, as this local church mission endeavor of Buck Run Church soon evolved into a full-fledged evangelical mission organization, The Romanian-American Mission (RAM), now engaging in mission activity in six Eastern and Western European countries. And growing!

One cannot overestimate how important was the simple but faith-full obedience of the three preachers who were willing to take the dare of simultaneous *missional messages* to change their sermons on that Sunday in June, 1995. It became conclusive proof not only to the Lord's church, but to a watching world that "God is," that Jesus is the living Lord of the Church, and that Christ leads by His Spirit those who are willing to walk by faith the way of the Cross!

The incredible news is that the Father also confirms His missional confirmations when we faithfully obey them. One thrilling story to illustrate from the remarkable Romanian venture for Christ in '95.

A few days later in Pascani, Rob and his wife Tonya felt led to take their witness to the streets. As Rob began to share with any who would listen the fire of heaven fell and an astounding happening of God took place. Suddenly, the spot on which they were standing became holy ground and the glory of the Lord was poured out upon them. The place became saturated with the holy presence and power of the resurrected Christ.

Scores of people were drawn to the gospel witness and called out to the Lord for His mercy and grace. So many were coming that Rob and Tonya divided the crowd into two groups in an attempt to handle the situation better and get names and addresses for follow-up. It was a futile effort. They lost count of the numbers who trusted Christ when they reached around 200.

A powerful religious figure in that city was seen running angrily toward the crowd when, amazingly, it was if he had hit a glass wall that knocked him backward. He turned and went back the way he had come. Policemen were sent to stop the event and disperse the crowd. They ended up on their knees, confessing Christ. Some nearby construction workers in their hard hats dropped what they were doing and were seen peering over the fence at their building site. Tears were cascading down their cheeks as they, too, became touched by the tender, loving, precious Spirit of God.

In Acts 2 we are told that the Father speaks to and through His special-called people, the Church, in special ways when they become indwelt by His Holy Spirit.

Missional Messages and Spiritual Gifts for the Last Days

When the Day of Pentecost came and the Spirit of God was poured out on the fledgling Church of Christ, this Scripture in Acts 2 tells us that the disciples began to speak miraculously in foreign languages they had never learned. The phenomenal sound that resulted must have seemed like Babel being revisited. It soon attracted a multitude of folks who had come into Jerusalem from many countries for the sacred feast. Obviously, they began to wonder what in the world was going on. And they asked the Apostles in fact just that.

The Apostle Peter stood up in the midst of the crowd and gave an interpretation of this strange happening. It is significant that Peter in his reply to those seeking an explanation did not focus at all on the strange feat of speaking in unlearned languages. Rather, he pointed out to the multicultural, multinational group of Jews that had gathered and witnessed this miraculous display of multiple languages, that this was actually God's signal that the last days had come upon them. The last days in God's timetable for human history when His Spirit would be poured out on, not just a select few, but on all people, that is, upon all those who would call upon the name of the Lord and be saved. More than this, Peter declared that God would again speak to His people after having been silent – so the Jews taught – for 400 years!

Peter then introduced three specific channels through which God would communicate to all His people during the last days. These three were well known because they were incased in the Old Testament writings and influenced greatly the religious practice of Israel. But even when they had been an active means of divine disclosure in years past, only a few select people were known to have been favored with the possibility of utilizing them to hear the voice of the Lord. Peter reminded the gathering of the words of the prophet Joel who had said many years before that, during the last days, *all the people of*

The

God would enjoy these three means of hearing from Him through the activity of His Spirit on their lives.

The three means of receiving *missional messages* from the Lord were revealed to be words of prophecy, visions, and dreams. Now, it is quite understandable why Peter and the Apostles would choose to share this message in many different languages. It was necessary so that all the people there, persons from countries throughout the Roman Empire, could hear this word from God in their own native tongue. The message to them is found in Acts 2:15-18 (NLT):

> "These people are not drunk as you suppose... No, what you see was predicted long ago by the prophet Joel. In the last days, God says, 'I will pour out my Spirit upon all people. Your sons and daughters will prophesy. Your young men will see visions, and your old men will dream dreams. In these days, I will pour my Spirit even on my servants – men and women alike – and they will prophesy . . . (And) everyone who calls on the name of the Lord will be saved.'"

Over the past several centuries, the Church has, for the most part, ignored these three spiritual means of hearing from God, especially in the Western World. Traditional Christianity in the West for many years now has tended to summarily discredit the role of words of prophecy, visions, and dreams in the life of the Church. Many who are unsympathetic to those who claim legitimacy for these forms of divine disclosure point to bogus claims, self-promotion, and spiritual pride among some of the practitioners. Such objections are understandable. To a point. To be honest, however, you and I surely know that these same abuses may be found from among adherents of all forms of Christian expression, whatever their tradition.

While Peter does not use the word, "gifts," to describe the extraordinary means of hearing from God, it is obvious that he is referring to special gifts of the Holy Spirit. Much as the Apostle Paul does in Romans 12, 1 Corinthians 12, and Ephesians 4. And while Peter here mentions only three supernatural enablement's for those filled with God's Spirit, Paul makes a more extensive list of certain of these gifts the Spirit gives for the building up of the Body of Christ and its members. Paul moreover asserts that everyone in whom the reality of the Spirit is present possesses at least one of these gifts. Peter appears to indicate that the three gifts Joel predicted for the last days would be made available to all who called upon the name of the Lord and who would become His.

Both Peter and Paul are at one with the primacy of prophecy among all spiritual gifts, with Paul stating emphatically that this gift is to be desired above all others. One wonders, at the same time, if the phenomenon of dreams and visions Peter refers to may be significant means of "knowing" that are included in Paul's understanding of what he termed the gift of knowledge. Might such knowledge not be an experience similar to the one John had on the Isle of Patmos when God revealed to the Apostle the meaning of what was taking place currently in the church as well as what would be taking place up ahead? Might it not be understood as a message in the form of a call to the church to prepare, while encouraging the people of God with the fact that the Father will have the last word in all things when His children have a cross laid upon their shoulders?

Let's take a closer look at these three special spiritual gifts, these means the Father uses to reveal Himself at critical times to us last days' disciples, to be passed on to the Church. *Missional messages* all.

We'll take our first look at the gift of dreams, which is obviously out of Peter's order in his sermon on the Day of Pentecost. With your understanding, it will allow me to share happenings in my own testimony in the chronological order in which I experienced them.

Missional Messages Through Dreams

Dreams are amazing vehicles through which the Father sometimes chooses to speak to His children. Following my massive heart attack upon coming to Brandon, I was struggling with what I must do to access the healing, restorative power of God in my life. Indeed, to find the miraculous dimension to the spiritual walk I was searching for. In Dr. Peale's book, I discovered how the Lord could liberate me from my bondage to physical impairment, fear and sense of failure. After I became willing to surrender everything to Him and ask for the Holy Spirit's filling of my life, my prayer was answered.

As I mentioned earlier, that experience of surrender and filling was prefaced by a message God sent me through a dream Gail had a few nights before. On the morning after in question, as Gail and I took our daily walk through the neighborhood, I asked her if in her early morning quiet time God had given her a message to give me. She thought for a moment and said, "Well, no." Thinking about it further, she offered this: "You know, I had a most interesting dream last night." "Tell me about it," I urged. So she did. Gail dreamed that I had a serious illness – an incurable illness. It seems that my body was producing blood clots, the production of which could not be stopped. The doctors said that if somehow the blood clots were not checked immediately I would die. In the dream we then learned that some medical doctor had made a breakthrough in treating this problem. He had invented a bracelet-like contraption to be worn around the wrist, like a wrist watch. If it were faithfully worn it would stop blood-clotting. The person affected would get well. In the dream, we both were excited because we knew that if I got one, I would get well.

There was one catch, however. The device would cost $2 million dollars and the insurance company would not pay a dime of it. In the dream, Gail didn't flinch at all when she was told how much one of the bracelets would cost. She was overjoyed that it was possible to obtain this instrument because it would prolong my life of service and purpose for God and His kingdom.

In the dream, we sold absolutely everything we owned, withdrawing all we had in the bank as well as liquidating what stocks and bonds we had. Family members likewise made sacrificial contributions. Friends chipped in, especially those at church. When everyone pitched in, we were enabled to obtain this priceless treasure. We rejoiced that God allowed us to purchase this gadget that you needed to live and serve the Lord.

After sharing the dream with me Gail asked, "Did God say anything to you in the dream?" Without hesitating I replied, "Yeah. He did!" "What?" she inquired.

"Well," I began, "for one thing, He reminded me of the parable Jesus told in Matthew 13 about the merchant whose goal in life was seeking valuable pearls. Who on one occasion in his travels stumbles onto the largest, most beautiful, most expensive pearl in all the world. The merchant wanted that pearl more than anything he had ever wanted in all his life. So he went back home, liquidated all of his holdings and assets, and returned to buy that one pearl. He succeeded because he became willing to pay the price. The cost was everything he had!"

"So," Gail asked again, "What did God say to you through my dream and the Scripture He just gave you?" A light came on immediately in my soul. "You know, Gail," I replied, "It is apparent that He is making plain the cost of that which I had asked Him for that special night before we left Monroeville. What I told Him I would pay any price for. The thing I most desired on earth: The miraculous presence and power of the Lord, living in and through me." "And," Gail continued, "The cost?" I then verbalized what I now know to be true: "It will cost me my life completely surrendered to Him and His will, all I am and have on the altar of sacrifice."

The Father had finally brought me to the place where I knew that in my commitment to Him, there must be nothing left of what I have, so that I may have absolutely everything He has and desires to give.

I made that commitment then and there that day to pay the price. As a result, I received the magnificent fullness of the Father's Presence in my life.

Upon searching the Scripture for enlightenment on this thrilling experience, I soon realized, however, that I must make this commitment anew every single day if Christ's presence would stay warm and dynamic within my life. For the most part I have sought to do this. Haven't always done it, needless to say. But when I have, I have seen the glory of the Lord poured out so mightily that, on some occasions, I have almost been unable to bear it!

Jesus said, "If anyone desires to come after me, let him deny himself, and take up his cross daily, and follow me. For whoever desires to save his life will lose it, but whoever loses his life for my sake will save it." (Luke 9:23 NKJV)

Paul taught that we must, "Keep on being filled with the Holy Spirit."

From this *missional message* from the Father to me, issued one of the favorite sermons I love to preach, "The Pearl of Great Price." You will believe me when I tell you that it was one of the first sermons the Father led me to preach once I got back into the pulpit in Brandon. In the introduction to the sermon I shared this remarkable dream, and how God spoke to me and revealed the extraordinarily wonderful dimension our relationship could and would have. And how available it was for everyone. You know that it's available for you, too, don't you?

The Father has chosen dreams as an avenue of spiritual giftedness to convey significant *missional messages* to you and me who truly believe and are willing to obediently share them with others in Christ's body, the Church. I continue to be both amazed and wonderfully blessed when the Father chooses to speak in dreams and allows His Spirit to give them interpretation.

I am aware, nevertheless, of the danger inherent in the telling of dreams and their felt interpretation to others, for such can easily represent nothing more than an individual's fanciful speculation and the promotion of his or her personal agenda shared with others as a word from God. For that reason I have concluded it to be of utmost importance to follow certain guidelines that seek to distinguish between true messages from God and those that might be the projection of one's own prejudices or desires. Consider the following:

First, it seems obvious – at least to me – that we cannot seriously attempt to make every single dream we have at night a message from the Lord. For one thing, we are told, we do not remember nearly all of our dreams. Moreover, in many cases, those that we do recall are filled with such a complex jumble of mixed images and emotions that it seems quite unreasonable that God would choose to send us a really important message in a form so difficult to interpret. As a rule, I make little or no to-do about a nighttime story unless when I awake I am "gripped" by the clarity of the dream and with a sense that there is gravity and magnitude to it. A dream that will not let me go!

Second, I then begin to talk to the Father about it and implore Him to make known the meaning of the dream for myself and for others with whom He may desire it to be shared. It is a matter of "seeking Him out" in earnest prayer, even with fasting if necessary, to ascertain His divine will.

Third, once the Father has given what I feel to be His message in the dream, I seek confirmation of the interpretation He has laid upon my heart. Jesus taught that a matter is established by the testimony of two or three witnesses. It must be true of dreams and their interpretation.

To illustrate, I call your attention back to the dream God gave Gail that she, in turn, shared with me concerning the blood clots that were threatening my life. God's confirmation to the dream, and how I felt led to interpret it, was found in these three witnesses: (1) The immediate recollection the Spirit gave me of the Parable of the Pearl of Great Price, found in Matthew 13:45-46; (2) The gift of Dr. Peale's book received about the same time, with that preacher's situation closely mirroring mine; and (3) The experience of being bathed spiritually in warm oil, from head to toe, when I made the commitment to truly pay the price of total surrender for the longing of my soul.

If God does not choose to give clear confirmation to a dream, we must by all means not pursue it as a *missional message* however provocative it may seem to us. There's such a thing as *contramissional messages*, as we have seen. The Enemy would like nothing better than to have you and me deliver a confusing word to God's children and make them prey to his devious devices!

God has used dreams to speak to people as far back as Joseph in the Old Testament who interpreted the king's dreams which, as a result, led to Joseph being placed in a position to make a difference in the lives of many, indeed an entire nation. He continues to use *missional messages* in the form of dreams, to speak in particular to persons who need to know our Savior and cannot receive the Gospel through any other means.

Reports from Christian missionaries and church leaders at this very moment do not cease to amaze us as they share what is happening in countries that have been closed by radical Muslims and other groups to mission activity by Christ-followers. In places where Christians are tortured and killed for their faith and the worship of God is being systematically stamped out, there are few opportunities for the disciple of Christ to share His faith without his entire family being subjected to torture and to death. However, something remarkable is taking place. Some of these henchmen of evil are being communicated with through dreams whereby they are presented with the claims of Christ. And wholesale numbers are embracing our Lord!

My first visit to Romania in 1994 was an incredible one. Gail and I saw God move in unprecedented ways, even in dreams. Our entourage pulled into Bucharest and stayed one night in a hotel until the next day when we were sorted out into homes in the capital city. Bill Davis of Henrietta, Texas, president of Church Starts International, had invited our team to join his in planting several congregations in the area. Bill was anxious that Gail and I stay in the home of some outstanding Christian leader in the country.

When we arrived Bill began to tell me about the wonderful family who had invited us into their home. Sounded great. The next morning at breakfast, however, Bill relayed to us that the family with whom we were staying had to go out of the country on business and wouldn't be able to host us. But, he said emphatically, that we had another outstanding Christian family who wished very much to have the Jacksons in their home. "Wonderful, Brother Bill," I replied. "It matters little where we stay if there is a bed to stretch out on!"

When the hosts and hostesses came to pick up our team members and get them to their houses for a week, no one showed up for Gail and me. We were the last to be claimed. It was after noon that day before we knew who, where, what, and why.

Finally, Bill came to tell me that the second place where we were to lodge had also fallen through – another emergency of a sort. But he promised that this third family who had agreed to take us was one of the finest in the country. They were Nicu and Aurora Vandici. Nicu was at that time a part of the leadership of the Voice of the Gospel radio station. Today, he is the Executive-Director of Transworld Radio, a Christian radio station that blankets the entire country of Romania and parts of Europe.

Bill was right. The Vandici's were and are some of the finest Christians – and gracious hosts – ever we had met. It was mid-afternoon when we arrived at the Vandici's apartment. Aurora had prepared us our first Romanian meal which we took great delight in eating while, at the same time, enjoying fellowship with these new friends.

Shortly after we had sat down for our meal there came a loud knock at the door. Nicu excused himself to accommodate whoever was there. It was a big man. Mr. Popovici. Nicu did not know the gentleman, as he lived in an apartment a couple of high-rises over in the neighborhood. The following is the gist of what transpired at the door:

Mr. Popovici told his story. It was fascinating. He told Nicu that he had not slept in three nights. He said that each night he had a dream telling him that a stranger was coming on that

135

particular day – Saturday – to this particular apartment. It was a person who would tell him about the Book. When he finished sharing his dream with our host, Nicu pointed over to the table where I was seated and told his visitor, "That is the man!"

Nicu invited him in to await the conclusion of our meal. I had the great joy for over an hour following the meal to tell Mr. Popovici about the Book. More than this, to share with him the wonderful Man of the Book. When the Spirit gave the green light I relayed how a person can know this remarkable Jesus. Mr. Popovici wanted badly to know Him. Before he left that afternoon he became a believer, giving his life to Jesus Christ.

Two days later, a similar thing happened in an apartment, in one of the high-rises, in the home of a believer. She had invited her neighbors in for fellowship. Approximately 20 ladies crowded in a small room. With me was my gifted interpreter, Brother Sorin Covaci, youth minister at Holy Trinity Church in Bucharest at the time, now the pastor of a Romanian congregation in Troy, Michigan. When we arrived most of the women were seated and were chatting with each other. After Sorin got the group's attention, I began speaking. One dear lady excitedly interrupted: "I have had a dream this week. In that dream I saw the faces of two light-haired men coming and telling me about Jesus. *You* are those two men!" It should not surprise anyone that this lady as well as most of the others in attendance gave their hearts to Christ. *Missional messages* from God accomplishing their purpose!

Missional Messages Through Prophetic Words

We have already touched on the importance of prophecy as a gift of the Spirit to the follower of Christ in these last days. As we have seen, prophecy in the New Testament is considered the gift Christians should seek as a first priority so as to be used of God to deliver His message to the Church and be a blessing to others. This avenue of hearing God seems to be the highest form of Pentecostal giftedness after the Holy Spirit is received.

All of us are agreed, I suppose, that there was a sacred office of Prophet in Old Testament Israel as well as in the New Testament Church. Some believe that office still exists and should be maintained in the Church along with that of the Apostle. Others contend that, with the canonization of the New Testament, the witness of the Prophet and the Apostle became codified in the Bible, thus the office became no longer needed in the ongoing development of the Church's life and mission. Moreover, since Peter at Pentecost declared that the last days have now come and the Spirit has been poured out upon the Church (all persons, men and women, even slaves) who come to accept the Christ are gifted to prophesy. Little need for special professionals in these fields!

The Apostle Paul, who was named among the prophets in the church at Antioch and who suggested that some members of the Body of Christ, the Church, are given the gift of prophesy, encouraged everyone in the Church to seek this spiritual gift. It is evident from Paul's writings that messages primarily of "gloom and doom" that we hear especially on television today from those who say that God has given them a word for the Church (interestingly, often recited in "King James" language) is not God's intention in prophecy for the last days. He wrote in 1 Corinthians 14:3-4 (NLT): "One who prophesies strengthens others, encourages them and comforts them.. . .

One who speaks a word of prophesy strengthens the entire church."

When I was in college and seminary a distinction was drawn between the prophet as "foreteller" and a "forthteller." So gun-shy were we of anything that smacked of Pentecostalism, with its emphasis upon the reality of the Holy Spirit – the living presence of the Lord Jesus continuing in His Church – that those who taught us passed quickly over the "foretelling" aspect of the gift to make certain we knew that "forthtelling" was probably the best understanding of the prophetic task as affects the Church today.

While there is most assuredly the element of "forthtelling" in the understanding of prophesy, such as, "speaking out for Jesus," or "preaching the Gospel," within the power of the Holy Spirit, one must not overlook the element of "foretelling." Those who prophesy have the ability when, under the influence of the Spirit of God, to address the future in ways that bring encouragement to the downhearted, hope for a better tomorrow, and a promise of God's Presence shaping everything up ahead for good to those who love Him.

Such edification causes the believer experiencing broken-heartedness, disappointment, defeat, and hopelessness, to catch a renewed spiritual breath, determined to go forward to fight the good fight of faith and thereby to expect victory. Even to celebrate it in advance!

I have shared with you something of the health problems I encountered while pastor of the First Baptist Church of Brandon, Mississippi. Following my heart attack God gave me unusual energy for the task He had assigned me there.

Nevertheless, I was never quite well. In and out of the hospital, with issues stemming from an injured heart and doubtless my failure to do what the doctor told me to do.

In April of 1984 I began a series of five hospitalizations over a five-month period. Some extremely serious. The fifth time my condition spiraled into depression. Deep depression. Indeed, so deep that over a fourteen-month period I was almost a non-functioning human being. During this time Gail and I could not even carry on an extended conversation. We could exchange small talk, but that was about all. "The weather's nice today." "Yeah." "What's for lunch?" "Good."

The doctors placed me on total disability and told me that I would not be able to cope with work the rest of my life. FBC Brandon, again, cared for us like few congregations would have done. They asked that we stay in Brandon and allow the church to minister to us. I knew that would never work. That a relationship of pity could emerge from their genuine love and a catering to a former pastor would not be healthy. Nor would it be fair to whomever might come as the new pastor. So, we made plans to move. But, where? After a year, back to Monroeville!

In the meantime, at 47 years of age I wondered if I were washed up altogether as a pastor. That same yellow recliner in the darkest corner of our den housed me again, where I threw myself a pity-party every day. I was fearful and hopeless all over again. "Father, what can I do? Give me some word of encouragement. Some word that the remarkable journey we've been on does not end here!"

Gail received a phone call from my friend, Evangelist Gary Bowlin, who along with his family had made their home in our congregation. He asked for permission to come by for a brief visit with me. Gail told him no, that I could not carry on a conversation with anyone. He then asked if she would give him one minute. "Gary," she answered, "I'll give you one minute, but no more."

Gary was soon there and was ushered into the room where I was seated. The word he bore was brief: "Brother Bob, God has given me a message to give to you. Will you receive it?" I replied, "What is it, Gary?" "Brother Bob, God has told me to tell you that the greatest days of your ministry are before you!" I replied, "Gary, I don't understand it but I receive it as a word from the Lord." What a blessing and encouragement those prophetic words were. I accepted them by faith. They kept me going, looking for that something special the Father was going to do to enable the desire of my heart to become a reality: that He would make my life a miracle for His glory and the pleasure of Christ and His Kingdom.

I wish I could tell you that this word of prophecy, this *missional message* from the Father was like swallowing a pill and the next day everything was fine. It wasn't. But it became an anchor for my prayers, my faith and my hope, while the Holy Spirit continued the process of changing me and shaping me into the image of Christ, a finished product that is certainly a long way from completion. And will not be completed until I see Him face to face one day. But, thank God, changes in spiritual formation began to take place! And have continued. Praise His holy Name!

I was out of the full-time pastoral ministry for five years. You may find it hard to believe that those years were some of the most wonderful years of my life. Occasionally, someone will say to me, "You must live with the regret of having to be placed on the shelf for five years, right in the prime of your life!" My response always is, "To the contrary. I wouldn't trade those years for anything in the world!" You see, I learned more about the Father, His will for my life, about prayer and the Holy Spirit, in those five years than all the other years of my life and ministry put together. How I thank God for them. And how I thank God for those words of prophetic encouragement Gary Bolin delivered that enabled me to hold on 'til God got all things ready for opportunities unlimited and unbelievable ahead. And got me ready, too!

The Father uses us frequently to deliver prophetic words that honor Him and bring glory to His Name while we share a message of encouragement to others. Dr. Eddie Davison is the outstanding senior pastor of First Baptist Church in Hamilton, Alabama. We have been friends ever since he held a similar position at the Camden Baptist Church, the flagship Baptist congregation in Wilcox County, Alabama. At the time, I was serving a temporary stint as a director of missions for the Bethlehem-Pine Barren Associations of Baptist Churches in Monroe and Wilcox Counties. The churches there went out on a limb and graciously asked me to serve with them while I was healing from the cataclysmic breakdown of health I suffered while pastor of the FBC in Brandon, Mississippi.

Gail and I had moved back to Monroeville following our four-year stay in Brandon where I was repeatedly in and out of the hospital and finally placed on total disability at the ripe old age of 48.

We had been back in Monroeville about three years when I was asked to serve in this mission capacity. The Monroe County association was by far the largest and I gave four days a week in the office in Frisco City. I devoted one day a week to the Wilcox County churches going there each Thursday to meet with their small group of pastors, for fellowship and encouragement.

On my Thursday venture I usually arrived at Camden Baptist around 10 am to fellowship with Eddie. Often times, if he were not busy, we'd have lunch together. We grew to be close brothers in Christ during my two-year hitch as missions director.

When I arrived on this particular Thursday I sensed something was terribly wrong with Eddie. His demeanor gave him away. He was in the valley of despair. He poured out his heart to me immediately when I asked what was obviously troubling him. The deadline for getting income tax returns into the IRS was only a few days away and he had absolutely no money to pay his taxes. Some unusual expenses had depleted his finances. He was humiliated. Embarrassed. "What can I do, Brother Bob?" He inquired almost pathetically.

Eddie and I talked awhile. I encouraged him with words about the faithfulness of God, the God who rarely shows up early but is always on time in behalf of His faithful servants. I prayed and asked the Lord to meet the needs of this beloved man of God who was faced with a crisis not of his own making.

I was on my way out of my friend's office following the prayer when I stopped, turned around and without thinking blurted out, "Eddie, remember this: Jesus has been known to put tax money in a fish's mouth!"

When I arrived in Camden the next Thursday I didn't know what to expect. The tax deadline had passed. What a joy it was to be greeted by this special friend who was sporting a smile that literally went from ear to ear. I knew that our Lord had intervened and rescued His devoted servant. I simply asked, "How did He do it?"

He then told me the remarkable story. On the Sunday night that had just passed, one of the young deacons in his congregation, Phillip Sims, had called to explain ('fess up?) why he had missed church that day. He had been involved over the weekend in a big fishing rodeo in North Alabama. Phillip then relayed to his pastor the extraordinary thing that had taken place. "On my way to the lake something inside me said, 'If I win this rodeo I ought to give the prize money to Brother Eddie.'"

Know what happened? Phillip won the rodeo. He told his pastor that every time he reeled in a fish, he kept saying, "This one's for Brother Eddie! This one's for Brother Eddie!" I suppose you can guess the rest of the story.

What a mighty God we serve! How He longs to show Himself faithful to those who dare walk with Him in trusting belief and obedience. How He desires to speak through the Spirit of His Resurrected Son to you and me: to encourage us, to challenge us, to elicit our trust of everything up ahead to Him, promising to always be there when we arrive. And on occasions He reveals how He's going to do it!

Fast forward with me to an incident that took place in December, 2009 when I was rushed to the hospital in Decatur with another heart attack, my fourth that we have record of. Every single doctor attending me told me that I must go back on statin drugs. My cholesterol was sky high. Always has been. I had been on statin drugs before. They just about did me in. In fact, they ate up the calf muscle in my left leg. Even with those drugs my cholesterol was too high. I was adamant. No more statin drugs for me.

When I went to my family doctor for a check-up following this last heart attack, Dr. Reddy became serious with me and lovingly told me that I must go back on statin drugs. I politely said, "No." Then, out of the blue a word came from within me that I had not thought and I abruptly said, "My dear friend, I'm not going back on those drugs because, as a witness to you to the power of my Lord, the living resurrected Christ, I am claiming that my God will heal me and lower my cholesterol into numbers that are normal and acceptable to you!" Dr. Reddy, a wonderful man and great doctor, originally from India and an adherent of a non-Christian religion, simply shrugged his shoulders.

March 11, 2010 I was involved in an automobile accident that sent me again to the hospital for several days. When Dr. Reddy came in the next morning to report on blood work and other tests they had done, he said, "I've got some things to tell you." "First of all" and he began to smile, "Your cholesterol is 139." "Do you know why, my dear friend?" I asked. He then just looked up and pointed to heaven. Hallelujah! I now have ongoing opportunities to share my faith with this excellent physician. There is, as you might suspect, much more spiritual intensity to our conversations.

Missional Messages Received Through Visions

Peter also said in his Pentecostal sermon in Acts 2 that as a result of the pouring out of the Spirit upon the Church, young men would "see visions." Visions appear to be means through which God chooses to speak to His church and us, its members, giving us creative and exciting directions in the way that we should go for a victorious journey in fulfilling His will. It is a picture or graphic or scenario implanted somehow, somewhere in our inner spiritual optic center, that lays out the Father's plan for us up ahead and His call to a commitment to that plan.

After my breakdown of health in Brandon, God took me back to Monroeville, Alabama for four years of healing and preparation for the monumental, thrilling task He had prepared for me ahead. In time, my friend Micky Kennedy created a chaplain's job for me with his Monroeville Telephone Company. Counseling employees and their families out of the backdrop of my own trials and pain, I found myself much more sensitive and concerned about those who were hurting. And I found that God had given me much more to offer them from the Bible as well as from my personal experiences than ever I had had available to me before.

The Gullett's Bluff Baptist Church, just out of Camden, gave a worn-out preacher a chance when no one else would. They allowed me to preach again after a three years' absence. It was here that God changed my preaching style from one that was glued to a manuscript and shackled to the pulpit, to one of no pulpit, while preaching without notes. The freedom became exhilarating. My wife said that my skills in communicating the gospel increased 1,000%. Thank God! I needed improvement.

Still do! The people at that little country church became angels of God to Gail and me. We received from them hundreds of *missional messages*, many of them prophetic, that gave us great encouragement in a time of need.

I have previously told about my time as a director of missions in Monroe and Wilcox Counties that briefly followed my Gullett's Bluff experience. All part of the healing process as God continued to prepare me for those promised "best days of ministry before me." I have always considered that wherever I might be in God's will at any given point in time, and whatever He might have me doing, was surely the "best days" for me. But I could never have imagined at this point in my journey just how tremendous were the things God had prepared up ahead for my life and those of my family – and friends!

One morning in my quiet time in April, 1990, an unusual thing happened to me. I received a message emblazoned somewhere, somehow, in my empty cranium. The only handle I have been able to hang on it is the word "vision." These words appeared: "Return and Build the Temple!"

I didn't make much out of this command at first. But it appeared again the next day in my quiet time. And the next. And the next. "Return and Build The Temple!" It was dawning on me that, once again, the Lord was up to something. But, again, I didn't know just what. I began to beseech the Father for further delineation. He told me as He had done ten years before in Monroeville, "Get into my Word!"

In studying through the book of Micah, I was drawn to chapter four. It talked about the Temple, how it would be established as the highest hill around. And that people would stream to it.

My eyes were riveted to verse 8, in the NIV, that said: "As for you, O watchtower of the flock . . . your former dominion will be restored to you."

"Oh," I mused. "This means that I will become pastor of a former church for a second time. But where? All my former churches have shepherds and seem to be doing fine." The next morning the vision came again: "Return and Build the Temple!"

Who would have ever thought that the following Sunday my pastor, Vince Whittington, would resign FBC Monroeville to accept the pastorate of First Baptist Church, Oxford, Alabama? I found it interesting that the Monroeville congregation was making plans for a new facility. Friends of ours began to come to us and asked if we would consider becoming their pastor again. "Return and Build the Temple?" In Monroeville? The church and town I loved so much? What day did they want me to start punching the ol' time clock?

It was a perfect arrangement for Gail and me. Seemingly. We had just completed building our dream house there. (Though Gail says it was more like a nightmare house. And I have concurred.) We had moved Gail's mother there to an assisted living facility. We were only 40 miles from my dad, who loved having us near in his old age.

But God was not in our return to FBC. We made it a matter of prayer for several weeks and simply could not get peace about it. Finally, on a Wednesday afternoon before a meeting of the pastor search committee was to take place that night, at which time we were told that my coming back to Monroeville was to be addressed, I hand-delivered a letter to my good friend, committee chair George Heard, withdrawing my name from consideration, stating that God was not in this move. They were shocked. Steve Stewart, who was on the committee, told me at lunch one day shortly after I moved to Decatur, that at the time he thought it to be a foregone conclusion that I would come back as pastor.

The next morning I greeted an old friend. You guessed it. That same old vision, "Return and Build the Temple!" It kept coming back until Sunday night when I received a phone call from another dear friend, Z.T. Lester, in Frankfort, Kentucky. "Brother Jackson," he began, "our church is in the initial process of adding on to our building. Our pastor unexpectedly resigned this morning to go back home to Virginia. While this is by no means an official word – we haven't elected a pulpit committee yet – a lot of folks wanted me to call and find out if you would consider coming back to lead us again?"

At that very moment I had the same experience I had after reading Dr. Peale's great book nine years before. A feeling of warm oil being poured on me from the top of my head to the bottom of my feet. I knew it was the Holy Spirit. I said right then and there, "Yes, Gail and I will come back!"

I have in this writing waxed effusive in praise of the congregations in Monroeville and Brandon. All deserved, and more! In pages up ahead I will be pleased to share with you something of the magnificent love affair that Gail and I had with Buck Run Church that stretched over many years.

Gail and I went back to help "Build the Temple." The fourth chapter of Micah became the prophetic picture of much that would take place at Buck Run on this our second time with them. "People will stream to it." Keep in mind that Buck Run was a village church in the Forks of Elkhorn community, five miles out of the capital city. Nonetheless, people started pouring in from towns in all directions. The plans for a new addition had to be changed three times to keep up with the growth of the congregation. Over a stretch of two years people kept coming even though there was not even a sign on the premises identifying the church. (One of our members misjudged the driveway into the small parking lot and knocked the church sign down. It was not replaced until we moved into our new sanctuary across the highway!)

For two years Buck Run was one of the fastest-growing Baptist churches in Kentucky. After about four years, it became the largest congregation in the city of Frankfort and Franklin County on Sunday morning. Thom Rainer, president of LifeWay, wrote one of his pioneering books on church growth, *Eating the Elephant.* In it he devoted an entire chapter to the phenomenal things God was doing in our church. He entitled the chapter, "The Miracle of Buck Run." It *was* a miracle church because of the great God who was moving among His people through His living, Resurrected Christ. It *was* a miracle church because the people faithfully listened to His voice and obediently sought Him and His will out as He spoke.

This material on *missional messages* may appear to be unnecessarily long. Nevertheless, its extensive length is deliberate. It is important that we who would participate in this promising journey understand that, if we pray earnestly and fervently for guidance in what God would have you and me and our churches do, and we believe that He will answer our prayers, there is a constellation of ways He can and will choose to speak to us to make His will known. Let us not overlook any

149

one of them. And if we can and will choose to believe, let us not be shocked when He utilizes one or more of them as confirmation.

Let us listen. Listen. Listen. And not close any door. The Father desires so much to lead you and me to His living, resurrected Son, Jesus.

May we not miss out on this tremendous opportunity by turning a deaf spiritual ear to the multiple ways he might choose to speak.

Chapter Six

Seek Him Out in the Workings of His Mysterious Providence

"And we know that in all things God works for the good of those who love Him who have been called according to His purpose."
Romans 8:28 (NIV)

Significant faith ("And we *know*!") understands that, while God's ways in His providential care and governance of His Creation are past finding out, He nevertheless discloses Himself – His glory, His love, His will, His power – in certain mysterious acts that may be comprehended and engaged in by those who earnestly seek Him out.

"We know" this because of our love relationship with Him through Jesus Christ, His Son and our Savior. "Know" is the word for knowledge that is gained from an intimate relationship between two interacting parties.

It is, for example, like the knowledge a husband and wife have of each other that is not ordinarily known by another because in the intimacy of marriage there is a disclosure of self that only the two persons living together can fully know.

Thus, in Romans 8:28, the Apostle Paul is declaring that we who are in an intimate love relationship with the Father through Christ "know" for certain that He will take whatever situation we find ourselves in, or whatever we may be facing and, in His time and in His way, turn it into that which is good for us. We know, moreover, that He will use such turns of events to further His divine purposes in and through our lives for His glory, for the edification of the Church, Christ's Body, and for our development in faith and obedience. We "know" it because it is being disclosed to us in remarkable, mysterious ways.

"In all things." God is working behind the scenes, most times *in cognito*, in absolutely everything that happens to you and me, in everything you and I encounter, moment by moment, day by day. As he does, He demonstrates His care for us and reassures us that He is in control even when it may appear He is not.

What are some of the "all things" in which the Father works to demonstrate His love, His purpose, and His power to us who truly believe and are committed to obey the Spirit's dictates in each instance? What are some of the "all things" in which we might expect the Father to be at work, showing up in surprising moments and in serendipitous ways to validate the reality of His Providence?

Consider the following that come to mind which, I realize, do not comprise an exhaustive list.

He May Be Found in the Coincidental

> "Now by *chance* a certain priest came down that road. And when he saw him, he passed by on the other side. Likewise a Levite, when he arrived at the place, came and looked, and passed by on the other side. But a certain Samaritan, as he

journeyed, came where he was. And when he saw him, he had compassion." Luke 10:31-33

All persons experience the coincidental in life. Obviously we do as Christians, but with a decided difference. We who are believers look for the Father within those coincidences. When we do, we discover Him there, setting the stage for His glorification in the event as well as in the lives of those caught up with us in the mysterious happening. Let's take a look at a couple of examples.

On Sunday, August 21, 2010 Central Baptist engaged in what was billed as a one-day "Harvest Revival" with Phil Waldrep preaching. It was a most unusual, spirit-filled occasion in which the emphasis was, interestingly, on baptism. In 55 years of pastoral ministry I had not encountered anything quite like this. It was a well-done and effective spiritual affair.

Without fanfare or pressure the evangelist geared his messages around the call for persons to come and be baptized – that very day! First of all, it was a call to come and trust Christ as Lord and Savior for those who had never made this commitment and to seal the decision in the waters of baptism. "See, here is water. What does hinder me from being baptized?" The call was, moreover, to those who had been contemplating the initial step of obedience to Christ, following their surrender to Him sometimes in the past, but had simply not found the courage to publicly take a stand for Him in baptism. It was also addressed to adults who had been baptized as children, who had admitted later on to themselves, perhaps to others, that they did not at that earlier time fully realize the ramifications of true commitment to the Lordship of

Jesus Christ and now desired baptism as a true and devoted follower of the Christ.

The emphasis on coming for baptism at the end of the service was unique. The Holy Spirit took control and 36 persons responded, 31 of them being baptized for the first time since giving their hearts and lives to Him. Most of them adults. Praise the Lord!

A large number of other commitments were registered on this blessed day. Some came to transfer church membership from other congregations. A significant number came to "rededicate" their lives to Christ. Jesus Christ was very much alive in His church on this day through the evident presence of His Holy Spirit moving the church and its members to new spiritual heights of intimacy with Him.

Rob had all things well prepared for the service. Disposable baptismal garb was on hand for as many as 50 people who might come to embrace baptism. Volunteers were ready to assist those being baptized. The church staff and their spouses, along with the deacons and their wives, were ready to counsel one-on-one those responding to the altar call.

Problem was, a lady who was a visitor in the congregation came forward at the conclusion of the second service, visibly moved by the Holy Spirit – sobbing and shaking – and there was no wife of a deacon or staff member available to counsel with her. They were all engaged at this time in talking and praying with respondents. Rob quickly panned the congregation and spotted Penny Fitzgerald seated close to the front. He knew her to be a godly lady and capable counselor. The pastor pointed to Penny. She knew what the signal was and immediately left her place to come and assist this visiting inquirer.

Coincidence or not? Many will call Rob's momentary prompting to select Penny Fitzgerald to counsel this particular guest of our church to be but a coincidence. People of faith will see the unmistakable providential hand of God reaching into a situation needing His direct intervention to work behind and within that situation, to bring all things together for His glory and the goodness of His favor upon a lovely lady who needed it at that special moment.

Coincidence or not? What do you think? On the Wednesday night prior to the one-day harvest revival, Penny was at church along with her family. The evening Bible study groups for all ages in the church had just concluded. Moms and dads were claiming children from their respective areas of church life while husbands and wives awaited each other's class to disband, if they happened not to be in the same group.

Penny was busy getting her chickens together for the trip home when she spotted a lady standing by the escalator. She recognized that she was probably a visitor, so she made a point to walk over to introduce herself and welcome her to Central Baptist Church. Guess what?

On Sunday, when the visitor came forward seeking that "something significantly more" in her relationship with Jesus Christ, the Spirit of God directed Rob to pick out a person she had met on the Wednesday night before to counsel with her. Rob was quite unaware of any connection. The respondent and Penny discovered they had much in common.

This dear lady – let's call her Sally – was adopted as a child. Sally has been struggling with a strong desire to reconnect with her biological parents but does not want to hurt her adoptive parents whom she loves dearly. She brought this issue to the table when she and Penny began to talk. Do you think it strange that the Father nudged Sally towards Central Baptist on a special Sunday whereby she was coincidentally brought into a counseling situation with Penny Fitzgerald, the *mother of four precious adopted children?*

Come and See, Jesus Christ is Alive! in His church! In the coincidental that happens when He is made to be Lord through expectant prayer and radical faith – that is, again, trusting belief and obedience. The coincidental for the believer is always missional in nature. t is the set-up for you and me to show forth God's love, grace, and purpose to another person yearning, consciously or unconsciously, for a special touch from Him.

It took place on April 15, 2003. We were enroute home from Romania. Our party had just boarded the plane in Amsterdam headed for Detroit, our flight's second leg on a jaunt back to Lexington, Kentucky. Our plane was packed – only two empty seats on the jet. Would you believe it – one of the empty seats was next to mine? Jumping Jehoshaphat! How I began to excitedly plan to enjoy the extra room for writing, my favorite way of making something positive out of a long trip over the ocean while sitting back in the plane's cattle car!

We were primed for takeoff when for some unknown reason things were put on hold. I understood why when I heard the door in the front of the plane open and a young lady walked in. I was relieved when she took the empty seat on the other side of the plane. I heard the door slammed shut and I thought to myself, "Phew. Saved by the bell!" "Not so fast my friend," I heard a familiar voice say to me in my inner being. About that time another young lady appeared walking down the aisle. My aisle! I knew what it meant. She would be my traveling partner for the next eight hours.

Her name was Petulah Redwood. A beautiful young Jamaican-born lady who had, nevertheless, homesteaded in Manchester, England. The other young woman who had boarded the plane just before her was her sister. The two of them were on their way to New York for some kind of family gathering as I recall. I wondered out loud how two sisters could get on a plane in Manchester England bound for New York and end up on Northwest flight 67 from Amsterdam to Detroit?

Petulah's story was remarkable. The sisters had arisen early on that Tuesday morning to board a plane from Manchester to London to connect with a direct flight into New York City. For whatever reason when they got to Heathrow they had either missed their flight or it had been cancelled. Subsequent flights were booked for the day. The only possibility of getting to New York in time for their family event was to catch a flight to Amsterdam and hope that they could get there in time to take flight 67 to Detroit and then hitch another ride to New York.

The sisters decided to take a chance. They arrived in Amsterdam within a few minutes of the departure of NW flight 67. Someone called ahead to our plane. They were told that our aircraft would wait about five minutes for them but no more. Petulah said they ran every step of the way from where they had deplaned to our gate of departure. They made it. Just barely. Here she was sitting in the seat next to me.

Petulah was a delightful young lady. Open to talk. An interesting conversationalist. After we discovered who each was, the Lord said, "OK, Bobby boy! Here she is. She's yours – and mine!" I got the message loud and clear. I asked the Father for words that would be fitly spoken.

I began by appealing to divine purpose. The following represents a rather accurate account of our conversation. I said, "Petulah, even though it may seem coincidental to you, might you consider the possibility that it's not by accident that you have been seated by me today." She replied, "Yes, I'll accept that possibility." I continued, "As a Christian, I believe God arranged this moment so I could tell you how very unique and wonderfully special you are to Him and the remarkable plan He has for your life." She responded, "You know, I've always wondered why I'm here in this world." I added, "Well, God has so uniquely fashioned you – He has made no one else like you, nor will He ever – and conditioned you by what some mistakenly call the 'accidents' of time and place, that you may uniquely change the whole course of human history if you so choose. That opportunity is conditional, however. You must put self to death – your own desires and agendas in life – and invite Jesus to come in to live and reign in your very being. It is He who actually works through you to make a difference in this world, a difference that is good, right, and just."

"I'd like to think my life could be used to make a difference," was her reply. "May I share with you," I asked, "How you can come to know Jesus Christ personally by letting Him in to make that difference in your life while you watch Him make a difference in those around you?" "More than anything," she confessed.

158

I spent the good part of an hour approaching this witness opportunity sharing, first, what Jesus Christ has done in my life. More than this, what He is *presently* doing in my life and, consequently, what I knew He could do in her life. I told her about His amazing grace that channels into our lives through the conduit of radical faith. I talked with her and explained the matter of repentance. I then confronted her with the cost of discipleship. Without blinking an eye, she said that this is what she wanted for her life. Right then and there she trusted Jesus Christ as her Lord and Savior and entrusted all she was and has to Him.

We parted ways in Detroit. I don't know if I'll ever be blessed with the joy of seeing her again this side of heaven. I wish at times I could at least hear about her journey of faith. About what the Lord is doing in and through her life. Obviously God doesn't want me to know. Perhaps it is because I don't need to know. But, dear reader, would you do me a favor? If by coincidence you ever run across a Petulah Redwood, Jamaican-born, Manchester resident, now citizen of the Kingdom of God, would you please let me know? It would be such a blessing to get some word about her. Maybe you might bear enough information that would enable me to reconnect and learn the results of another of the Father's remarkable, coincidental working out of His Providence in my life – and hers!

Sometimes God adds a bit of humor to His behind-the-scenes activity in your life and mine. When Rob was called into vocational ministry he moved from Troy, Alabama where he was working as a pharmacist at Big B Drugs, to Birmingham where he enrolled in Beeson Divinity School at Samford University. Birmingham afforded Rob the opportunity to fill in for a huge pool of pharmacists needing days off, etc. It helped him provide the means to go to school.

Rob was only one year at Beeson before he was called as my associate pastor at Buck Run Church in Frankfort and transferred to Southern Seminary in Louisville. While in Beeson, however, he was called in September 1990 to pastor a precious little congregation, the Antioch Baptist Church out in the country from Double Springs, Alabama. Rob served there only eight months before moving to Kentucky, but the tiny church experienced a tremendous spirit of revival during that time. Fifteen souls were baptized. That number led their entire association of churches. Not much water splashing in baptistries that year in that county! How about in your county this year? How about in your church?

Several of the fifteen baptisms came from one family. That family had an elderly aunt in the hospital in a neighboring town that they wished very much for their pastor to pray with. On this particular Sunday they asked Rob to go to the hospital and pray for Aunt Fannie. They told him that Junior, their 12-year-old son, would go and identify Aunt Fannie for him. Rob and Junior went that afternoon after church. Following lunch, of course!

When they got to the small town hospital Junior pointed out to his pastor that Aunt Fannie's room was the first door on the right down the hall. They got to the room and looked in. "That's her. That's Aunt Fannie," Junior exclaimed. So they prepared to enter the room. "Now," Junior cautioned, "Remember, Aunt Fannie is deaf and can't hear it thunder. Only in one ear can she make out any sounds. It's the ear over there next to the window. You'll just have to cup your hands up to that ear and yell as loud as you can."

Rob approached the dear lady's bed prayerfully. She had her eyes closed. Was she at death's door? He followed instructions to a "T." He went to the designated ear, cupped his hands and shouted as loud as he could, "AUNT FANNIE!! THIS IS BROTHER ROB JACKSON!! AUNT FANNIEEE!!"

The lady in the bed moved her head back slightly on the pillow, cocked one eye up as if in shock – or disdain – and appeared scared to death.

The lady's son walked in about the time all the shouting began and Rob asked him, "Is this Aunt Fannie's room?" Laughingly, he said, "No, this is my mother, Mrs. Terrill, from in town here." Apologizing profusely, Rob nevertheless engaged the lady in conversation. Surprisingly, she opened up and talked freely and frankly to this strange young man and admitted that her soul was not right with the Lord. Rob then began to share how she could have the confidence that all is well with her soul, when peace and joy indescribable could be hers. Mrs. Terrill admitted she wanted that and as Rob tenderly led her into the Presence of Jesus Christ she entrusted her life into His matchless love and care.

The son was elated. He told Rob that he was a believer and had prayed for his mom's spiritual condition ever since he had become a Christian. He had prayed that God would send a minister or someone else who would get next to his mom and lead her to Christ. Then, with a chuckle, he confessed, "I never would have believed that it would be some young, crazy preacher that God would use to scare her half to death!"

Whatever happened to Aunt Fannie? She was in the next room down. Junior had made a mistake. Besides, she was comatose. She would not have been able to have received his visit or his prayers anyway.

Was it coincidental that Junior failed to check and make sure he had Aunt Fannie's room number right? Was it coincidental that he led his pastor to the wrong room to a lady Rob doubtless would never ever have had an occasion to meet? Was it just coincidental? Not on your life! How about the activity of a providential Father who is at work in, behind, and through all that happens to His faithful children? The Apostle Paul said He brings about that which is good for those who devotedly love Him and He works out His holy purposes through their lives.

I must admit that I do not have all the answers to how God works His intentions out through the coincidental happenings that amaze us just as they bless and mature us. I have discovered, however, that earnest prayer is often involved somewhere back up the road before the coincidental takes place.

I recall that in 1996 as we prepared for our third missionary junket into Romania, now as a full-fledged, independent mission organization (RAM), we felt the Lord leading us to include a medical team with each evangelistic and children's team. The only problem was that we couldn't get a single medical doctor to join our excellent nursing corps, in this our first attempt to provide a truly holistic approach to doing missions in Romania and beyond.

We prayed. Prayed. Prayed. Asked. Begged. Pleaded. Appealed to doctors of our acquaintance and ones we didn't know. The answer we kept receiving seemed always to be, "Not this year. Maybe later." We continued to pray. The prayer bond spread from those individuals involved with the Romanian-American Mission, to their friends and Sunday school classes. Buck Run Church and FBC Brandon led the way praying as congregations. Then it happened, coincidentally.

Gail and I had been to South Alabama to check on my dad who was in the nursing home. We had caught an inexpensive Southwest Airline flight from Louisville to Birmingham where we rented a car and drove on down to my hometown of Flomaton, on the Alabama-Florida line.

On our return, we boarded the plane in Birmingham and made our way back to Kentucky. After we were seated, a big guy strolled in with his family and sat immediately in front of Gail and me. He looked like a cowboy, clad as I recall in a western shirt, jeans, belt, and boots. For some reason I became intrigued by this fellow and desired to know more about him.

Loquacious me, I found reason to engage him in small talk. I discovered that he was Brian Wells from Springfield, Kentucky. That he and his clan were returning from a family vacation in San Antonio, Texas. We were not more than 15 minutes outside of Louisville when I finally got to the usual question that comes somewhere in a first conversation with a stranger. I leaned around from my aisle seat to where he was seated ahead and asked, "And what is your line of work, Mr. Wells?" He turned his head toward me and said, "I'm a medical doctor." "Well blow me down!" I said excitedly to myself, quoting the famous expression of the one and only Popeye. But I only said aloud, "Oh."

After a few moments of silence I said to my new friend, "Dr. Wells, have you ever been on a mission trip?" "No," was the reply. "Have you ever thought you'd like to go on one?" I asked again. "Yes, I have" he answered. I then began to get down to brass tacks, "Would you like to go on one in mid June?" "I think so," he responded.

My heart was beating 90 miles per hour as I began to share briefly the ministry God had led us to engage in and how he could play a pivotal role in helping us reach hundreds of Romanians with the love and grace of Jesus Christ. Dr. Wells said as we were coming in for a landing, "I think I can let you know tomorrow." That would have been on Sunday.

I called everybody and his brother I thought would stand with us in prayer over this strategic matter. We waited all day Sunday. Didn't hear from the good doctor. I don't know if it was Monday or Tuesday that I called him. He apologized for not getting back in touch but then made one of the sweetest announcements ever I heard. "I'm going. Count me in."

What a great mission trip emanated from this chance (?) meeting with Dr. Wells. Over the years Brian and his wife, Kathy, became dear friends of Gail's and mine. Indeed, they became great supporters of RAM.

After a few years, God began to speak to this wonderful man of God. "What about the poor who need medical care in your own area?" As a matter of significant faith – trusting belief and obedience – he opened a free medical clinic for the poor in

Lebanon, Kentucky and operated it for eight years. Several years ago Dr. Wells closed the clinic and made possible the free care for the poor in his expanded medical practice in Springfield. May the Lord be forever praised!

Did this work of Christian compassion in Lebanon begin coincidentally? Not on your life. We must go back to the many prayer warriors who, over a period of months, touched the heart of a loving Heavenly Father concerning the need for our RAM organization's first medical doctor to aid in our efforts to reveal Jesus Christ to a hurting, impoverished people.

As a result of untold numbers of prayers, the Father began to instigate certain dynamics of time, place, situations, and individuals that played together and eventually issued into the working out for the good of those who devotedly loved Him and were willing to be faithfully used by Him and His purpose.

"Come and see," Jesus Christ is alive in His Church! What a thrilling invitation. It can be your thrilling invitation if you choose to put self to death, embrace a cross, stay in prayer seeking the Father out while fully expecting Him to do the surprisingly remarkable thing in your midst.

He May Be Found in the Incredible

> "But as for me, I would seek God, and to God I would commit my cause – who does great things and unsearchable, marvelous things without number." Job 5:8-9

When I went as pastor of Buck Run Church for the first time, I was a student at Southern Seminary doing my best to keep all As in my classes so that I might qualify for the Ph.D. program. I discovered that there are more hoops to jump through than simply making good grades in class. For one thing, the student must possess a reading knowledge of Greek and Hebrew as well as two other languages, in my case German and French. I'm not gifted in languages.

One test that many of the guys of my generation feared was the essay exam. It consisted of only one question that was asked of the student that could come from anywhere: all he had covered in the M.Div. program, all assigned readings or from anything that might be religiously relevant in newspapers or periodicals – professional or secular. Some would take off an entire summer or a semester just to bone up for this exam. The aspiring doctoral candidate was given three hours to write one essay covering everything he knew on the subject.

I had worked and studied hard during my seminary pilgrimage. On this one occasion, however, I simply had not had time to get ready for the essay question, busy at this strategic moment moving to Buck Run as the new pastor and dealing with some unexpected, distracting issues.

It came time for the essay exam to be given and I was about as ready for the test as was   Cumberland College when they faced Georgia Tech in that memorable football game, on October 7, 1916. Remember the score? 220 to 0! What was I to do? Punting was out of the question. Too late to call the game off.

On the Sunday before the essay exam was to be given on Monday, Gail and I and the children were invited to eat Sunday lunch with our friends, Buddy and Jeanne Costigans. While Jeanne was putting the final touches on the meal, I happened to spot the new issue of *Time* magazine on the kitchen counter. It was the April 8, 1966 issue.

The cover both shocked and intrigued me. The color of the cover was solid red with big black letters emblazoned on the front. The words were in the form of a question: "Is God Dead?" It had just begun to make the rounds that three so-called American theologians, Altizer, Hamilton, and Van Buren, were suggesting such. I had done no substantial, in-depth reading on the subject because not much had been written for publication up to that time.

I picked up the magazine and read the article before we gathered at the table for the meal. As I read, the Lord said to me, "This is it. Your question will come from here."

From my graduate readings and seminars I was aware of the intellectual sources from which this idea had come. So that night after church I developed some thoughts in my mind around a topic I felt certain we would face, "Trace the historical, philosophical, theological, and ethical antecedents to the God is dead movement."

When I arrived at the coffee shop on Monday morning I saw a number of the fellows pouring through notes, quizzing each other, etc. They turned to me as they had done to each other upon arrival. "Bob, what's the question?" I gave it to them. "What?" they rejoined almost in bewilderment.

When we went into the classroom, the professor in charge had his graduate fellow come in and write the question on the board. Wow! Wow! Wow! The wording was exactly the same as had been given to me that had found lodging the night before in my mind: *"Trace the historical, philosophical, theological, and ethical antecedents to the God is dead movement."*

Well, I passed. In fact, I knocked the thing out of the park. Home run. Don't know about any of my buddies. But I left the campus going home to Frankfort ecstatic. I was also wondering at the same time why in the world the Father would do this for me! I began to seek God out in this wonder-full happening. "Where is He in it? What is He seeking to do? What is His message to me? And to others?" I asked Him aloud, "Father, what would you have me to do as a result of this unbelievable grace gift? How can I make certain You, Lord, become glorified through it all?"

Driving home, I also thought back to my first days entering Southern Seminary in the fall of 1959. I had felt the leadership of the Lord in my coming to this great institution ever since I was a boy, fascinated by an extraordinary Bible study in my home church led by Dr. Norman McCrummen. Dr. McCrummen was the young pastor of FBC Atmore and recent Ph.D. graduate of Southern Seminary. He was a genuinely humble man and yet at the same time, a brilliant and gifted teacher. I thought to myself, "One day I want to be a Bible scholar like him." I also remembered the battery of tests we had to take before entering Southern: psychological, aptitude, educational achievement level, etc. I recalled the post card I had received a couple of weeks later from Dr. Peyton Thurman, Dean of Admissions, that summoned me to his office.

What a marvelous man was Dean Thurman. A Southern gentleman in the truest sense. A man of humility and grace. And wit. What he told me that day didn't exactly tickle my funny bone, however. It didn't change what I thought of him one bit. He invited me to have a conference with him in response to an answer I had given to one of the concluding questions asked in the testing.

The question asked the incoming student in effect was, "What do you see yourself doing after graduation from seminary? What are your career goals?" My answer was: "I plan to go immediately into the Ph.D. program so as to not limit the opportunities I may have in ministry to and for the Lord, whether it be teaching on the college or seminary level, serving in a denominational position, or pastor of a large church."

Dean Thurman was kind. He always was. He sought to be gentle. He said ever so tenderly, "Bob, I have looked at your test scores and your stated career goals. I think you are being overly ambitious. What we are seeing in your test scores is a good C student. Oh, you might make an occasional B, but you should not expect many. As I said, you are a good, solid C student." "Now you need to know," he continued, "C students make some of our best pastors. But to try and push yourself toward something higher than this, in our opinion, is unrealistic and could lead to serious health problems or even in your leaving the ministry."

I thanked the dean for his kindness. I wanted to tell him he was wrong. But I was brought up to believe that one never contradicted or argued with his elders. All the way home to our apartment in Seminary Village, I thanked God for the plans He had for me, and the ways and means I knew were at His disposal to see these plans through, whatever the twists and turns the road up ahead may take and the obstacles that may be placed in my path.

Now here I was, seven years later, about to enter the doctoral program. I had a long way to go in meeting this academic challenge but I knew for certain, following the essay exam, who was guiding the journey.

You will understand when I tell you that I had to fall back on this incredible experience time and again during the days following. All the way to and beyond graduation.

It happened the first time after my supervisory committee, comprised of four of my professors, approved my prospectus for the writing of my dissertation. Another professor, under whom I had not studied, who was considered the authority on my subject matter at SBTS, shot me out of the saddle before I even to the starting gate.

I had developed a new hypothesis on the literary composition of the New Testament Book of James while teaching a course on the subject at a Howard College Extension Center. I had explored the hypothesis in a couple of M.Div. classes. Encouraged by several professors, I had pursued different perspectives on the subject in as many doctoral seminar papers as possible. I spent at least four years of painstaking work with the New Testament text reading, pondering, writing toward what I was certain would be my *magnum opus* one day. I was sure my work was going to be a major breakthrough in New Testament studies. Would I ever more be the talk within scholarly circles! My, my, my!

I was riding high in my own estimation when, "Bam," I found myself hard on my derriere, with the horse on which I had been traveling running away from me. "Whoa, Nellie!" Too late. Nellie was gone. It seemed that either it was back to the ranch or back home to the farm – though, to be truthful, I was never a farm boy. Just a product of the most wonderful small town in America, where just about everybody showered me with love and had great expectations for "one of their boys." They made me feel as if I were going to be somebody special one day. I already was, as all of us are, in that we're special to God. I just didn't know how or in what way. Didn't understand how it was being worked out. But for now my question was, "What am I going to do? Which way am I going to turn?"

While I was moping around, crying in my root beer, the Father spoke to me, lovingly, as to a small child. "Bobby, when are you ever going to learn that, if you ever hope to claim the prize, you've got to dance with the one who brings you to the party? If you hope to traipse in the Spirit, you've got to keep in step with the Spirit."

It was several years before I would finally understand what the Lord was seeking to say to me and do in and with my life. Until I did learn, He simply said, "Remember the incredible thing I did for you when you took the essay exam?" I had to keep coming back during those days to that incredible activity of the Father working mysteriously behind the scenes, causing the good to eventually come to fruition in my relationship with Him and His purposes for my life.

After the dust and emotional debris had settled from the wind of the Spirit's attempt to blow me on course with Him, another storm hit. I had gotten back to the ranch and gotten on somebody else's hobby horse with a dissertation I was not interested in and had a difficult time writing. But I "played the game" as doctoral students were at times heard to say.

My second prospectus passed my committee unanimously, as did each written chapter, until I finished the dissertation. All that remained before walking the stage and being hooded was defending the dissertation before the graduate committee. Would you believe that before we could get this meeting scheduled two of my supervisory professors went on sabbatical and were replaced? One of the replacements was – guess what? – an "authority" in the field I had written on. Not only did he ask that I rewrite portions of my dissertation but he demanded that I write an entire chapter just on his publications. "Good golly, Miss Molly!"

I did as I was told. I must admit the dissertation was strengthened appreciatively. I should have used this scholar's work to begin with. I must also admit, however, that this experience was a burr under my saddle for a long while. I simply could not understand how all this could have happened to me. And for what purpose? Have *you* ever felt like this?

I thank God for that incredible happening in which He revealed Himself six years before I reached the academic finish line. Still didn't comprehend it. I didn't really "get it" until nine more years would elapse in that transitional time just before leaving Monroeville and just after arriving the first time in Brandon.

It was then that I first came to understand and expect the unexpected on a regular basis from a loving, providential Heavenly Father. Indeed, in retrospect, it was then that I began to recognize that, when I thought Him to be absent and I all alone, He was there all the time. Working behind the scenes, doing the incredible. I just couldn't see it.

The reason I could not see him more profoundly at work, I discovered, is that I had never come to the place of truly embracing the Cross, especially when it was thrust upon me. I'm still in the process of learning its reality, its magnificence, its power, its rewards, its joys, its glorification of the Father and the Son through the Holy Spirit.

Come and See, Jesus Christ is Alive! In His people. In His Church. Doing absolutely incredible things. A watching world is waiting to see the reality of it all. The great invitation awaits its empowerment from your embrace – and my embrace – of Christ's Cross. Indeed it awaits the embrace of each of our churches. How incredible will be the results of such commitment. When prayerful expectancy joins radical faith in foolish total surrender.

He May Be Found in the Miraculous

> "Believe me when I say that I am in the Father
> and the Father is in me; or at least believe on the
> evidence of the miracles themselves. I tell you
> the truth, anyone who has faith in me will do
> what I have been doing. He will do even greater
> things than these, because I am going to the
> Father. And I will do whatever you ask in my
> Name, so that the Son may bring glory to the
> Father . . . . Jesus did many other miraculous
> signs in the presence of His disciples, which are
> not recorded in this book. But these are written
> that you may believe that Jesus is the Christ, the

Son of God, and by believing you may have life in His name." John 14:11-13; 20:30-31(NIV)

When you and I observe or experience the miraculous first hand our initial response should be to seek the Father out within the extraordinary event through significant faith – trusting belief and obedience. What is the Father saying to me? And to us? What of His will is He desiring to disclose? What must it challenge you and me and our churches to be? To do? To accomplish for His glory?

I find it somewhat miraculous that, at one and the same moment I began to pen these words on the miraculous, news began swirling around me about a miracle taking place that was touching, not only the populace of this country of ours but, also, people around the globe.

Who wasn't impacted in some way, at some level, by the story of the assassination attempt on the life of Congresswoman Gabrielle Giffords of Arizona? A lady who, before the accident, was an unknown outside her own state, and who overnight became known affectionately as "Gabby" by you and me and multiplied millions around the world. While we mourned without understanding the senseless loss of six precious lives in a sick man's rage, we nevertheless marveled over the miracle that took place before our very eyes.

The shot heard around the world was fired about two feet from Gabby's head, the bullet entering the temple and blowing out the other side of her skull, passing first through her brain. Praise God she survived this ordeal and, more than this, she baffled the doctors with her increasing indications of full recovery. Some medical specialists stated that it was a miracle of unprecedented proportions. That only the intervention of a divine Being could have made it possible.

While you and I are rejoicing over her remarkable recovery, we are made to wonder what this miracle really meant. What was God seeking to say, not only to each one of us, but to a callous society that has treated the miraculous as nothing but fabrication of the superstitious mind? It is not the purview of this writing to engage in social and psychological analysis of this horrific shooting. Nevertheless, at least two things may be said as a result of our observation.

First, in a world filled with insanity – both individual and corporate – we must find a way to come to peace as a people, or we will soon go to pieces as a society. The Church of Jesus Christ offers the Way! Let us pursue its presentation with everyone, everywhere, with all diligence. Second, hopefully, it will cause people, including many skeptics in the church who have to this point dismissed the idea of the miraculous, to pause and reflect on the meaning of that which neither science nor human reason can adequately explain. Now is a marvelous time to begin this reflection and conversation.

The Presence of the Miraculous

For those with open eyes and an open mind, the miraculous may be observed throughout the Universe. It may be seen as the providential activity of God in behalf of His children and His purpose in and through them for their world. It is His periodic breakthrough into human history at crucial moments to reveal His love and care, to exercise His governance in putting back in order that which has gone awry because of adversarial forces at work seeking to undermine His purposes.

As Seen in Creation. Most Christians will agree on the orderliness of Creation as the amazing results of a dazzling miracle that only a Being with wisdom and power far beyond what humankind could ever fashion or maintain. The Psalms are replete with the awe-struck description of a God who hung the stars in space. With billions of those babies dangling like beautiful Christmas ornaments on a giant tree, it is difficult to escape the fact that it took a miracle of indescribable magnitude to pull off this feat. Immanuel Kant said, "Two things fill my mind with ever increasing new wonder and awe: The starry heavens above and the moral order within."

While this Creator we call God is active in the world He has created, some would say primarily through the natural laws He has established for its maintenance, He often breaks through the natural with His supernatural activity that no one or natural law can explain, to call attention to His Sovereignty, His Authority, His Will, and His Providence. To make Himself known as the Center, as well as, the Circumference of the reality of life.

"The heavens declare the glory of God and the earth shows forth His handiwork." He is the Creator of all that is. His activity is miraculous for it is unexplainable. Except by the special understanding significant faith grants to us!

As Seen in Christ. The presence of the miraculous is observed on earth nowhere more clearly than in a person whose life has been radically transformed by the power of God – the power that raised Jesus from the dead.

Scripture teaches that when we receive Christ into our lives as Savior and Lord, the process of transformation takes place.

Every aspect of our psychosomatic being begins to change and we increasingly take on the likeness of Jesus Christ. Jesus said that it is a miracle of being "born again" or being born from above, a radical transformation of nature, character and personality that cannot be effected other than by the power of God's Spirit. No amount of personal reformation, psychological counseling, medical treatment or rehabilitation can bring about this remarkable conversion of one's total being.

Paul tells us in 2 Corinthians 5:17 (NIV): "Therefore, if anyone is in Christ, he is a new creation, the old has gone, the new has come!"

This new birth is occasioned when, through significant faith, one puts self to death (through confession and repentance), embraces Christ's cross, while surrendering everything he or she is and has to follow Him obediently. Those of us who have embraced this radical life and life-style know the remarkable difference the power that raised Jesus from the dead can make in one's life.

David Ruth's story a few pages back is an example of the tremendous victory Christ's resurrection power gave him when he turned everything over to the Lord. Things in his life that had him shackled and enslaved, things he sought deliverance from but could not effect, all gave way when Jesus Christ marched onto the scene and David bowed before His Lordship. His daughters noted how old nefarious habits vanished without his even being aware; without his even attempting to put them aside in his own strength. David said, "It was a miracle." The greatest miracle one can experience. It is God doing the impossible in a human life!

Another little song I learned as a child in church said it so simply – and powerfully:

Things are different now, something happened to me,
Since I gave my heart to Jesus,
Things are different now, And it's plain as can be,
Since I gave my life to God.

Has your life undergone this transformation? Is it taking place even now? Is the Holy Spirit changing you into Christ's likeness in ever-increasing wonder? If not, it is imperative that you take steps to allow the Father to work His miraculous magic in your life. Please be aware of the fact that you can never expect to help your church pulsate with the powerful life of a Resurrected Savior unless you have allowed Him, in fact, to come alive in your life!

As Seen in the Church. The Church, we are told by Paul, is the Body of Christ, the continued re-presentation of the Living Lord in the world. As such, it is the continuation of His life, ministry and purpose among and before those who are perishing. This Body has the evidence of the Holy Spirit obviously breathing within and energetically moving it along, so as to make known the Risen Christ who ever reveals His dynamic, powerful Presence in human history. The miraculous becomes an inevitable characteristic of the supernatural dwelling of God among His people.

The miraculous element of faith-life takes many forms. The unexplainable happening – that beyond human reasoning – has been shown to be a reality in the Church of Jesus Christ in numerous ways, as realized earlier in the story of the Central Baptist congregation in Decatur. More needs to be said of what

God has done and is doing in the life of that church – and in other congregations – to elaborate on the miraculous element, in particular, in the healing ministry of the church.

The Church as the body of Christ that continues the life and ministry of Jesus in the community where God has placed her extends His healing ministry there among His people. The passage in John 14, found above, is just one of many scriptural references that remind us that the church, collectively, and we who make it up individually, will be empowered for that witnessing role of healing in the community – according to our faith!

The Apostle, again, points to "gifts" of healing that the Spirit of God gives to the Church. "Gifts" plural, not just "gift" singular. There are different healing gifts. These gifts are given to various persons in the Body of Christ to bring God's mending, restorative power upon those within it with special needs. There are, for example, individuals with the gift of healing damaged emotions or broken relationships, such as we see embodied in Christian counselors or sensitive souls in the congregation. Some possess the gift of physical healing, such as medical doctors, pharmacists, nurses, special therapists, etc. There *are* those, moreover, who sometimes are seen to possess special spiritual giftedness to bring to bear God's healing touch on most all conditions of brokenness and illness.

I personally feel that pastors whom God places over a flock are gifted by a special anointing of the Spirit to care for the sheep. They are spiritually equipped to give the flock leadership and direction for the journey, to feed and water them for their nourishment, and to protect them from ravaging danger. Then, to paraphrase the Psalmist, the shepherds "Anoint their heads with (healing) oil" when they are bruised and hurting.

If, as I suggest, the gift of healing is given to the pastor why, you may ask, is there not more evidence of it in the life of the flock? I think it is because, while we who occupy the pastoral offices of the church have been given the gift, we do not always "unwrap" the gift, through significant, radical faith – trusting belief and obedience! At least, that was my experience.

Most ministers, for example, in some fashion seek to utilize this special giftedness when visiting parishioners who are sick. Usually it is through a prayer that the healing power of the Father is sought.

As previously stated, I stepped down as associate pastor of Central Baptist Church, Decatur, when my three-year contract terminated on November 1, 2010. I continued, however, to cover the hospital for Rob on occasions when he was out of town until our new associate pastor arrived on the field at the end of December.

On the afternoon of December 6, Gail and I visited Darlene Rains in the Parkview Hospital, following surgery that had been performed that morning on her left foot. Her testimony is perhaps similar to many church members who along the way, under various and sundry other situations, have experienced the Father bringing to bear the miraculous on their bodies through the mediation of His pastoral ministry in the congregation.

Before surgery on the left foot Darlene had for some time experienced a great deal of pain in her right hip. Interestingly,

180

following surgery, she had no pain in her left foot. But, the pain in her right hip was severe and had become exacerbated as it ran down her right leg. Indeed, it was so intense that she could hardly lie in bed. Strong medication could not even take the edge off the pain.

After our brief visit, I prayed expectantly in Jesus name – in His stead – that the Father would touch His child with healing. Darlene recounts that the moment Gail and I turned and walked out of the room, the pain turned and walked out of her body! And it hasn't returned since. Blessed be the God who cares for us, His children, and heals us!

God, of course, is Sovereign and far wiser than any of us about what our greatest needs are. Therefore, He does not always grant what we ask for. I have found nevertheless that when I pray in expectant faith and He does not at that time give what I beseech Him for, He always gives something better or, at the very least, prepares those of us involved in the prayer event for something exceedingly better ahead. All for His glory!

This is true because, as I have observed, there are different levels of healing. The very lowest level of healing is the *physical*. You and I are healed of our often infirmities from time to time by our Father only to get sick again. Since our bodies are constantly in a state of decomposition and decay, subject to the incessant ravages of age, circumstances, overindulgent lifestyles, accidents of life, and the impingement of hostile, evil forces that are seeking at every moment to destroy us, we can never experience total healing in our journey through this world. Not until death claims us do we experience the *highest healing*, the transition from this imperfect human state into the state of total wholeness, to be found only in the presence of our Eternal Father.

In the meantime, God heals but on different levels, always desiring that we find His healing on the highest level of our most important need.

Above the level of *physical healing*, for example, are the levels of *relational and emotional healing*. God at times fails to heed our pleas for the healing of our bodies so that we can discover the greater joy of having impaired relationships restored. Let us never forget that true Christianity is about relationships. If it is anything, Jesus taught, it is about the complete surrender of all we are and have in a love relationship with God and neighbor. Moreover, Scripture teaches that if there is something amiss in our relationship with another person, something is surely amiss in our relationship with God. Consequently, the blessings of God cannot rest upon us in the here and now nor in the hereafter! A sobering thought.

Like so, the lower level of healing in the *physical* is sometimes denied us for the sake of the opportunity to encounter the higher levels of *moral and spiritual restoration*. The Apostle James reminds us how integrally tied together are all the impairments we experience in the *physical, moral, and spiritual dimensions* of our being. He tells us in 5:14-16 (NLT):

> "Are any of you sick? You should call for the elders of the church to come and pray over you, anointing you with oil in the name of the Lord. Such a prayer offered in faith, will heal the sick, and the Lord will make you well and if you have committed any sin you will be forgiven. Confess

your sins to each other and pray for each other that you may be healed. The earnest prayer of a righteous man has great power and produces wonderful results."

God allows illness and pain to continue their pillage of our bodies at times to awaken us to the need of a higher level of healing, that of the brokenness that sin has brought about. Such physical illness gives us an opportunity to discover the greater need of our lives and to hear *missional messages* from God revealing to us what is the more glaring evil that is destroying our very souls.

George heard that I had returned to Buck Run Church for a second time, following a sixteen year hiatus. We had been friends during my first pastorate there. However, he had left the church and turned his back on the things of God shortly after our family moved to Monroeville, Alabama. He was for all practical purposes lost to God and the Kingdom purposes for his life. He had a family member call me and ask me to come visit him in the King's Daughters Hospital in Frankfort. He was dying. His body was eaten up with cancer. Its progression had crossed the point of no return. He wanted me to come and pray for his healing!

We had a tearful reunion that day in his hospital room. He talked openly about his situation and about his impending soon departure from this life. About his fear of what lay ahead of him. I sensed that there was something far deeper plaguing him than just his battle with cancer and his fear of dying. We moved gingerly into the realm of relationships. I inquired of him who in his family or close circle of friends was creating an unholy anxiety in his mind and in his heart. He broke down and cried. "Brother Bob," he intoned, "I have a brother, Jim – you know him well – with whom I have not spoken in over three years." I said to my long-time buddy, "George, you know, don't you, that this estrangement from your brother is worse than your cancer? It's eating away at your soul. And creating this unrest and anxiety about where you are right now at the close of your journey. It is that which is keeping you away from God, His love, His grace, His forgiveness, and His assurance of wonderful things that can lie ahead of you." "George, unless you make things right with Jim they will never be right with your Lord and you will not be able to claim security in God nor ownership of that which you desire up ahead."

I prayed that morning for George's healing, making it very clear that I was praying for his greatest need, the healing of his heart and of his relationship with his brother. I was unable to return the next day to the hospital, but the following day, Wednesday, when I returned to George's room I noted a different man. Yes, his body was still wasting away. But there was a calmness noted in his countenance, punctuated by a smile on his face that told me the whole story of what surely happened the night before, when George called Jim to come to his bedside.

There the two brothers embraced in tears and asked that each would forgive the other of whatever had caused their alienation. It was a remarkable time of healing. And from that moment on, until God took George by the hand and lifted him out of this vale of sorrow and tears, there was no longer any anxiety, no regrets, no longer anymore physical pain, only the glory of the Lord encompassing a fellow who chose to come back home to his God. It happened when he came by way of the cross, putting self to death – in the confession of sin and repentance – so that he and his brother could thereby live together in forevermore love!

How amazingly related are the things of the heart and the things of the body.

Her name wasn't really Thelma, but to protect the family we will call her by that name. Her story, nevertheless, is altogether real and true. She was a member of one of the churches that I have had the joy of serving as pastor. She came to my office one day quite distraught, with her emotions out of control. I knew that Thelma was an alcoholic. She had been in and out of treatment, gone to first one doctor and then to another. Tried everything that anyone else told her might work to no avail. She wasn't all that old, but her problem made her look twenty years older. She came to me as a last resort.

Thelma asked if I would pray for her. She wanted desperately to be healed. Obviously, her abuse of alcohol had created serious problems for her marriage, her family, her life in the community, especially within the church fellowship. I told her that I did want to pray for her but first, I wanted to ask her a few questions.

I asked Thelma if she would tell me about her childhood. She hesitated for awhile, skipped here and there going nowhere in particular with her story. Then she burst into uncontrollable crying. She admitted what I had suspected: she had been sexually abused growing up. It was by her father. The abuse lasted until she left home. I asked her if she had ever forgiven her dad. She said, "No, how could I ever forgive a man like that?" I asked her if she had ever considered that her unforgiving heart had created so many of her problems and caused her to live a life with alcoholism? She told me that she had never linked those things.

I shared with Thelma about the power of forgiveness and the danger of the unforgiving heart. I relayed to her from Scripture how our forgiveness or unforgiveness of others actually dictates the forgiveness or unforgiveness of God towards us. She grasped the concept clearly, though it was difficult. To forgive a father like that would, in effect, be like taking up a cross and putting self to death in order to receive the liberating power of the Holy Spirit.

I closed our counseling session by making a suggestion. I asked her to consider going to her father's grave and there to pray that her heavenly Father would fill her heart full of His love for her dad. And then verbally and sincerely forgive him.

Thelma came back to my office a short time later and told me what had happened. She had done what I suggested. She had travelled across the state to where her father was buried. There she got on her knees and asked her heavenly Father to fill her with love for her dad. She told me with joy effervescing from her soul, "It was wonderful, Brother Bob! I started crying while on my knees telling my father that I loved him and forgave him for what he did to me!" She told me that, almost immediately, her desire for alcohol left her. She now felt good inside herself. Things were getting increasingly better in her relationship with her family. God was now so dear and precious to her life.

I haven't heard from or about Thelma in a long time. But for years following this incident she was still basking in the

Sonlight of God's love and forgiveness and living proof of the miraculous, healing power of the resurrected Christ.

I have found in my own experience how God at times postpones our physical healing until we return to His special assignments in our lives, repenting of our disobedience and committing ourselves obediently to the tasks He has given us. A healing on quite a higher plane.

2010 was a painful year for me. Blissfully painful. I was hospitalized six times, once with a heart attack, once because of an automobile accident, with the other four being related to the first two incidents. For a guy 74 years of age I guess some might suggest that the wearing away of one's body shouldn't be thought to be too unusual. But it was. Because, you see, the verse of Scripture God gave me for my 2010 yearly message indicated a year of smooth sailing. Or so it seemed.

My personal message from God was printed on a little card taken quite coincidentally from the desk of Paula Brown, the lovely Christian lady who assisted me, of all things, in getting my medical insurance records straight at the main office of BlueCross-BlueShield in Birmingham! Here's what the card said, in Psalm 32:8 (NLT): "I will guide you along the best pathway for your life. I will advise you and watch over you."

Here I was lying in a Decatur General Hospital bed for the second time with legs that had been severely damaged in the automobile accident. The injury to the legs had caused profuse internal bleeding following the accident, at first unnoticed by the doctors who were busy as bees attempting to make certain that my ticker was ticking properly. This unchecked loss of blood caused my blood pressure to drop out of sight. Because of this, I passed out at Big Bob Gibson's Bar-B-Que Restaurant and almost departed this world before the medics could get me back to the hospital. For several months both of my legs and ankles were swollen, the left one almost twice its normal size, with an army of blood clots patrolling up and down both legs. They seemed to act as guards to prevent agents of healing from getting in and establishing a beachhead in the areas that needed desperate help.

One clot was the size of a lemon in my left leg and was threatening the future use of this limb. Dr. Glenn Ward probably saved the leg with an emergency surgical procedure that removed about one-half of the clot. The other half, attached around a main nerve, was determined to be in too dangerous a place to remove.

As I lay in the hospital bed on that March day, 2010 following surgery, with both legs and left foot in constant pain, I reexamined the Scripture the Lord had given me a couple of months earlier to serve as a reminder that year of His providential guidance and care. I began to question, "Father, how can it be said that you have really guided me along the best path for my life? In taking the shortcut home from my early morning exercise workout, how could my choice of the narrow Red Bank Road have been your choice for me?"

To understand my accident, it is probably necessary for you to know that the narrow shoulder on my side of the road was filled with wet leaves that had been soaked following a couple months of rainy weather. It caused the front and back tires on the right side of my car to sink down about four inches on the curve when I sought to move to the shoulder and dodge the gentleman coming toward me, who rounded the bend on my side of the road. I lost control of the car and greeted head-on a small but sturdy tree. The car was totaled. "How for heaven's sake, Father, could that have been your best guidance for me that morning?"

I continued to reexamine Psalm 32:8 with this question: "Father, you promised to watch over me and to advise me. Lord, I need some advice. Tell me how you were watching over me. What is the meaning in all this?"

In that moment God did advise me. He sent me a *missional message* couched in a Scripture verse that I had pondered through the years but whose truth I had not been able to get a handle on. The Father said, "Remember Hebrews 5:8, the verse that has long had you puzzled?" "Yes, Lord," I replied. He said to me, "That verse is for you. Ponder it for awhile. Listen for my voice in it as you seek a word of guidance."

So I did. And, God's *missional message* to me in Hebrews 5:8 began to make sense.

The verse speaks about our Lord Jesus and His obedience to the Father. It says, "He learned obedience by the things He suffered."

I confess I do not understand everything the writer may have had in mind as it relates to the life of our Savior. However, the Spirit made it perfectly clear what it should mean to me. Follow my story:

Two years prior to the occasion of this hospitalization the Father had given me an astounding commission. In an early morning devotional time, as I was carrying on a casual conversation with Him, He dropped a bomb on me. Like a bolt out of the blue He said, "Bobby, I want you to set down in writing everything you have seen me do. Everything in your life, in your ministry, and in the lives of those who have shared with you the pilgrimage I have had you on in this world."

I was shocked. I must admit that I have had four or five books rattling around somewhere in my vacuous noggin for many years. But I had been so busy with pastoral duties, while also leading the RAM mission organization, that I thought I would put off a writing career until I reached a ripe age of say 81! How foolish of me to have ever thought such. The Father, however, interrupted my neat little misguided plan.

I was also *frightened* by my Lord's commission to me. It's one thing to fancy yourself writing a book. Quite another to really do it. I immediately got cold feet. For one thing, I developed pause about this new charge because of what the Father had asked me to write. *Everything I've seen Him do!* The fact is, I have been privileged in my long ministry to see God in His Holy Spirit do some of the most unbelievably awesome, incredibly miraculous things one could possibly be granted to see. (As has Rob in his briefer ministry!) I have not often talked about them. After all, I am a *Baptist* Christian, you know.

Not many Baptists believe in what some feel are the spooky things of the Spirit. It's okay to believe intellectually in the Holy Spirit, as in the Creed, or in a Confession of Faith, as long as you keep Him there in His place. Like in a box. Like, say, in a coffin! I thought, what will some people think if I place all these things down in writing?

All during this time I was suffering physically. At times, in excruciating pain. I prayed constantly that God would heal my body so that I could get on with the numerous responsibilities He had given me.

Return now with me back again to Decatur General Hospital where we were before this last excursion. Dr. Ward had removed the large blood clot from my leg. As I had been prepped for surgery, God had begun to prep me for something far different. Once again I brought up to Him the Scripture verse He had given me to demonstrate His providential governance and care of my life for the year 2010. As related above, I began to ask God where all the pain and suffering fit into His promise to me for that year. As you recall, He directed me to Hebrews 5:8. "He learned obedience by the things He suffered." He told me to ponder it in light of all I had encountered.

Immediately the light went on. It didn't take me but a few moments to get the message. The Father said, "Bobby, you have not done what I told you to do two years ago. *I instructed you to tell all the things you have seen me do!*

A personal testimony is the most powerful tool the disciple of Christ and His Church has to offer a watching world that stands in need of a witness to the Living Lord. Folks who are searching for reality in the Christian faith desire more than just a book of "how-to's" based on some formula for success. They want more from us than only what we can tell them someone else said or did or experienced. I must say, at the risk of offending some, that the outside world wants to hear more than a bunch of scriptures you and I can quote to them. *They want to know what you and I know to be true about Jesus Christ!*

191

Because of what we have experienced and seen Him do. How He has changed our lives and is making a difference in our interactions with others and the way we are responding positively to the vicissitudes of fate and fortune. They want to see and feel and experience the resurrected Lord in our lives and in the life of His Church.

Our Lord's instruction to the Gaderene tomb dweller whom He had made whole is instructive about what is fundamentally involved in the Christ-follower bearing His witness. Said He, "Go home to your family and friends and tell them what great things the Lord has done for you." Mr. Jones, if you have truly met the Master and are enjoying an intimate daily walk with Him, and are witnessing His remarkable, living presence in your life, you will find it extremely easy to share Him with a new friend or a stranger. Most folks outside the church are open, even anxious, to hear true stories of a truly alive God. When you do share your real-life testimony, the chances of your neighbor inviting the Lord into his or her heart and life are exponentially increased.

A miraculous healing took place in my hospital room. Not the immediate healing of the body – though that would come. It was in a much higher healing – *the healing of a disobedient spirit*. Ever since that time I have been writing like crazy, especially since stepping down from the pastoral ministry. The Lord encouraged me to continue to pursue with Rob a book for the Church of Jesus Christ. The writing would not be built around stories of God's activity that we had merely heard or read about. It would instead embody occurrences that we have experienced and personally know to be true about the Lord of the universe and the things He continues to do in and through His people, His Church. We now seek only to present a matchless Heavenly Father and His marvelous Son, Jesus Christ, working through an incredible, powerful Holy Spirit.

The Purpose of the Miraculous

Some question why miraculous activity is a must for the life of the Church today. Why would the Lord of the Church feel it necessary to abrogate the laws He established in the beginning that have given structure and governance to His creation and an orderly life for you and me on earth? The Apostle John in chapters 14 and 20, cited above, has answered this question rather clearly. Note three reasons.

To Bring Glory to the Father. Our Lord Jesus suggested in John 4:13 that the reason He performed miracles and, consequently would enable you and me in the church to do them in His stead, was to "bring glory to the Father."

How fundamentally different is this stated purpose of miracles in the church from what we regrettably find espoused today in some Christian circles. The emphasis too often, as Leonard Ravenhill said, about some evangelism that is done today, is purely humanistic. It's all for the glory and pleasure of man. The "Have you had your miracle today?" syndrome brings a spiritual arrogance to the church that is divisive and deadly. It can cause new converts as well as immature church members to believe that the experience of, in particular, a healing event in their lives makes them more spiritual than others and more special to God than those who have not had a similar type experience. Such an attitude is satanic!

Jesus did not always heal everyone He came in contact with. But, when He did heal – and it was often – He did it to bring glory to the Father. Not to congratulate a man or woman on their favored place in His Kingdom.

Eddie Scheler, dear friend and brother of Rob's and mine, is the dynamic young pastor of the Saint Paul's Lutheran Church in Decatur, one of the outstanding Christian congregations in our city. Several years ago Eddie had a miraculous healing that sometimes he shares to point others to a God who is very much alive, caring of His children and is worthy of all our worship, praise, and devotion.

On November 1, 2003, before dawn, Eddie was hunting when he fell about 15 feet off a deer stand out of a tree. While he landed on his feet, his right leg caught the force of the fall. The sound of the crack he heard upon impact was thought by him to be a broken leg. It turned out to be 4 inches of crushed and disintegrated tibia and fibula just above his ankle bone. He knew he was in trouble when the surgeons subsequently pointed out that the x-ray was picking up no bone mass at all in that part of leg. It was as if the bone had disappeared. The surgeon said that what he found there were thousands of little fragments and splinters of bone.

God's providential care in this accident was revealed in a number of miraculous turn of events. For starters, Eddie woke up early on this day in question and decided to go hunting. Alone. He slipped out without telling anyone where he would be hunting that day. And he forgot his cell phone. Think what might have been had Eddie lain on the ground in that remote place indefinitely, gripped in horrendous pain.

How gracious the Father was to nudge Eddie's friend, Ben Troutman, and his nephew Nate, to get up that morning and decide to take a walk, in hopes of bagging a turkey. It was the first time Ben had been out in the woods all fall. They had not planned to go that morning but, again, "something" just waked them up and told them to go. A remarkable set of circumstances changed the direction of their turkey search so that they were at just the right place, at just the right time, to hear their friend, Eddie, when he called out for help.

Eddie likes to make the point when telling his story that "God never arrives too early nor does He arrive too late!" His timing is perfect, as are His providential workings in behalf of His children. Until Ben and Nate appeared – surely sent by the Lord – Eddie held on by praying the simple little plea from the liturgy, "Lord have mercy. Christ have mercy. Lord, have mercy." Throughout his ordeal of surgeries and painful recuperation he clung to one of his life verses, Romans 8:28 "We know that God works in all things for the good of those that love Him and are called according to His purpose."

The hospital to which Pastor Eddie was taken on the morning of his accident had no orthopedic surgeon on call. It "just so happened" that unexpectedly Dr. Shebir Bhayni appeared on the scene. He gave God's good servant a shot that knocked him out and kept the pain at bay for the next 24 hours. Enough time to set the leg in a splint to allow the swelling to go down so that the next orthopedic man would have the best chance for possible surgery.

On November 3, Eddie was taken to Pittsburgh, Pennsylvania to the Forbes Medical Center, where Dr. Spencer Butterfield and his medical team were noted to be at the forefront of those who handled these kinds of cases. Dr. Butterfield, as he prepared for surgery, described Eddie's shattered leg as "horrific." Eddie, an avid runner, asked the doctor if he would ever be able to run again. Dr. Butterfield said that he could not promise anything except that he would probably walk with a limp and, very possibly, with a cane.

On November 6, the Butterfield Team did a 3 ½ hour procedure that consisted in placing two 6 inch plates and 20 screws in the leg. The doctors said they would be permanent fixtures. There forever! The pain over the three months following surgery was almost unbearable. For four months the preacher could not place any weight on the leg whatsoever. In fact, during this time of intense pain, the only time there was relief was when prayer intercessors would come and lay hands on his leg and pray! Sometimes they would come to the house, sometimes at church, but each time the pain was completely relieved as they prayed. The medication really didn't help much, but Eddie discovered what he already knew, that more powerful than any medication are the healing hands of God upon His people!

No doubt because of the prayers of people across the nation who were praying, but also as a direct result of these intercessors, through the summer and fall of 2004 Eddie's walk began to get noticeably better. It became increasingly evident that he would not walk with a limp nor need a cane. He began to run, up to five miles an hour on the treadmill. One day in April, 2005 after a workout on the treadmill, he noticed that there were red marks along the leg where the screws had been placed. A trip back to Pittsburgh revealed what Eddie's wife, Trish, said she had known all along: he had a loose screw! In fact, 20 of them.

An unbelievable "something" had happened. An x-ray revealed that the shattered bones had miraculously grown back together so strong and in such perfect proportion to the other bones in the leg, especially the ankle bone, that it was beginning to push the screws out. Surgery was scheduled. All the "permanent" hardware was removed. What the surgeon found was shattered bones put back together again and made whole!

Dr. Butterfield remarked following surgery: "You must have somebody on your side." Eddie smiled and said, "I do. A wonderful Lord, a great wife, a praying congregation, and a gifted surgeon."

Now, Pastor Eddie runs as fast and as long as he ever did. He also jumps just as high. Not in church, of course! However, at times when he thinks on the Father's miraculous providence, in particular on what He did for him in and through the hunting accident, he leads his congregation like an exuberant cheerleader in reading another of his life verses, Psalm 75:1: "We give thanks to you O God, we give thanks for your name is near; (we) tell of your wonderful deeds."

The miraculous element to our Christian faith is always experienced for a definite reason. Primarily, to bring glory to the Father. Christ is committed to bringing glory to the Father through His Body, the Church and, thereby, provides remarkable happenings in the life of His people as prompters for His worship, adoration, and praise.

To Engender Faith Among His Disciples. In John 14:11, Jesus admonishes the Twelve, "Believe me when I say that I am

197

in the Father and the Father is in me; or at least believe on the evidence of the miracles themselves."

Faith is measurable. Because we who follow the Christ are on a continuum of growth, all of us at different levels of becoming-like-Christ, our faith is likewise at different stages of becoming like His! Some have much faith. Some have little. Jesus at times seemed to be exasperated that His disciples had so little. He made clear that the depth of one's faith determined how much of the Spirit's miraculous power would be released in his or her life.

Just as "iron sharpens iron," nothing enhances one's faith like companionship with persons of faith. Unless, however, it is either the experience or the witness of God's miraculous power poured out on an individual or on an entire congregation of the faithful at a crucial, strategic moment in time.

We have recounted a number of incidents of the miraculous intervention of God in the life of Central Baptist Church as He sought to inspire the congregation to attempt the impossible for Him and His glory in the move to a new campus. Each miracle built increased faith in the lives of its membership in general and in an increasing number of individuals in the congregation. One such incident involves a prayer for specific healing that took place on a Wednesday night, May 31, 2006. It was precipitated by Dr. Glenn and Jennifer Ward's desperate plea to their pastor to intercede for Jennifer at a most difficult, dangerous moment in her life.

You will recall Donna Campbell's "faith trek" to the prize Easter egg so that she could give to the building fund? Remember, too, how she prayed to find the egg not only so she could give, but so that God would be glorified and her children would see the results of believing prayer and have *their* faith deepened? Well, Jennifer Ward's story likewise grew out of her heart's desire that her children see God alive and at work so that they might believe in the Lord and trust Him with all of their hearts and souls.

Her story begins when she had a transformational experience with the Lord in her thirties. She and her husband, who, likewise, about that time, had experienced a miraculous change in his life, submitted their lives and their marriage to the Lord for His glory and His will. They were raising their three children, Will, Ben, and Jena Beth with the commitment to "bring them up in the saving knowledge of the Lord" and to be an example to them. Following their conversion, Glenn and Jennifer involved themselves in numerous ministries in the church and were using their health-care careers to serve Christ in mission work around the world.

Jennifer prayed fervently for her children every day during their teenage years that God would deepen their faith and that they would never question who He was. At times she worried about their relationship with the Lord. One morning she was so burdened that she pled with God to strengthen their faith *even if He must use her health to do so!*

Oddly enough or, as she says, perhaps by God's design she forgot that prayer. A couple of months later she awoke like any other day and went out to work in her garden. At lunch she came in exhausted. While preparing something to eat she had a sharp pain in one side of her face. She took Tylenol and thought little about it but as she returned to work the pain returned. By night fall the pain was unbearable. No relief to be found. In just a few days the pain had gotten so severe she could no longer function. She could not even bear a single hair brushing her face or her tears to roll down her cheeks.

Jennifer was diagnosed with *Trigeminal Neuralgia*, commonly known as "Suicide Disorder," a neurological disorder that is extremely difficult if not impossible to treat. It's an incurable disease. The medications she was given made her sick and did not mask the pain. A neurosurgeon was consulted. He told them what Dr. Ward already knew: A surgical procedure, a craniotomy, was the only thing that might help, but it was extremely dangerous at the very least. It was known to leave patients zombie-like, with the permanent loss of mental faculties.

Glenn and Jennifer knew that there was no one else to turn to except their Lord. They came to Rob on that Wednesday night during family night supper and asked if he would pray that God would heal her without her having to undergo such dangerous surgery. Rob said yes, of course. He immediately went to his office and got the vial of olive oil he uses for anointing those who come to him for healing prayer, in obedience to James 5:13-16.

Rob had a message prepared for that evening's mid-week service. He nevertheless sensed in his spirit that this night was to be a signal moment in the life of Central Church, a congregation that was learning to walk by faith. So he scratched plans for the sermon on his way back from his office. When he mounted the pulpit he announced to the congregation that "Tonight, God is leading us to have just a service of healing prayer!"

You could have heard a pin drop. This is a Baptist church, you know. While Rob had on occasions anointed with oil those who had come to his office for prayer, he had never publicly called for such a service at Central. Never even mentioned one in his first 2 ½ years as pastor.

When Rob called Glenn and Jennifer to the altar and informed the church that he would anoint her with oil, lay hands upon her head and pray that God would heal her, the silence became deafening! Jaws dropped so low, so fast, that it was a thousand wonders there were no facial injuries recorded that night in the congregation!

The pastor invited those who desired to join him at the altar in laying hands on both Glenn and Jennifer, while praying over them, to do so. Though it doubtless seemed a little strange at first, many in the congregation came forward and, in faith, beseeched the Lord to bring healing to His precious servant, Jennifer, so that through her life and in His church He might be glorified before a watching world.

It was a God-moment. The Holy Spirit came in power upon the service and baptized the congregation in His gracious love. *By Friday, Jennifer was pain free!* Praise the Lord! Since that moment, Jennifer has used every opportunity to praise God, not just for her healing, but for His answer to her fervent prayer. Although her children were not present at that service, in the ensuing days – and months and years – they have witnessed the miraculous hand of a mighty God doing what only God can do. They will never be the same. Neither will the church.

Jennifer's healing was not the only touch of the Father on the lives of persons in the Central congregation that May night, 2006. Following prayer for the Wards, the pastor invited others who desired the anointing of oil and prayer to come forward. A number of members came.

I do not know the names of all who asked for the Lord's healing in that remarkable service, nor just what kind of healing they experienced. I am aware that Ruby Newby, wife of our associate pastor for senior adults, came forward and found the healing grace of the Lord efficacious for her. Following heart surgery she had developed a constant hacking cough that had lingered interminably. Prayer and medicine seemed not to help. After several days following this special service and prayer for her, the cough left.

Jason and Amy Ratliff's story was different but also Christ-honoring and inspirational. They came that night to the mid-week service, a young couple who had struggled with infertility for a number of years. They so much desired a child. Had consulted with doctors, gone through all kinds of tests and the results were the same. Chances of Amy conceiving, even with the assistance of a fertility clinic, were not encouraging.

When Rob stood up and announced that Wednesday evening that things were going to be quite different from the norm, that it would be a dedicated service for prayer and laying hands on those with special needs and hurts, Amy and Jason looked at each other. With tears welling in both of their eyes, they knew at one and the same time why they were there that night. During the service Jason stood up and asked for prayer in support of their desire to have a baby. The pastor invited them to come down to the altar where he proceeded to anoint them with oil while the congregation joined him in the laying on hands and praying for this precious couple.

Amy did not get pregnant right away. It happened just over a year later. Nevertheless, she and Jason made a remarkable commitment that God honored. They decided to forgo any medical options and simply put their trust in the Lord, to be submissive to His will, to whatever would bring glory to Him. As a result, God sent them a beautiful little girl, Reynolds, who is a blessing to her mother and dad and their families as well as to her church family. More than this, Reynolds is a constant, visible reminder that miraculous are the offspring of significant, trusting faith. And faith continues to beget faith at Central. And God continues to honor it!

To Elicit Faith From Unbelievers. When, in John 20:30-31, the beloved Apostle reminds us that Jesus performed far more miracles than were recorded in His book, he gave the reason why he had included those that he did: "That you may believe that Jesus is the Christ, the Son of God, and that by believing you may have life in His name."

What is the one book of the New Testament that a church most frequently chooses to place in the hands of an unbeliever? The Gospel of John! It appears in these verses above that, from the beginning of the Christian movement, this Gospel with its remarkable stories of Jesus' miraculous healings was utilized for the evangelistic, missional task of the church. Indeed, the very wording of the verses indicates that the book, now read, would have been in the hands of an inquirer into the Faith, a seeker after the Truth.

The Father today continues to perform miracles in and through the Church, the Body of Christ. The miracles are signs that point unbelievers to Christ, the living, resurrected Lord. One who can and will set them free from their bondages and sins and give them the life He enjoys – Eternal life!

My daughter, Jeannece (Neece) Luhrs, who resides with her husband Dennis in Frankfort, Kentucky, is a woman of significant faith –trusting belief and obedience – and prayer. Because of this the Father at times allows her to see Him do remarkable, unbelievable things.

In June of 2002 her 17 year old son, Jake Hart, was in the University of Virginia Medical Center in Charlottesville, Virginia. He was awaiting surgery to remove two tumors on his pituitary gland, a serious procedure. Practically all of Jake's immediate family was there. Because of the cramped hospital room, all of us took turns in visiting in Jake's room.

The night before surgery, Neece and Dennis had left the room to get supper when they came in contact with two very distraught women in the elevator. They were crying and kept repeating, "Our sister, our sister" like a mantra.

As one woman looked up, Neece simply inquired, "What's wrong with your sister?"

Between sobs the story unfolded. The previous night, their sister had gone for a swim in her backyard pool. After swimming, she headed to the bathroom where she collapsed. Her family called 911 and she was rushed to the hospital. Unfortunately it was determined that she was in a vegetative state with no apparent brain function. A hopeless prognosis was given and the family was devastated. Just as they were finishing telling Neece and Dennis in a few brief words about this sad situation, the elevator door opened and each headed their separate ways. At the prompting of the Holy Spirit – a *missional message* indeed – Neece called out to the women, "I would love to pray with you for your sister if you would like." Surprisingly, they were open to the suggestion and they exchanged hospital room numbers.

When Dennis and Neece returned to the hospital and were getting settled in with Jake, a woman knocked on the door and entered with the question, "Are you the lady who is going to pray for my sister?" As Neece shook her head yes, she began a silent, fervent prayer for the Holy Spirit's leadership. In her own words, her prayer was along the following lines, "What am I going to say, Lord? I have no words for this family. What kind of prayer would even be appropriate for this situation? Lord, I am over my head but I believe that You impressed upon me to offer prayer, so I ask that you get me out of the way and You pray the prayer – through me – that You want spoken to this family."

Neece was led by the unnamed sister who opened the door to a larger area that was literally brimming with people – perhaps 30 or more. "Help, Lord!" was all she had time to mutter when the matriarch of the family came up to her, embraced her, and through tears thanked her for coming. As they all joined hands, Neece began to pray. To this day, she admits that she doesn't remember exactly what she said. The words were not her own. They were the Lord's! She only remembers that she prayed that God would be glorified in the situation as He saw fit.

After the prayer, and many hugs and tears, my special daughter headed back to Jake's room. A third sister whom Neece had not previously met followed her out the door. After thanking her for the prayers, she explained something of the family situation. It seems that her parents were believers and that she and her sisters had grown up in a Christian home. However, all of the siblings except this one lady had fallen away from God. Moreover, there was division and discord in the family.

Neece handed the sister a page of Scripture verses on healing and suggested that she, as well as the other family members, take turns reading the Scriptures out loud all night long while pleading with God for a miracle in her sister's life. She thanked Neece who returned to Jake's room where the family began preparing for his surgery the next morning. The Father blessed so incredibly with a successful surgery for Jake. He blessed even more remarkably in the life of this unknown family down the hall. While our family awaited Jake's return to his room from recovery, the third sister and her immediate family knocked on the door. Neece almost hates to tell it but she admits that, at the moment, she wondered if the sister were still alive. The news she gave Neece was glorious. God touched this family. They followed her advice and read those Scriptures all night over their sick sister. How God worked! A number of the family members during the night were saved, broken relationships were restored and their sister remarkably improved. Their sister was healed and, the next morning, sat up in bed! Last Neece heard, the family was moving their sister to a rehab center.

Neece has regretted that she did not exchange contact information with this family. She has often wondered how they are doing. But, more often, she has wondered how many other opportunities she has missed to be a conduit of the Holy Spirit because she failed to heed His promptings.

In the Father's providential care and guidance of His people He at times moves within their midst with miraculous power to bring about physical healing so that other, higher healings will be effected. Indeed, so that faith will be elicited in the hearts and lives of unbelievers and salvation may come to their souls!

Keep the invitation clearly in your heart and on your lips: Come and see, Jesus Christ is alive! In His Church. Among His people. For He is miraculously working all things out for good, for His glorious purposes, especially for those who need evidence that elicits faith in the heart of the unbeliever.

Chapter Seven

Seek Him Out in Life's Disappointments

"So Jacob served seven years for Rachel, and they seemed only a few days to him because of the love he had for her. Then Jacob said to Laban, "Give me my wife, for my days are fulfilled, that I may go in to her.' And Laban gathered all the men of the place and made a feast. Now it came to pass the evening that he took Leah his daughter and brought her to Jacob . . . (And) it came to pass in the morning that behold, it was Leah."
Genesis 29:20-23, 25 (NKJV)

Life is filled with disappointments. Some great. Some small. All are discomforting. Sometimes devastating. The Good News is that God may always be found in the disappointing, working out His providential care for us, when we earnestly seek Him out in faith.

The story of Jacob working for Rachel posits for us some salient truths to ponder whenever disappointment comes our way.

All of Us Have a Rachel in Our Lives

Jacob had taken the first stage out of Dodge. Well, actually, out of the land of the Philistines! Wanted posters were posted at every watering hole between there and his destination, Haran, the home of his mother Rebekah's family. A price was on his head. His brother, Esau, was out to get him because he had stolen his birthright.

Haran offered him a safe place to hide out for a while. So Jacob took off. What a lucky dude he was to run smack dab into the most beautiful woman his eyes had ever laid hold of.

She was a knockout! The Genesis writer described her as "beautiful in form and appearance." That is, her body was statuesque and her face was a perfect 10. She was the Julia Roberts or the Angelina Jolie of her day. Without as many blemishes, perhaps. Or perhaps more! When Jacob saw her he was so moved that he burst into tears and planted a big one right on her kisser.

Her name was Rachel. She just happened to be the unmarried daughter of his Uncle Laban, with whom he would be staying. What a set-up for spending an exile! Talk about suffering for one's sins! This would almost make you doubt that such ever happens. If this is Purgatory just how immeasurably wonderful must Paradise be?

Rachel was the pinup girl thumb-tacked to the walls of Jacob's imagination, one he always dreamed he would someday find. The one he would pay any price to have – even to working seven years for, if need be. Now, here she was!

Would you not agree with me that all of us have a Rachel in our lives? From time to time we do. "Rachel" stands for whatever is revving our engines up at any given moment of time. She is the beautiful heartthrob for whom our being burns with desire. She is the dreamboat that our minds keep drifting toward all during the day. She is the "Moonlight Sonata" whose melody enthralls us and dances with us until we fall asleep.

Who is Rachel? She is our highest aspiration in certain moments of our life. The goal we seek above all else. For the child, it's the dream of becoming a teenager. For the teen, it's the magic age of 16, when a driver's license is to be had; maybe, even a car.

Rachel is making the team. Scoring the winning touchdown. Being selected cheerleader. Marching with the band at Mardi Gras. Being invited to the prom. Getting a diploma. Going off to college. Receiving a coveted sorority bid. Landing an unbelievable job. Marrying the right person. Finding a church that is warm and inclusive, that "accepts me just like I am." Learning more about God and His Word. Finding real purpose in life. Having a *true* friend. Being blest with a child, while helping her become somebody special. Enjoying good health. Having enough stashed away for a rainy day, a season of flood and the wintertime of age.

Who is the Rachel in *your* life? or whom you would pay any price, make whatever sacrifice necessary for her to be your own? You have a Rachel, don't you? Of course you do. You always will. She's an inescapable part of your humanity and mine.

Without Rachel, you and I would amount to little in this life. And accomplish less. But there's something else to consider.

The Father Does Not Always Give Us Rachel

When Jacob arrived at the family place in Haran he found that Uncle Laban had another daughter, Leah. She was nothing like Rachel. From the picture that may be drawn of her from Scripture, we see an unmarried, older young lady who is homely, unattractive and, perhaps, even cross-eyed. If it were not politically incorrect to say so, she was probably your stereotypical old maid daughter who had no suitors. And who had absolutely no chance of ever having one.

When Jacob fell in love with Rachel, he asked Laban for her hand in marriage. Unc agreed, as you know, with one stipulation. Jacob would have to work seven years for him before he would allow a wedding to take place. When that time was fulfilled, Jacob pressed the matter and Laban threw a big feast to negotiate the wedding contract.

Keep in mind the custom of the day. Marriage was thought to have been completed once physical union was consummated. The feast, which could last sometimes up to two weeks, was the big event of the wedding. It was the gigantic prelude that led to that precious, sacred moment when the bridegroom and bride came together as one. The banquet included rich delectable food and good wine, music, and dancing. That night, somewhere around midnight, when the party finally came to an end, the bridegroom departed to his chamber and awaited the arrival of his darling bride, escorted or sent by the father.

Again, the custom was that the groom would not see his bride's face on the day of the wedding nor during the wedding night. It was not until the morning after the consummation that the groom had the joy of seeing his bride's lovely face for the first time as his wife.

That was a breathtaking moment for Jacob. Think of the drama, the anticipation, the joy welling up in his heart the next morning as he took his bride's veil and slowly began to lift it.

Then, imagine what must have been his feeling when the veil was fully lifted and there she was: *Leah!*

What had gone wrong that he had missed out on Rachel, the desire of his heart, and had ended up with her unwanted sister? It was a matter that Laban, the father, just didn't want Jacob to have Rachel. At least not at this time. He wanted his new son-in-law to have Leah instead. So Jacob got Leah. Just plain and simple.

Now, let's talk of disappointment.

My call in January 1966 to become pastor of the Buck Run Baptist Church the first time around was a dream come true. I had prayed for some time for a "choice" student pastorate, one that would offer me a challenge in the pulpit, develop my pastoral skills while providing a place for my family and me to live until I finished Southern Seminary.

Buck Run was about as choice as could be found. Founded in 1818 by the famous pioneer preacher, John Taylor, Buck Run was nestled in the historic village of the Forks of Elkhorn, situated picturesquely on the banks of the lovely Elkhorn Creek.

The church had an illustrious past. A number of notable men of God served as student pastors there, going on following graduation from the seminary to prestigious pulpits, influential denominational posts, important teaching positions and missionary assignments. Besides that, my friend Ken Hoffmeister, whom I admired as a tremendous scholar and man of integrity, had just completed an outstanding pastorate at Buck Run and, on his way to write for the Sunday School

Board (now LifeWay), by way of a pastorate in Florida, had recommended that I follow him as shepherd of the flock.

Buck Run in my mind was the ideal situation. To be brutally honest, as much as anything else, it would allow me to "put all my begs in one ask-it!" I was at that time driving a school bus two shifts, morning and afternoon, for a Catholic elementary school in Louisville. Besides that, I was working as stock boy and janitor of an antique shop.

I was also serving as pastor of the Beechridge Baptist Church in Shelby County, a wonderful little country church. All three jobs combined earned me a big fat income of $90 a week. Buck Run said they would match that figure. What a thrill it would be to take some of the stress off the difficult schedule I was keeping while pouring my heart and soul into my seminary adventure.

Besides, the pulpit committee had waited a year on me which, of course, made me feel rather important! They had come to hear me preach at Beechridge the first Sunday in January, 1965, and unanimously invited me to preach a trial sermon at Buck Run. I had only been at Beechridge a couple of months and didn't feel I could ethically leave after such a short time. But Buck Run had secured the services of Brother Claude Boozer, retired minister, to serve as interim pastor. He was doing a good job. The church was in no hurry.

The committee came again, one year later, this time to our apartment in Seminary Village and invited Gail, the children, and me to come before the church. We were ready! Anxious! Excited! It surely was God's gracious leading.

"At last, my love has come along." I couldn't wait to get to Frankfort and embrace the Rachel of my dreams. But after the deal was sealed and we moved on the church field, I lifted the veil and guess what? There was *Leah!* "Father," I cried out, "what have You done to me?"

What *had* He done? Well, for one thing, He had plopped us down to live square dab in the middle of nowhere, five miles from town, and three miles from the closest shopping center. I left early in the morning for school and came in late in the afternoon, sometimes at night. Gail and our two small children, Robbie and Neece, were stuck in a sea of loneliness and helplessness, without car or any means to get anywhere, to get anything.

What *had* He done? He had moved us into a converted cement block car garage with no inside walls or insulation, a cement floor and one coal oil heater in the center of it all. You need to know, however, that Gail and I had chosen to live there, but that's a part of a remarkable story just up ahead.

What we did not bargain for was the nice man who volunteered to paint the place, who chose not to paint the walls the color we had picked but found a good buy on some other colored paint. Likewise, he found a tremendous bargain on some vinyl tile squares that he put on the floors. Just looking out for the church, of course.

Neither had we bargained for the serious water problems we would encounter. It was so cold in the rooms surrounding that heater in the little hallway that in the winter the water froze from time to time in both the kitchen and the bathroom. The meandering Elkhorn Creek, which flowed so stately behind our house, that was incredibly beautiful, was also deadly. Polluted with raw sewage. Not safe for human consumption. We had a chlorinator on our well pump.   Sometimes it worked. Sometimes it didn't. This was long before bottled drinking water became a gleam in some entrepreneur's eye!

What *had* the Father done?   I suppose my greatest disappointment was the discovery that He had led me to a church in which not everyone liked the new preacher. Can you believe that?

Now it wasn't like there were a whole heap of folks against me. It was basically, as far as I ever knew, just one man. But did his opposition evermore cause me pain! He just happened to be the church training director, the father of the church pianist and soon to be father-in-law of the minister of music. He was also the teacher of the only men's Sunday school class in the congregation, whose lectern he used, I was told, to air his opposition to the new pastor.

This dear brother was also church treasurer. My agreement with the church was that I would receive my $90 salary each week. We needed it. Big time. When Buck Run said they would match my combined income we failed to take into consideration that my expenses would be more in Frankfort since I would be driving 100 miles round trip to school, four days a week. Finances were *real* tight!

I didn't get my pay check the first week on the job. Thought they had just decided to pay me bimonthly. When I didn't get my check the second week I began to wonder what was going on. I called the chairman of the pulpit committee that had brought us to Buck Run and asked him about it.   When he inquired with the brother about why I had not received my pay check he got this reply, "Because he doesn't deserve it!" The deacons had to meet to instruct the treasurer to write the check.

My first year at Buck Run was the toughest ever in my long ministry. In fact, I came under such stress that I developed a point ulcer. But it was a learning experience. Actually, a re-learning experience as I – like you – have encountered a myriad of disappointments in the journey through life.

Just none of the magnitude and impact this one had on my life and that of my family. Here's the lesson that I'll never forget: regardless of how lofty are our dreams, how earnest are our prayers, how determined is our work, sometimes the Father chooses not to give us Rachel. At times, when we lift the veil, we discover He has given us Leah!

You have learned this lesson, haven't you? In a disappointing friendship, marriage, job choice, investment? In a church relationship that has let you down? In the direction your child has taken in life? In the realization that your nest egg for retirement is not hatching enough chickens? The list is endless. Too late to pine for Rachel. Looks like Leah is going to be your bedfellow for the duration!

The good news is that when disappointment comes it's time to celebrate, to be of good cheer! The story of Jacob's disappointment points to another lesson. One that is remarkable. Don't miss it. It will wonderfully change your life. And untold numbers of lives through the years, if you will accept its premise while giving yourself to the love of Leah.

Father Knows Best

For many, this advice is as outdated as the radio and television series of the late 40s and early 50s featuring the Anderson family of Springfield, USA. Please don't be deceived by the fallacious thinking of modernity. It is as true now as it was in the 50's. Indeed as it was in every generation all the way back to the Garden of Eden: "Father knows best!"

It was surely true in the Rachel-Jacob-Leah love triangle. We hesitate to give too much credence to the cunning wisdom and trickery of Papa Laban. After all was said and done, however, Jacob may have wished for an opportunity later on to thank his father-in-law for his marriage to Leah. Because what began as a major disappointment in his life became over time a great blessing.

The blessing of course emanated from God, the *Heavenly* Father, who orchestrated the remarkable story of Jacob, one of the patriarch's for chosen Israel. Who, along with Abraham and Isaac, became the progenitors of true faith. The Father's providential hand may be seen in the coincidental meeting Jacob had with Rachel at the well. It may also be seen in the Father's reward of Jacob's obvious embrace and care of Leah, his growing appreciation and love for her through the years.

Just what does the Heavenly Father know that will enable you and me find victory, joy, and fulfillment in our disappointment?

He Knows That We Need Leah! Just as we earlier stated that all of us need a Rachel in our lives – someone or something that keeps our motors running full blast, stoking our motivation to continually reach beyond our grasp, just so, we also need a

217

Leah. One who will love us unconditionally, care for us unreservedly, and fulfill us eternally.

You may be thinking: "Bob, this is a different kind of Leah you seem to be talking about now than the one I have had thrust upon me." Maybe. Maybe not. Perhaps the reason you question this is that you have not given your unwanted Leah a chance. As a believer in God's providential care and leadership of your life, you may have not accepted your Leah as God's great grace-gift to you. You possibly have not chosen, as Jacob did, to embrace her and to love her with an appreciation deeper than just infatuation. You probably have not given her opportunity to love and care for you, to strengthen and enable you to grow in ways that Rachel never can or will.

Your problem and mine often times is that we fail to understand how important it is to "take up" the cross that has been thrust upon us, for Jesus' sake. To commit ourselves to earnestly seek the Father and His will out in a given situation. To put self to death and consider, at least until the Father releases us from it, that this is what He wants for us at this particular time so that He might reveal His glory through us. So that His resurrected power may come alive within you and me and touch others who need to experience His remarkable presence and power.

The fact of the matter is that Rachel was doubtless far more difficult for Jacob to live and deal with than was Leah. The picture we see of her in Scripture is not flattering. She must have given Jacob *some* kind of time.

She was her daddy's baby girl. He had named her, "ewe." She was his little "lamb." She was doubtless spoiled beyond measure and when you add this to her ravaging beauty, it is understandable that life and everyone in it gravitated around her and her every wish. We see in the Genesis story that she was jealous, could throw temper tantrums and, like many beauty queens in today's world, she chose to be independent even of her husband at times. When she left Haran with Jacob you don't find exactly the same submission to and love for him as you did in, say, the beautiful story of Ruth and Naomi, mother-in-law and daughter-in-law. Rachel may have said, because the situation had demanded that they leave, "Wherever you go I'll go. Wherever you lodge I'll lodge. Your people will be my people." But, she surely didn't say, "Your God will be my God!" She may have sung "I'm Bound for the Promise Land" when she left Haran, but on the way she stole her father Laban's household idols and planned on doing her own thing religiously regardless of Jacob's position as patriarch of Israel!

While Jacob was infatuated with Rachel's beauty and loved her to her dying day, there was no indication that Rachel loved him in return. H. V. Morton wrote, "Rachel remains one of those women with nothing to recommend her but beauty. She is bitter, envious, quarrelsome, and petulant."

I find it, therefore, not hard to believe that over time Jacob found Leah to be far more wonderful to him than Rachel. So much so, he even asked to be buried by her. In Genesis 49:29-31 (NKJV) we find this charge to his sons as he faced death, "*I am to be gathered to my people; bury me with my fathers in the cave that is in the field of Ephron the Hittite, in the cave that is in the field of Machpelah, which is before Mamre in the land of Canaan, which Abraham bought with the field of Ephron the Hittite as a possession for a burial place. There they buried*

*Abraham and Sarah his wife, there they buried Isaac and Rebekah his wife, **and there I buried Leah.**"*

It didn't take me a lifetime to realize that the Father knew best when He gave Buck Run to me. Just a little over a year or two at the very most. From the word go I embraced Leah as God's special treasure for me. I sucked up the difficulty and disappointment that was mine at the first and accepted her with deep appreciation. In choosing to lift my cross I saw God doing some amazing things in my life. Even in dealing with the brother who opposed me I found myself not seeking to retaliate or to defend my disagreements with him. Instead, I chose to be as kind and courteous and as caring of him as I possibly could. In a little over a year God led him to choose another congregation in which he could be happy serving our Lord.

Over those earlier years and the many years of our relationship that followed, as we worked and played together, as we struggled and prayed together, as we laughed and cried together, as we dreamed and believed together, as we dared and celebrated together, there developed a love affair to remember between pastor and people. A love affair words cannot adequately describe.

I know this: after I received a Ph.D. in December, 1972, though I had numerous opportunities to engage so-called "greater challenges," I found myself not wanting to leave. Our family stayed on at Buck Run eighteen more months. Until we were called to First Baptist Church in Monroeville, Alabama.

Many years later, during those five years I spent in Monroeville the second time around, after having been placed on total disability in Brandon, I often wondered just where God one day might take me to experience the promised "greatest years of your ministry up-ahead." I confess that I flirted around with many dreams of this and that Rachel. But when the Father led that marvelous lady to call me back a second time to Frankfort, I knew that my heart belonged to Leah!

I hope that you in your moment of disappointment are finding what I have found to be true in mine. That the Father always knows best. He knows that you need Leah!

He Knows That Through Leah's Offspring You and I Will Experience His Greatest Blessing. God desires to bless His children. And He does. But the story of Jacob and his two wives reminds us that those who embrace unwanted Leah are blessed far greater than those who choose to make love to Rachel.

God had promised Jacob, as He had his fathers Abraham and Isaac before him, that He would bless him, that his seed would be more numerous than the sand on the seashore and that, through his offspring, all the people on earth would be blessed (Genesis 28:13-15; 22:17-18; 12:2-3). Know which of Jacob's wives made possible the fulfillment of the promise? Not Rachel. It was Leah! But Leah had to undergo some changes in her life before the great blessing of God could be visited upon her. And on the lengthening issue of her life.

Keep in mind that Jacob was not the only one who had to deal with disappointment. Leah did also. She didn't handle it well either. For far too long she moped around controlled and victimized by the disappointment that her husband didn't love her. In the naming of her first three sons it was obvious that

221

she was totally self-absorbed with her plight. Each name, Rueben, Simeon, and Levi, carried with it the connotation of "Poor me, will he now love me?" (Genesis 29:32-34).

In my opinion, whatever other purposes her choice of names served, they surely caused the family to slosh around in her pity puddle 24-7. Misery loves company. Leah made certain that symbols of her misery were present everywhere anyone turned.

Between the third and fourth child something remarkable took place in Leah's life. A change that indicates significant spiritual conversion and growth. No longer do we find her totally turned into self, dwelling on her disappointment. She now has turned the focus of her life on God, seeking to discover His will in her situation. In so doing her life begins to reflect liberation, joy, and fulfillment!

The words of Genesis 29:35 (NIV) are telling, "She conceived again, and when she gave birth to a son she said, 'This time I will praise the Lord.' So she named him Judah."

A remarkable turnaround had taken place. Leah had discovered the meaning and power of the cross and resurrection, many years before our Savior embraced the old rugged cross of Calvary for her sins, yours and mine. She had learned that when one puts self to death and through radical faith submits to the will and good pleasure of the Father, an incredible new life is born. And amazing are the issues from the womb.

She named her son Judah. Who was Judah? The head of the clan through whom came David, Israel's greatest king. From

David's line came Jesus of Nazareth, the Savior of the world. Through Jesus Christ you and I and a multitude too numerous to count have come into the family of God. Through this family you and I have been, and continue to be, heavenly blessed. Beyond belief!

"Father knows best." He knows that you and I need Leah, for through Leah's offspring will come by far our greatest blessing. And His divine purpose for humanity will be realized.

When I came to Buck Run that first time and encountered my Leah, I was doubtless not the only party having to deal with disappointment. There surely were those in the church who had to deal with it, too! With the initial unrest that attended my coming it would have been unnatural if there were not some in the congregation who wondered whether or not the church had make a mistake in calling this particular pastor.

Nevertheless, both pastor and people realized right away that the only way to experience the blessings of the Father was for both parties to embrace each other in love, seeking by faith to discover His will in our marriage. Then to be obedient in the doing of it. This we did, and that which issued from our decision became more than amazing! Jesus said, "Wisdom is justified by her children."

Buck Run was aware that housing for the pastor was a major issue. In fact, the leadership asked that I come and lead then in building a "nice" parsonage. As a student that would have been the easiest thing to do during our stay there. But I could not get peace about this proposal seeing that the largest subdivision in Frankfort, Indian Hills, was just developing less than two miles from the church, with over 1,000 houses on the drawing board.

Buck Run was not ready for this golden opportunity. The church building had only four Sunday school rooms. The old sanctuary was like a dark dungeon, atrociously ugly, and in my mind would never appeal to those young families moving into well-appointed new homes.

Gail and I prayed about the matter. We told the committee our decision. We were ready to come but not to build a new parsonage. We were committed to live in the little block house. We would come if the congregation would commit to doing whatever was necessary to reach the Forks of Elkhorn community as well as East Frankfort for the Lord Jesus. The church bought into the vision!

Once there, plans began to be made to refurbish the historic sanctuary and add to it an education wing with kitchen and fellowship hall. After about a year of getting ready we fired away at this target full bore. Preliminary plans were approved and we were primed to take the next step.

It was then that I began to get uneasy about moving forward until we consulted our neighboring congregation, the Calvary Baptist Church, just across the creek. Calvary was the result of a church split in 1948, when a significant number of Buck Runners left to form a new congregation. They built their building literally "just a stone's throw away."

After several weeks of discussion and prayer, our deacons voted unanimously to send a confidential letter to the Calvary deacons asking for a meeting to discuss our separateness and what it must mean to the Lord and our witness in the community. Moreover, since both churches, almost identical in size, were planning building projects, we asked for their counsel on what entrenching our division would mean to the cause of Christ. On May 22, 1967 a five page single-spaced letter was mailed to our deacon brothers in Calvary.

Calvary deacons met on May 25 to discuss the letter and returned a fraternal message indicating their prayerful concern and interest. On July 6 the two deacon bodies gathered in the basement of Frisch's Restaurant in one of the more Spirit-filled meetings I have experienced in my ministry. Men embraced like I have never seen before. They shed buckets of tears. After a lengthy prayer session, a Bible presentation addressing the matters at hand was presented by my good friend, Tom Sawyer, pastor of Calvary and traveling buddy of mine each day to the seminary.

The discussion moved to the reunion of the churches which Buck Run proposed for consideration. Our deacons made it clear that we were not asking Calvary to come back as members of Buck Run, nor return to the historic property. We were proposing that our congregations explore the possibility of a new church, under a new name, to be located on some neutral site in the community. It was unanimously agreed that the matter under discussion – that had been miraculously kept secret – be brought to the attention of both congregations following morning services on Sunday, July 16. And that several months be given both congregations to pray about and discuss the issues, with a secret-ballot vote to be taken simultaneously at both churches on a date to be determined.

The vote as to whether or not formally explore the reunion of the two congregations was held on Sept 24, 1967. Buck Run voted in favor by the margin of 76 to 3. Calvary stopped the negotiation by a narrow margin.

The leadership of both churches was sorely disappointed. Buck Run members were deeply disappointed. But something miraculous happened to Buck Run that ended her disappointment. She soon discovered that when she voted to die, she voted to live. When she became willing to give up 149 years of rich, colorful history, God began writing a history for her that became incredible, if not unbelievable. When she embraced the cross, the Resurrected Jesus Christ came alive in her midst, among His people. And a watching world began to be drawn to this something special that the Lord was doing.

Architectural plans were immediately made ready for bidding. The cost of construction, including add-ons, parking lot and furnishings, totaled approximately $100,000. This was 10 times the church's annual budget of $10,000! The congregation didn't blink an eye. We crafted our own homemade financial campaign and $45,000 was raised in pledges for the first three years.

A ground breaking ceremony took place on November 10, 1968, in our sesquicentennial year. We dedicated the new building and remodeled facilities on May 17, 1970. Over that 18-month period we saw God perform miracle after miracle. Church membership grew rapidly. Money began to come in at such a rate that, when we dedicated the building, we had enough surplus in the bank to put a third down on a lovely new house for the pastor in Indian Hills. Because of her faith and obedience the congregation got her "nice" parsonage and a new church facility to boot!

Some of you may wonder what happened to the little cement block house that for a number of years became the precious home for Gail, Neece, Robbie, and me. Over time she also became well loved. Many happy days and nights were spent in her company. Thankfully, we were able to save the old girl. She got converted and graced by the congregation to continue her life as a member of the Buck Run family. The decision was made to expand her sphere of influence by making her part of the new building and turn her into a new fellowship hall. Following her facelift she began again to serve up delightful delicacies, now for the entire congregation, that continued the culinary excellence Gail's kitchen had been noted for.

How I had grown to love my Leah! In my eyes she had become far more beautiful and wonderful than the Rachel of my dreams. Thank you, Father!

Dear reader, you can come to love and embrace your Leah as well. If you will, the children that will issue from your marriage will be many and marvelous. And wholesale numbers of persons grappling with disappointment in your community, will be drawn to you and your family of faith, and find great delight in the Living Lord in your midst.

He May Be Found in Life's Trials

> "My brethren, Count it all joy when you fall into various trials, knowing that the testing of your faith produces patience. But let patience have its perfect work, that you may be perfect and complete lacking nothing." James 1:2-4 (NKJV)

What do you do when life caves in? When your heart gets broken into a thousand pieces and seemingly can't be put together again? When tragedy strikes and dark black crepe is draped around the walls of your soul? When you get impaled upon a cross because of circumstances beyond your control? Perhaps, because of the mean-spiritedness of another who wishes you no good? Or as a consequence of your own rebellion to the will of God? What do you do when the torrents of the rampaging flood waters of Jordan sweep you away from your moorings and your feet can't find the bottom?

Just what *do* you do? Know what the Word of God tells you – and me – to do if indeed we are believers? It tells us to celebrate. That's it. Throw a big one. It tells us to laugh! And sing! And dance!

James expresses it like this, "My brethren, count it all joy when you fall into various trials." How in the world can he say this? Because he knows something profound about the providential maneuverings of God. Like Paul also knows, as seen in Romans 8:28. Both of these giants of the faith know that in the depths of our distress and despair God may be found. Doing some unbelievable things. Turning things around for our good while working out His magnificent purposes through our lives.

When precisely in life's trials can a person of significant faith expect to discover God and His transforming grace? The Apostle James is instructive.

When Being Under Attack

James tells us that we should consider it indescribable joy when we "fall into" various kinds of trials.

It is interesting that the Greek word for "fall into," *peripipto*, is the same word Jesus uses in His parable when describing the man who "fell among robbers" (Luke 10:30). He was literally surrounded by thieves who attacked him, took everything of value that he had, beat him unmercifully, and left him for dead. Thank God, before death could have the last word the good Samaritan comes along and rescues the helpless victim of the attack.

Two things are suggested in the story Jesus told that doubtless had an influence on James' thought.

First, the good Samaritan is surely the Christ-figure in the story. He comes to bring us love, grace, mercy, and salvation during the various attacks that come against us. We can count on Him. He will always come to our rescue. For that we should rejoice exceedingly even while being attacked. Of course, as Jesus tells the story, the Samaritan is the prototypical Christ-follower who, for the glory of God the Father and the sake of Jesus Christ, continues our Lord's mission to "rescue the perishing, care for the dying." Like a good neighbor!

Let us remember what we must be about. Let us not forget what our Lord modeled for us when He took up His cross of sacrifice so that those who had been attacked and left for dead along the roadside might live! And to have reason to experience His joy like you and I do!

Second, the attacker is Satan (and his henchmen). Numerous New Testament verses link Satan to the attacker. Jesus surely was referring to Satan when He said, "The thief comes but to steal, kill, and destroy."

The Appearance of Satan. Peter reminds us to be ever sober and vigilant because our adversary "walks around like a roaring lion, seeking whom he may devour." The Apostle is not suggesting that the diabolical one "looks" like a lion. Just that he stalks us at all times like a lion, prancing around in nervous anticipation, waiting for the precise moment when we will be the most vulnerable to his attack.

Actually, when Satan comes to attack you and me he does not always appear the same. He takes up residence from time to time in whatever form or economy that opens up to him to use in confronting us. There are "various" kinds of trials as James reminds us. Satan uses whatever vessels are at his disposal for his attacks. Whatever presents him with the greatest chance of undermining and destroying God's good work in our lives.

Sometimes our adversary finds an empty, unguarded abode in human flesh and blood to occupy and utilize to launch his personal attack on you and me. Such was the case of the men who robbed the guy in Luke 10. Here were men who, somewhere along the way, had opened their lives to the adversary. Over time, he overran their innermost beings and enslaved their wills to do his bidding.

We should ever be mindful of what Paul teaches us in Ephesians 6:12, that we "wrestle not against flesh and blood but against . . . the invisible rulers of this present darkness . . ." When we keep this thought uppermost in mind we will be enabled to respond as Christians to those who attack us. To those who seek to do us in with lies and personal vendettas, who seek to rob us of our good name and reputation, who stab us in the back while smiling (or, frowning!) to our face. We can begin to approach the attacker and his attack against us, as Jesus Christ did, when we realize that it's not the person we see who is the enemy and the source of our pain. It's the one we can't see who has somehow been allowed to crawl in that person's skin – either temporarily or permanently – to work the works of darkness through his or her enslaved personality.

So how does the person of faith respond when surrounded by the attacks of others? In absolute hilarity and joy! Because he sees immediately who is the true source of the attack and realizes Jesus has already defeated this enemy. Moreover, the believer "knows," as John would say, that "He that is in (me) is greater than he that is in the world." Therefore, he will have no fear because God is at work in and through the difficult event, promising victory that's on its way for those who are His faith-full and obedient followers.

One of the most treasured goodbye presents I ever received in my coming and going in the pastorate, came from my dear friend, Evelyn Gardner, when I prepared to leave Buck Run Church for the last time. Evelyn, who had grown up in Buck Run, was at this writing the church clerk and business manager of the congregation. She came into my office while I was packing my books.

"Bob," she said, "I just wanted to say something personal to you." "I have known you for a long time. (It was actually 37 years at that time!). There's one thing I want you to know that I have admired about you through all these years." "Fire away, Ev," I responded, "I'm delighted that somebody has at least *one* good thing to say about me!" I continued, "You aint' gonna lie just because I'm leaving, are you?" "You know me better than that," she retorted! I did. I do.

Evelyn stated that the thing she would remember me most for was that I always remained the same person regardless of the situation I was confronted with. When faced with adversity as well as success. She said she appreciated in particular the fact that when someone was rude to me, even downright hostile, I never sought to retaliate, but seemed to always respond to the antagonist with love and kindness. That when difficult issues became a source of conflict in the congregation and things got tough – as occasionally they do in the best of marriages – I could be heard walking the halls, singing or whistling some happy tune.

"How do you explain it?" She asked. "Quite simply," I replied. "It's a matter of faith. It's the certainty the believer can have that the Father has absolutely everything, at all times, under control!"

Some of you who are reading this may wonder just what are the things you and I can know for certain when facing difficulty and encountering trials of various kinds and degrees. Trials that come to us in human form.

Well, for one thing, we "know" that if we are the ones who have precipitated the attack the enemy has launched against us in people-skin, that the Father will discipline us through the ordeal and use this discipline to continue to change us even more likely into the image of Christ. A reason to celebrate indeed!

We also "know" that if the other person is the one who has come to be an instrument of hurt and destruction in the hands of the enemy, God will take care of him or her. "Vengeance is mine. I will repay," says the Lord. Therefore, we need not worry about that guy or gal with the dagger that has cut deeply. Nor do we need to help the Lord out in seeing that the attacker gets his just due. We simply leave the matter and the person in the Father's hands, believing that He knows what's best for everyone – even our attacker. He, Himself, has promised to mete out whatever punishment is needed. Big-time cause for celebration!

Then since the Father in His providential care is "working in all things bringing about our good," we have reason to whistle, to sing, and to dance. We "know" that He's got something far more wonderful than anything we've known just up ahead for us! And the greater the difficulty and trial we endure, the greater the blessing He is working out for us!

Satan appears in many forms to attack us in his most advantageous way. The vessel he sometimes uses *is a set of circumstances,* often our situations-in-life. As James hints to us in verses following his section on trials and testing, the evil one can appear in the raiment of wealth and affluence, as well as in the rags of poverty. In either station he has a platform from which to attack us and seek to replace the Lord Jesus on the throne of our lives. Or to keep Him from ever ascending to this place of authority and rule in the first place.

As often as he can our adversary gains entrance into the powerful structures of institutions and does his dirty work through them, to inflict pain on God's children. The cruel despot who controls and enslaves entire countries is embodied and driven by no one but old Satan himself! Would you believe Satan at times is even ensconced in church congregations? Or in committees within a church? Or in religious organizations? Know any such animal? What would one look like to you? How would it act? What are the consequences when it begins to follow the dictates of the evil one?

Satan's most devastating blows against humankind by far come when he is able to invade Mother Nature's birth canal and utilize her contractions to wreak havoc and spread travail among large numbers of persons. Volcanic eruptions, cyclones, hurricanes, floods, tsunami are but a few of the natural disorders that Satan has a hand in spawning. One recalls from Job's experience that, while God gave permission for Satan to test and prove the righteous man's faith, Satan was given free reign to determine the means of the testing! (Job 1:12; 2:4-8).

Will, then, the adversary have the last word in the disaster and confusion he is able to create on earth? By no means! The contractions of Mother Nature are but the rhythmic countdown to a new earth God is preparing to give birth to just up ahead! And what is about to happen on a cosmic scale is taking place in microcosm each time tragedy strikes you and me and others within the family of faith.

The Act of God. "God is at work in all things" – that includes even in the horrendous things – "bringing about good for those who love him, who have been called according to His purpose."

It was in the wake of a powerful tornado that struck Frankfort at 4:50 pm, on Wednesday, April 3, 1974 that I came to realize how mightily the Father is at work in the tragic on behalf of His children. Approximately 120 houses were damaged or destroyed. The Capital City Christian Church suffered considerable damage. A major portion of the Evergreen Baptist Church building was demolished as was the parsonage.

I recall how persons, as they picked up the pieces of their lives, began picking up the jargon of the insurance industry in asking, "Was this an act of God?" I felt led of the Lord to address the issue on the following Sunday morning in the pulpit. Taking my text from Romans 8:28, I sought to point out how the providential hand of God was incredibly in evidence restraining the force of evil let loose on our community. How God indeed turned the deadly attack of Satan into something remarkably good for His glory.

I asked over and again the rhetorical question "Was this tornado an act of God?" I answered each time with a resounding "NO!" It *was* for us, as it was for ancient Job, an attack by Satan! Then I proceeded to show – at least to my own satisfaction, of course – just what was in that calamitous tragedy that enabled people of faith to see an act of God.

When no lives were taken in death by the ferocious wind that leveled the Tierra Linda subdivision, – *there* was an act of God! When the only thing left standing in many of the houses was a small jagged piece of a wall here or there, right where a family member in a split second fell to the floor – *there* was an act of God!

When neighbors who had not known each other before began to reach out to each other in love and to develop friendships – *there* was an act of God!

When folks who had drifted far away from the Lord came back home; when some who had never known the Savior gave their lives to Him for the first time in grateful appreciation – *there* was an act of God!

On the day following our great catastrophe (?), when roads began to be passable, I went across town to see my brother in Christ, Yancey Sanders, precious pastor of Evergreen Church.

What do you say at a time like this? Being moved by the gravity of the moment all I could mutter was, "Yancey, I'm so sorry!" To which he replied, "Bob, don't be sorry. Yesterday after it happened, a deacon in our church who had not spoken to me in over two years came and embraced me in tears, saying, 'Pastor, don't worry. Together we'll build it back!'" Now, *there* was an act of God!

Somehow, our Lord is borne along in the womb of the tragic, preventing the evil one from totally destroying those who love the Father while giving birth to something wonderfully new and grand in their lives!

The composite Scriptures under consideration are clear. It's time, brothers and sisters, for you to celebrate when you fall into the hands of those who begin to attack you from all sides. Those who would take what you have, beat you up pretty badly, and leave you for dead. The reason? There's a good Samaritan on His way to rescue you at that very moment! His name is Jesus.

As you celebrate your trials, remember that there are hundreds, perhaps thousands, all around you in your community who have nothing to celebrate because they have never met the Savior. Might you introduce Him to that special person, or persons, the Holy Spirit will guide you to during your earthly journey?

When Experiencing Shipwreck

It is to be noted that the only other place in the New Testament this compound wording, "falling into trials" may be found, besides in Luke's story of the Good Samaritan, is in Acts 27:41.

This verse is couched in Luke's account of Paul's shipwreck just off the coast of Malta. The reading in the NIV is as follows: "But the ship struck a sandbar and ran aground. The bow stuck fast and would not move, and the stern was broken to pieces by the pounding of the surf."

The Encounter. Dr. Luke appears to be utilizing a medical term here for trials, the word "affliction," (Cf. Thucydides and Dioscorides). From my own encounter with a major depressive episode that lasted over a period of several years, I recall how debilitating was this disease when I became grounded by a sense of helplessness, immobilized by fear, uncertainty and a sense of tragic loss of control. I then became sitting prey for many other illnesses to blow and beat against my incapacitated hull like howling winds and ravaging waves, breaking down my health, ripping it apart board by board!

Paul seems likely to have been going through just such a trial of depression in 2 Corinthians 1. He uses this word "affliction" in verse 6 to hint at the problem he was experiencing in verses 9-11. Here he admits that he was weighted down so heavily that he was like a beast of burden, with legs collapsed under him, totally immobilized by the weight. Indeed, he confesses that in this state he had the sentence of death stamped in his mind.

Did Paul's afflictions destroy him? Not on your life. He points out that the God in whom he trusted, who had delivered him from death many times in the past, was continuing to be faithful. Upon Him he trusted that deliverance was on its way. To be sure, the old soldier of the cross professes his faith that whatever up ahead would come and beat against his life would not destroy him. He believed beyond a shadow of a doubt that in such dire times he had a Deliverer who, like a midwife, would take him out of the womb of darkness and despair, hardship and pain, and give him new life. Like James, he understood that from his trials would come a new person, more mature and complete, for the glory of the Father and the enhancement of His holy purposes in and through his life.

I found this to be true in my experience. And if your life is facing this kind of shipwreck, I promise that you can find His deliverance for you as well. Trust in God is the key. That's radical faith and obedience. It means putting self to death while taking up your cross as if it were Christ's own cross, and allowing the Christ of the empty tomb to come alive in your life!

Obviously, the image of shipwreck to explain our trials goes far beyond the medical. It includes every single attack of the enemy that comes against us when we, like fish swimming in a barrel, without power or strength to control what is happening to us, fall prey to an evil marksman who would take from us everything near and dear, including our lives.

I find it also intriguing that the root word for "trials," *peirasmos*, is from the same Greek word that has given us our English word, "pirate." Have you encountered the infernal Black Beard in your voyage? What has he taken from you? What is he robbing you of at the present moment? Love? Joy? Peace of mind? Hope? Faith? Assurance? A sense of purpose?

Where are *you* just now in your journey? Could you, like Paul and his entourage, be experiencing a shipwreck so devastating that the storms that are beating against you are tearing the old ship apart board by board? With pirates standing by waiting to collect the spoils? If such is your case, please follow James' advice. Start celebrating. Start singing. Start whistling. Throw a party. As a symbol of trusting faith ask your loved one or friend who is going through this turbulence with you if you may have this dance! Then watch the Heavenly Father as He brings you through to something far more wonderful than you could have ever dreamed possible. Believe me. 've been there. Many times. And now, as before, I am hilariously celebrating!

The Encouragement. For those of you who may have experienced a shipwreck that has literally torn your life or your family apart, one that finds you still struggling to keep your head above debris-filled water, I wish to pass on to you a testimony of a friend. He gave me permission to share it with you with a prayer that it will enable you to find God in the womb of your tragedy and thereby discover that something remarkably new and wonderful He is seeking to give birth to in your life.

On Saturday night, April 24, 2010, a bomb exploded in the home of Greg and Donna Dorriety of Fairhope, Alabama that shattered their world. Their beautiful daughter, Elizabeth, who had turned 15 five days before, took her life in her upstairs bedroom.

Elizabeth was the most unlikely teenager for something like this to happen to. A freshman at Fairhope High School, she was a member of the Key Club, the swimming team, and the track and field team. More than this, she was a Christian young lady, a member of the St. Lawrence Catholic Church and very active in her youth group. She was much beloved by family and friends.

I have often guessed how dark it must have been "The night the lights went out in Georgia." I confess to you, however, I could never be able to comprehend how coal black dark it must have been the night the lights went out in the Dorriety home in Fairhope. Losing a child must be one of the most tragic of all tragedies. But – praise God! – as will be seen in Greg's testimony the lights came on again brighter than ever before. He and Donna caught a plank that God had provided from the shattered wreckage and made their way to a special island He had waiting for them. A place of safety with ample provisions for every need and an exciting new life of purpose and challenge.

In talking with Greg about his encounter of shipwreck he told me that there were "before" and "after" stories that needed to be told in order to understand what took place in their lives.

The "before" story is rather typical of a traditional Southern family. I've known the family through Greg's mom, Gwen, since we were young adults. She and her husband, Hurston, lived in Atmore, Alabama and we in Monroeville when first we met. She was an executive officer in the main office of the United Bank. Gail and I and our family have had a long standing friendship with Gwen and her family ever since.

The Dorriety clan moved to Daphne several years ago when Gwen and Greg became partners in an investment and financial planning firm. They immediately immersed themselves in the life of the community. They are what we in L.A. (lower Alabama) call "good" people. They are good citizens. They are good church members, not just church-goers.

Greg has been an active parishioner in St. Lawrence since putting down his stakes in the Eastern Shore area of Baldwin County. Not only has he been a faithful participant in his church he has also been a serious student of God's Word. Even before he faced his most difficult trial he was involved in a weekly interdenominational men's Bible study led by a Presbyterian friend.

Greg considered himself a Christian but he admits that there were some nagging doubts in his mind. At times it seemed that his involvement in church was more perfunctory than dynamic and real. Moreover, he said that he possessed the fear of dying. No assurance of salvation whatsoever.

Nevertheless, Greg sought to inculcate biblical principles in his lifestyle and especially in his business. He was – and still is – most fascinated by "The Prayer of Jabez," the prayer that the Buck Run congregation found to be so powerful when prayed under the instigation of the Holy Spirit. You will recall that this simple little prayer is found in 1 Chronicles 4:10. The words again in the NIV: "Oh, that you would bless me and enlarge my territory! Let your hand be with me, and keep me from harm so that I will be free from pain!"

Greg made note cards with this passage on it and placarded it around on walls and placed it on his desk. He prayed the prayer often. He now admits he only prayed it with visions of dollar marks dancing in his head!

God didn't bless him. He didn't enlarge his business. He didn't keep him from pain. Instead, Greg suffered the greatest pain in all of his life that night he encountered shipwreck just east of Mobile Bay.

Thank God there is an "after" story that followed the trial of Greg's faith. As a starter, he discovered he *had* no faith. He finally admitted that he really didn't know God! He had no personal relationship with Jesus Christ.

The day of the funeral for the Dorrietys must have been like Paul's first clear sight of the Island of Malta as that piece of wreckage he clung to became a life boat that began to take him to shore.

The funeral was amazing. St. Lawrence's large sanctuary was packed. Gail and I stood with perhaps a hundred or more outside. The tragic nature of the death notwithstanding, it was a triumphant service. An unusual spirit of peace enveloped the congregation. Elizabeth's brother, Will, a midshipman at the US Naval Academy in Annapolis, gave a moving eulogy.

After the service, Greg made his way with a close friend to his favorite spot to sit and reflect. It was outside the historic Grand Hotel at Point Clear. Obviously, his thoughts were on his precious daughter, Elizabeth. Suddenly, a male cardinal, Elizabeth's favorite bird, lit on the edge of an empty chair close to Greg and began chirping at him. Simultaneously, he noticed Winston Groom, author of *Forrest Gump*, and his daughter, Carolina, walking up the sidewalk. Instantly his mind replayed that scene in his favorite movie where Forrest stands over the grave of Jenny and finds closure and peace.

Greg said, "A great rush of comfort immediately came over me with a message of 'Everything is okay.'" He and Donna continue to receive numerous messages of confirmation like these as God speaks peace to their hearts.

Greg admits that there still are moments of anxiety, fear, horror, and depression. But these are being worked through and becoming less and less frequent, with less magnitude, because of the loving support of family and friends, professionals, and most of all, because of God! The God who was in doubt has now become real and is constantly sending love messages, (*missional messages*, I call them) through limitless means (animals, plants, people, sounds, smells, tastes, movies, books, etc.). Bible verses Greg says that he had heard or read many times now "jump off the page" to him with resounding meaning and purpose.

What happened? After the tragedy Greg and Donna sought the Lord and found Him to be waiting for them. His experience, he explains, was like walking on a dangerous tight rope over a deep, chilly, mist-filled chasm between two high mountains. It was scary. He feared he would lose his footing at any minute and fall off. He was terrified over what might happen to him if he did. One day on the tightrope he simply stopped, and trusted. Trusted his life and everything about himself to the Heavenly Father.

At that very moment he received an inner warm feeling that God had absolutely everything under control. It was an unbelievable transformational moment! The tightrope no longer held any fear for him. His feet became steady and his walk sure. He began to be filled with joy and ecstasy because the uncharted mountain over there was waiting for his exploration, challenge, and celebration. He became excited about the new world he soon was to discover.

Greg said that, although in the "before" story he never cared much about the term, his "after" story experience has caused him to use the concept of "being born again" as an apt image to adequately explain what has happened to him. He has become a new man in Christ Jesus! "The old has been put away, the new has come." No longer does he fear death because God personally abides with him at all times and gives him inner assurance.

With this new birth and new life has come a new perspective on the meaning and purpose of life. On why he is here and what he must do. In his recent testimony before the Eastern Shore's Outback Group he said, "One thing about a tragedy like this is that it redirects your thoughts, your senses, and your actions to such an extent that you have a completely different view of the world."

He continued before this Christian men's group to say, "We are each assigned our own set of circumstances. As an aside, I believe those circumstances have nothing to do with (one's) wealth, family legacy, social status, education or lack of it. Ultimately, I believe we are all here to serve a particular purpose for the glory of God and we will be here not one second longer than it takes to accomplish this task."

What is the task Greg and Donna have discovered that is part and parcel of their reason for being? It is to share the good news that Christ's living resurrected presence is available to make an extraordinarily wonderful difference in those whose lives have been shattered by tragedy. Their message is about the power of the Lord, efficacious for the healing of the afflictions of Satan's attacks. They are reminding everyone as they have opportunity that we have been sent here to bring glory to our God! Period. Everything else is extraneous.

The "prayer of Jabez" is still a life-verse for Greg. Seen now from a different perspective. The Father is indeed blessing this man unbelievably. But not necessarily with larger caches of money. Instead, the Lord is enriching his inner life day by day with a growing sense of His Presence, power, and promise of even greater things ahead. The Father indeed is expanding his territory. He is enlarging his life's sphere of influence by bringing numerous people across his path each day who need an encouraging witness for Christ. He is barraged with invitations to speak to Bible study groups (women and men), civic clubs, and church groups of many denominations.

Dear reader, if you are now going through trials of various kinds please take heart by the testimony of Greg and Donna Dorriety. From what they discovered in the midnight of their lives, a story that well corroborates the biblical message, your moment of despair may be turned into rejoicing. However, you must earnestly seek the Lord out in the tragedy, trusting expectantly that He may be found and is waiting to show you that something better for you just up ahead.

Now here is Jesus. The innocent Son of God hanging on a cruel tree. For you. For me. For your friends. For the stranger you have bumped into recently. For the Hispanic child out playing that you pass Sunday on your way to church.

Two guys are being crucified with Him. Both deservedly so. Both had embraced a life of thievery. Little had they realized that they were the ones who were being robbed repeatedly by the "pirate" until almost too late. Both men now the epitome of shipwreck. One of them rails at Jesus. The other senses something profoundly special and eternal in this man from Galilee. He cries out for mercy and grace as he submits himself to a new Lord: "Lord, remember me when you come into your Kingdom." And Jesus said to him, "Assuredly, I say to you, today you will be with me in Paradise."

That's what it's all about in the Christian's trials, isn't it? One day there's shipwreck. The next day there's Paradise! That is, for those who would seek Him out in the tragic encounter through significant faith. In the shipwreck God is discovered in the very midst of it all. Making the difficult understandable. Granting His wisdom to those who ask. Providing a reason to celebrate by defusing the power of the evil one with Christ's conquering power that He gives to those of us who by faith surrender absolutely all on the altar.

It all begins to add up, sisters and brothers, when you dare count it all joy!

Chapter Eight

Seek Him Out in the Uplift of the Cross

"Then he said to the crowd, 'If any of you wants to be my follower, you must turn from your selfish ways, take up your cross daily, and follow me. If you try to hang on to your life, you will lose it. But if you give up your life for my sake, you will save it.'" Luke 9:23-24 (NLT)

"My old self has been crucified with Christ. It is no longer I who live, but Christ lives in me. So, I live in this earthly body by trusting in the Son of God, who loved me and gave Himself for me." Galatians 2:20 (NLT)

Where in the world is God?

That seems to be an appropriate question. With Mother Nature writhing in excruciating pain, history convulsing and gasping for breath, and humankind on the brink of committing social, moral and spiritual suicide, you may wonder: "Where in the world is God?"

In light of our own individual predicament, with burdens, hardships and losses that somehow seem at times to be unbearable, the question for many of us appears to be justified: "Where in the world is God?"

The answer to some may seem simplistic. It is not. It is perhaps one of the most profound statements the Christian faith makes: God is wherever the Cross of Christ is.

247

We have explored above a number of arenas in and through which God may be discovered by persons of significant faith: in prayer and fasting, in sacred Scripture, in missional messages, and in the workings of His providential care and governance. In some instances faith opens our spiritual ears to hear God's Eternal Word. In others, it opens the windows of our souls to see and engage the power of God's Eternal Spirit. In the Cross of Christ our Savior, unlike in any other form, faith enables the sojourner to more perfectly comprehend and apprehend the *heart* of our eternal Father. "For God so loved the world that He gave His only Son, that whoever believes in Him should not perish but have eternal life." (John 3:16)

God is wherever the Cross of Christ is. Obviously, God is present everywhere! But He chooses in this world to make His abode in a more profoundly self-revealing way wherever Christ's Cross is engaged and lifted up. He is where the Word of the Cross is preached faithfully and obediently. He is where the fellowship of His Cross is shared by His community, through faith, in their participation in the sacraments or ordinances of the church. He is where the Body of Christ, the church, lives the crucified life obediently and is a visible witness of His heart and love before a watching world.

Where in the world is God?

He is present in the life of an individual who has become heart-broken over Christ having to bear His Cross alone and lovingly, even joyfully, lifts it for his Lord and carries it faithfully for Him as long as he has breath.

But, you may ask, how can we in the 21st century lift the Cross of Christ? Wasn't Christ's experience of His Cross a one-time unrepeatable event in history that took place more than 2,000 years ago? Indeed. Nevertheless when you and I choose to faithfully and obediently follow our Lord Christ it inevitably leads us – each and every day – to an experience of Gethsemane and Calvary.

In our Gethsemane we choose whether or not to embrace the will of God, the consequences of which are looming before us. In our Calvary we willingly lay down our lives for the Father's will as revealed in Christ, so that He may live through us, for a world languishing in darkness and despair.

Simply stated, the cross that the vicissitudes of fate and fortune lays upon our shoulders, as well as the cross that we encounter weighing down on others at any given point of time, becomes the Cross of Christ when we lovingly, faithfully, obediently lift it up for His glory! We are instructed by the Apostle Paul in Galatians 6:2-5 (NIV): "Carry each other's burdens, and in this way you will fulfill the law of Christ . . . (yet) each one should carry his own load."

Too often we take these as sweet little verses that refer to doing nice little things for each other in the church during those adverse happenings that are common to humankind. Such as stopping by the funeral home for family visitation when a Christian sister or brother passes away. Such as taking a casserole by the home of a troubled friend. Or at the birth of a new baby. Such as sending a get well card when someone is sick in the hospital or dropping a note of encouragement to a friend whose husband or wife has left home and broken the vows of marriage. These are of course kind, Jesus-like deeds that Paul's familiar verses would include. They might also include a missional message from the Lord who tells each of us grappling with our own burdens to "hang in there, things are going to get better!"

These verses, however, while inclusive of special touches on special occasions that we *must* be about, speak to much heavier stuff. They point to a weightier responsibility than that which costs us little or nothing to fulfill. They speak to long term commitments. They call for a taking up of whatever is the cross thrust upon another and carrying it for Jesus' sake, however long it takes until the resurrected Christ in His glory becomes a reality in the given situation.

The phrase, "Carrying each other's burdens," in the Greek language is in the present active imperative tense, which suggests continuation. "Keep on carrying" the burden for the other. The word for carry, or bearing, is the word used in John 19:17 that describes Jesus carrying His Cross. Such a heavy weight He carried for you and me because of His Gethsemane decision. He made a commitment to put self to death so that others – you, me, our neighbor, as well as our enemy – might live. What a life-model for the disciple who would follow Him!

It is the picture we see again in the story of the Good Samaritan, as found in Luke 10. Once the two representatives of the Temple (Church?) took a look at the battered half-dead man along the roadside and realized it was going to take more than just a band-aid to take care of this fellow, they crossed over to the other side of the road and went on their merry way. But along comes a guy whose heart went out to the man in grave distress. The Samaritan was undoubtedly looking through the eyes of Jesus as he saw in this stranger a neighbor needing help. Serious help. And made a commitment to stick with him, to "carry" him, whatever it might take until the man was back on his feet again.

Not only did the Samaritan give immediate first aid, but he put the man on his own donkey (an extension of his wealth) and let it "carry" him to the nearest inn. There the good guy took care of the wounded Jew, spent all night with him making sure his new neighbor would make it. When it became apparent that he would survive, the Samaritan gave the inn keeper two silver coins, enough to "carry him" for two weeks. Then he made this commitment, "Whatever more you spend, when I come again, I will repay you (verse 35)."

The above is surely the essence, and the challenge, of Galatians 6:2. True love mandates that whatever it takes to lift the burden off the shoulders of the other who is down must be embraced by the Christ-follower!

At the same time, verses 3 and 4 remind us that the Christ-follower should not get so enamored with how strong he is spiritually that he neglects responsibility to take care of the cargo God has put aboard his own ship, to be delivered along the way at specific ports of call, determined by the Spirit of Jesus, for the glory of the Father. "Let him who thinks he stands take heed lest he falls" (1 Cor. 10:12).

Often overlooked in the parable of the good Samaritan is the fact that, after the Samaritan made certain the crisis had passed for the injured man and proper resources were provided to "carry" the man for an ample period of time, he left to take care of personal responsibilities. But he left with the pledge that he would return and pick up the tab for whatever else this new neighbor may have needed!

The Brandon Baptist Church is another remarkable congregation the Father allowed me to serve. It is a new congregation. Founded in 2003, I was called as her first pastor. I don't believe I have ever seen another church that embodied so closely the Galatians 6:2-5 model of cross-bearing. The congregation almost from the beginning committed itself to doing whatever it takes to lift the load off the shoulders of struggling people and of sister congregations. At the same time, it committed to giving careful attention to the care of her own valuable cargo, the people the Father was entrusting into her care, providing whatever was needed for them to become all God would have them be, at whatever cost.

Brandon Baptist members were meeting in the auditorium of Brandon High School in August 29, 2005 when Hurricane Katrina hit the Gulf Coast, the worst national disaster in American history. The Mississippi Coast was decimated. Since the church was in the process of constructing its first building, having concluded a miraculous fund-raising campaign marked by incredible financial sacrifices by God's people, it would not have been unreasonable if the congregation had assumed that it was doing all that it could for the Kingdom at the time. Perhaps taking a love offering with the promise to pray regularly for the situation might be all that could be expected of a two-year old fellowship of believers in their own building program. Not so!

The decision was made to commit to one devastated church on the coast and the hurting people in its neighborhood, to lift their cross and carry their burden with them until they were on their feet again! The Brandon congregation was raising money for its own building but felt led to ask for a sacrificial gift from its members to jump start the project on the coast and raised $30,000. In a word sometimes specifically used by Billy Foxx Swilley, one of the driving forces of this project, "Unbelievable!" It was indeed.

The Holy Spirit led the chuch to the Ingalls Avenue Baptist Church in Pascagoula. Soon Tom Kennedy, Kevin Dobbs, Robert May, Billy Foxx Swilley, Mack Honea, Bill Lee, Tommy White, and others were organizing teams going down not only on weekends but during weekdays as well. A host of able-bodied church members went when they could, cooking their own meals, camping out on mattresses on the floor of a room still intact after the big blow and water surges.

The first order of business was getting the houses in the neighborhood that were salvageable under roof and ready for occupancy. This work lasted for a number of months. But the focal point of the effort became the Ingalls Avenue Church building itself. As a starter, Ingalls Avenue needed to renovate the nursery so that families who came to worship in the gym would have their small children taken care of. Sufficient capital was raised to complete this job. And so it went, on and on. God's provisions through Brandon Baptist and other Christians got the job done.

I will never forget when the last $7,000 was given that completed the entire restoration project, after 13 months of laboring together in the Lord with the wonderful people of Pascagoula and others who came in to help. This check enabled the gym floor to be finished. It was a glorious occasion. The pastor of Ingalls Avenue, John Turner, also used that million dollar word when describing all that the fledgling Brandon Baptist congregation had done while, at the same time, building their own facilities at home. He told me, "It was *unbelievable*!"

Obviously there were other persons and churches that worked and helped on Ingalls Avenue during this critical time. However, for the Brandon Baptist Church, their involvement became total commitment in helping lift and carry the cross of a crucified sister congregation until it experienced resurrection. Their engagement was incredible to behold!

Brother Turner remembers special moments beyond the clearing of trees, the cleaning of debris, the hanging of sheet rock, the painting of walls, the laying of carpet throughout the building, etc. when Brandon Baptist seemed to be God's special gift for a special time. He told me that perhaps the first group that came into the community to see what could be done to make a difference was the BBC delegation: Tom Kennedy, Robert May, and Kevin Dobbs, associate pastor at the time. He stated that Brandon's delegation was an answer to prayer. When the delegation discovered the church lost all its video equipment, equipment was purchased. When they learned that Brother Turner had lost his transportation and had absolutely no means of doing ministry. Money was raised and Brandon Baptist gave him a car!

What a special moment it was when we delivered Pastor Turner's little red Ford Escort. I dubbed it the "Red Hot Mamma" and it elicited much laughter from time to time from persons in a situation that desperately needed a little levity.

It must not go unnoticed that, at the same time, the Brandon congregation was working overtime in Pascagoula, the Lord opened another door for ministry and told the church to walk through it. And they did.

Tom Kennedy, chairman of the mission committee, discovered the urgent need right in our own back yard. The Southside Baptist Church in west Jackson was the point of entry into a meaningful ministry to the homeless in a neighborhood that had undergone sociological changes on the west side of the capital city.

Southside Church was hurting big time. They had lost a large portion of their membership when the community began to change. There were, however, a small but dedicated few, led by Pastor Jeff Parker, who felt that the Father would have them stay and help make a difference in the lives of those who would remain as well as in those who may move into the neighborhood.

It soon became evident that homelessness was going to be a major problem facing that area of the city. All that would be involved in that kind of project would stagger the imagination of even a large church. Feeling the leadership of the Lord, Southside made a commitment to move into this ministry. With shrinking membership and a concomitant decreasing monetary base, it also became apparent to Pastor Jeff and those who stayed behind to lift the neighborhood's cross, that financial support from without was a colossal need.

Regrettably, little financial assistance came their way. For some time they operated on a short shoe string. Jeff went before the large Baptist association in Jackson to plead for help. Very little came. He was subsequently invited to speak to the annual meeting of the Mississippi Baptist Convention. His impassioned plea elicited more than a few "amens" but, again, little or no response at all.

Enter Brandon Baptist Church. The Father said, "Go!" The congregation said, "Here we go!" And off they went. Like a stable of thoroughbreds at Churchill Downs on Derby Day. With money they raised from within the congregation. With clothing and foodstuff. n the beginning, the men of the church – some women as well! – tackled the most pressing need of all. These dedicated folks, along with Freddy Harrell, who had not yet joined BBC, who brought his entire work crew, totally renovated the first home for homeless men, a building in deplorable condition.

It is noteworthy that this remarkable new congregation's very first formal budget was laced with significant provisions for missions and ministry around the world, including the Southside Baptist Church's ministry to the homeless! It's still there intact, as is their special partnership.

How did BBC do it? What caused them to think they could attempt so much just out of the starting gate? They simply believed. Let me correct that. They *radically* believed. And obeyed! They trusted the Father that, anything He led them to attempt, He would supply the wherewithal to see that it was done. Especially those endeavors that seem to be as big as He is!

Where in the world is God? When it seems He is nowhere to be found? Or when the challenge seems to be greater than is humanly possible to handle? He is where the Cross of Christ is. And when the Brandon Baptist Church chose to be a Galatians 6:2-5 congregation, lifting His Cross, the Father began to make

Himself known in and through that church. Powerfully. Persuasively. We began to see Him do some of the most miraculous things in our midst, especially in drawing persons to His Son Jesus Christ and His Church. Already a significant congregation when I arrived as pastor, I was amazed as I stood by and watched the Lord add more than 400 members in the four years I was blessed to be their shepherd.

Now, you may wonder where *you* as an individual follower of Christ may find the Lord for *your* life and situation. The principle is the same for the individual as it is for the congregation.

Found in the Uplift of the Cross of Sacrifice

The invitation of Jesus the Christ to follow Him, as again we see in Luke 9:23-24, involves taking up one's personal cross each and every day! When we do so faithfully and obediently we discover something incredibly astonishing. The Resurrected Life of our Savior becomes a Living Reality in our lives.

What is involved in this amazing discovery?

It Entails the Emptying of Self

In the call to discipleship, Luke reminds us that taking up one's cross is occasioned when that person "denies himself." We have been using the phrase "putting self to death" which is an apt, descriptive one. "The emptying of self" is also a most accurate description of what our Lord demands of us who would "come after Him" and discover the reality of His holy presence in our lives and in our churches. More importantly, for the sake of these conversations on Christ's witness through you and me in outreach through His Church, it is a crucial concept to help us better understand how Christ would reach the world through His crucified life.

The self-emptied life is the life modeled by our Savior for those of us who would follow Him. Theologians often speak of Christ's "self-emptying." I never cease to be moved when reading or hearing read that magnificent passage in Philippians 2:5-11 that speaks of the indescribable cross of sacrifice our Lord embraced for you and me and for all humankind, that He took up *even before coming into this world*! It took place in the majestic halls of glory when He made the decision to empty Himself of all the riches of His eternal habitation as well as His heavenly prerogatives, "Your attitude should be the kind that was shown us by Jesus Christ, who, though he was God, did not demand and cling to his rights as God, but laid aside his mighty power and glory, taking the disguise of a slave and becoming like men. And he humbled himself even further, going so far as actually to die a criminal's death on a cross. Yet it was because of this that God raised him up to the heights of heaven and gave him a name which is above every other name, that at the name of Jesus every knee shall bow in heaven and on earth and under the earth, and every tongue shall confess that Jesus Christ is Lord, to the glory of God the Father." (TLB)

Before describing Christ's self-emptying for our emulation, the Apostle admonishes us to let His attitude be in us. That is, let His inner mental disposition be in us as a blueprint for the engagement of our mission in the world. This blueprint prescribes the emptying life of self, taking up a cross of sacrifice while following Him in doing the will of the Father above all else.

The first disciples, with all their stumbling and bungling, nevertheless followed their Lord in two self-evident, sacrificial ways.

First, like Him, They Left All. Take the call of the brothers Peter and Andrew, then James and John, for example. It was no little response that these men made when, Scripture tells us in Matthew 4:18-20, they left their fishing business to follow Him. Theirs must have been a rather successful enterprise. Nevertheless, they gave it up in order to launch out on a journey, like Abraham of old, not knowing where they were going or what lay ahead. That sacrifice was a bold step of radical, obedient faith. They embraced a cross. They emptied self of all vestiges of earthly security to follow Him!

But notice this: James and John also left their father Zebedee! This was a gigantic step of sacrificial faith. It was disgraceful in biblical days for the son to leave home before the father had died. The son was expected to honor his father (and his mother) and care for his needs until his death. Besides leaving their father, these two fishermen were leaving behind their honor and the respect they had in the eyes of the people near and dear to them in their community. More than this, they were leaving behind the blessing of their father as well as their inheritance. In doing so, of course, they gained a far greater blessing from their *heavenly* Father and an inheritance that is out of this world!

What has been the cost of discipleship for you? I know a man well who, some twenty years ago, told his dad that God had called him to go to a distant land and preach the gospel. The dad, who lived close by, was both heart-broken and angry. He made a special visit to his son and told him that if he left he would be cut out of his will! It wasn't a difficult decision for the preacher to make. He had no other desire than to follow the Lord. But it was tough for him to leave a heart-broken, disappointed father whom he loved, in old age.

To take the claims of Christ seriously requires that, in following Him, you and I must take up a cross of sacrifice daily! It means emptying our lives not only of self but of the things of this world and of absolutely anything else that prevents us from doing the will of the Father. It also means emptying life of relationships we treasure that would keep us from following Jesus completely and other commitments that hinder total surrender to His Lordship. Have you emptied your life for Jesus?

Second, Like Him, They Gave All. One of the more neglected aspects today of the life of the New Testament community that Christ called together was their "self-emptying" in sacrificial giving. The eternal Word of God not only left His heavenly prerogatives to come to earth to do the will of the Father but He gave away all that the Father allowed Him to bring to earth for the doing of His will. It was the Father's unconditional love, incarnated in the Son and revealed in His life, that reached out to meet the needs of others. It was most profoundly revealed in Christ's self-giving love on the cross for the redemption of all humankind.

The early followers of Jesus gave up all rights to the ownership of the things the Father had placed into their hands. They began to see their resources in terms of God's entrustments. Clarence Cooper, pastor of Brandon Baptist Church, pointed out recently in an article that the early followers of Jesus did not speak of their *ownership* of things. They talked about their *stewardship*. They acknowledged that everything in the possession of a Christ-follower belongs to God and is to be held in trust until He gives the signal to give it away, under the Spirit's leadership. So the early church gave. Generously. Sacrificially.

Can you imagine what might take place in our churches and communities if we practiced what those early followers of Jesus did? What would it do to our current welfare system? How many more people would be touched with the reality of the living Christ in the life of His disciples and in the witness of His Church?

Luke reminds us in Acts 2:44-47 (NIV), "All the believers were together and had everything in common. Selling their possessions and goods, they gave to anyone as he had need. Every day they continued to meet together in the temple courts. They broke bread in their homes and ate together with glad and sincere heart, praising God and enjoying the favor of all the people. And the Lord added to their number daily those who were being saved."

Luke, again in Acts 4:32, tells us that the early followers of Christ in the Church lived lives of shared stewardship. In following their Lord's example, and being obedient to His demands of discipleship, they gave all they were and all they had so that the Father would be glorified and Christ might be made known before a watching world. As a result we are told in 4:33 that "With great power the Apostles gave witness to the resurrection of the Lord Jesus Christ." And His great grace was upon them all. So much so that people were discovering God in the lives of the believers and in the church and were *daily* coming to faith in Him! (Act. 2:47).

Just what happens when a person empties her or his life to embrace the cross of sacrifice? So much so that people in the world see Him alive and are drawn to Him?

It Affects the Experience of His Powerful Presence

When one empties life of self and takes up Christ's Cross in obedient, sacrificial surrender of everything to and for Him, a miracle takes place. That person becomes filled with His Holy Spirit. The Resurrected Christ comes alive within. And others see Jesus in the individual's life.

Two things must be pointed out concerning this experience of self-emptying. One, the Holy Spirit's Presence and power is experienced as a "filling" in the life of the disciple to the degree of his self-emptying. When there is much self-emptying, there is much evidence of His Resurrected Presence in one's life. Little self-emptying, little evidence of the Spirit. No emptying life of self, no Holy Spirit in evidence at all. Thereby, no saving relationship with Jesus Christ!

Dear reader, if there is no evidence in your life of the Holy Spirit, you need to do some serious soul-searching. Paul states in Romans 8:9 that where there is no Holy Spirit in one's life, that one does not belong to Christ! The problem of an absent spiritual presence of God in one's life is indicative that self is still in control, seeking to call the shots in that person's life. Ponder this question: "What of self am I still hanging onto that is keeping me from experiencing the Living Christ?"

Pastor and church leader, if there is no real evidence of the presence and power of the Holy Spirit in your church, you should also do some serious self-examination. What is it of self you and your people are corporately hanging onto that is keeping Him at bay in your body life? That is, keeping your community from seeing the living Christ in your congregation and being drawn to Him? And to His life-changing grace?

There is a second thing that must continually be underscored. The emptying of self in taking up a cross of sacrifice is a *daily commitment!* That little word, "daily," is one that is tragically omitted or at the very least ignored, in the American church's reiteration of Christ's invitation to would-be disciples. The journey with and for Christ is not a 100-yard dash. It is a long-distance run that stretches into eternity! Therefore, walking the aisle of a church and being baptized is not the end of the journey of salvation. It surely is not what Jesus had in mind when He issued the call to deny self, take up one's cross *daily* and follow Him. His intention was that those who would come after Him would take seriously the cost, pay whatever the price to follow Him *each and every day*! This is the only commitment that pleases God and allows Him to do what He desires to do for, in, and through the individual. It also is the only commitment that enables the believer to continually be filled with the powerful presence of the resurrected Lord!

A Case in Point

An example is in order to illustrate how the demand of Christ for sacrifice and cross-bearing may be actualized in the lives of those who may choose to follow Him. It is an example of leaving all and giving all so that God might be glorified and others might see Him alive in the life of the believer. And in the life of the church. So that persons may be drawn to Him and saved from the darkness of whatever kind that may engulf them.

This is the story of another of my dear friends. One of my true heroes of the faith. A man in whose life I and many more like me have seen the Living Christ and have been eternally impacted thereby. A man whose long life of ministry has been characterized by a cross of sacrifice which he has joyfully borne for His Savior and for the people to whom he chose to give his life in sacrificial service. I will then tell you about another friend of mine whose life was forevermore changed when he observed Christ in the life of this humble man of God.

Larry Baldridge, a Man Who Has Embraced a Cross of Sacrifice. I wish to introduce my story about this godly person with a statement made to me by Bob Fortenberry, retired superintendent of the Jackson, Mississippi public school system. Dr. Fortenberry said, "Preacher, you and I have been around long enough to know that, in the living of life, God blesses us with the privilege of getting to know a lot of wonderful, outstanding people. But," he added, "only a few great ones."

I think he is right. I *know* I am right when I tell you that one of the great ones God has allowed me to know is my long-time friend and co-laborer in the Lord from Pippa Passes, Kentucky. He is known as Lawrence Baldridge by the Appalachian poor he has spent a lifetime serving. To those of us in the "outside" world he is just plain Larry. Perhaps, you have never heard of him. Kentucky Educational Television did a documentary on this man of the mountains early on in his ministry. It was too soon. Too little. Those who may read this will now know and, I pray, will praise God with me for this special guy who has allowed his Lord to use him in profound ways to reveal the indwelling Christ and to bless the hearts of untold numbers in Appalachia. And also in Romania.

Larry was born seven weeks before me. Suffice it to say that both of us are beyond the "three score and ten years" God has promised to folks who come and go on planet earth.

Larry poked his head into history not many miles from where he has served the Lord and His people for more than 50 years. His parents were poor but proud mountaineers. His dad was a coal miner. Larry points out that, while poor, they didn't know it. He did know, however, that in many ways his family was rich. They never lacked for anything to eat as some did. They loved each other devotedly. His parents were godly people. Their faith tradition was that of the Old Regular Baptists.

The Old Regulars are hyper Calvinists, though most of them probably have never heard the name of John Calvin. To their satisfaction their understanding of predestination is "in the Book" and that is all that is important. These wonderful people do not believe in Sunday schools, formal worship, educated preachers, evangelism or missionaries. If God is going to save a person He'll do so without any human instrumentality.

If He chooses for some to spend eternity in hell, it's nothing anyone can do about it. The Old Regulars are a dominant religion in Appalachia. Larry has been effective because he knows them. They are his people. He is one of them. And loves them with every fiber of his being. He came to realize after he was converted during college days that such belief system is extremely dangerous and prevents wholesale numbers from ever being confronted by the gospel of Jesus Christ!

When Larry graduated from Garrett High School. he found his way to the Caney Creek School (Now Alice Lloyd College) in Pippa Passes, Kentucky, about six miles out of Hindman, approximately 25 miles from Hazard. It is an institution that would give him, like other Appalachian young persons, an opportunity to work his way through junior college.

While in college Larry was known for his wild living: drinking, gambling, and the like. In those days such a life style was a badge of real manhood for many of the boys in the mountains. His closest friend found Christ as Savior and Lord and, after several months of witnessing to his buddy, Larry was dramatically "saved" from himself and the attendant things in the world that seek to please self above all else but that end up destroying the soul. He soon became passionate in simply pleasing God.

In Caney School it was discovered that Lawrence possessed a prodigious intellect. He received a free ride on an academic scholarship to the University of Kentucky from which he graduated with a B.S. degree. Soon thereafter, U.K. awarded him a master's degree. The University of Louisville gave him an opportunity for further graduate work and he became recipient of a second master's degree. He also studied abroad in Europe.

Larry was, and is, a poet extraordinaire. In my opinion, at least two if not more of his poems deserve to be included in any anthology of American literature. I have no doubt that he could have earned a couple of doctoral degrees and have taught with distinction in some of the most prestigious universities in our country. That was not the goal of his life. The Father had other plans for him.

Somewhere along the way our Lord Christ put his hand on Larry and called him to preach the gospel. He enrolled at the

Southern Baptist Theological Seminary in Louisville. It was here that we met and discovered that we were close soul brothers, though we had come from backgrounds about as dissimilar as two could possibly have come from. I was drawn to him by the breadth of his knowledge, his impeccable integrity, and his utter transparency of soul that allowed the Christ to be seen within and without his life in unmistakable clarity. In his life I discovered where God is in the world!

It was at the seminary that Larry met Martha, a missionary kid, who had grown up in Brazil. A godly, lovely lady with no pretensions, no aspirations for worldly things or fame, whose sole desire is to serve her Savior, she is God's perfect helpmate for Larry. She has served faithfully alongside the husband she adores through all these years.

Larry graduated from the seminary with a bachelor of divinity degree (today, it is a master of divinity, MDiv). He also completed the course work for the master of theology (ThM) degree at Southern but did not fulfill the requirements for graduation,being prevented by one of the professors from writing his thesis in absentia. He had been called to come back home to his hills to serve as a missionary. He could not stay in Louisville any longer.

So he and Martha invested their lives in Appalachian Kentucky and in the beautiful people there. He was called as a missionary by the North American Mission Board. He also became pastor of the Caney Creek Baptist Church where he still serves. God has, moreover, allowed him through the years to teach courses in New Testament as well as in philosophy at both Alice Lloyd and the Community College in Hazard, Kentucky.

Larry served for a time as something of a talk-show host for a television program that aired throughout the mountains, discussing everything from current events and politics to religion. He became one of the most well-known figures in his part of Kentucky. Often urged to run for political office, he has steadfastly declined knowing that this is not what God has called him to do.

He has nevertheless involved himself as an activist in defense of nature's environmental garden in which he and Martha have lived and loved and raised three wonderful children. He delivered one of the more stirring speeches ever on the floor of the Kentucky legislature in Frankfort against the devastating practice of strip mining. He inveighed against those who were disfiguring the landscape, ravaging the virgin forest, and despoiling the hills of Appalachia, taking away their beauty and sounds of music!

If he has become one of the more well known figures of his area, he has surely become one of the best loved. He and Martha through the years have lived totally sacrificial lives for the people God planted them among. They have taken in the homeless. Clothed the naked. Fed the hungry – at their own expense. They have kept the lights turned on in many a poor person's house even when their own lights were flickering. Though Larry is a horse trader without peer, the things of this world and the trappings of affluence and success have had absolutely no allure for him or Martha. I read somewhere along the way, years ago, this haunting prophecy, "One day you'll meet a man for whom these things mean absolutely nothing at all. Then you'll know how miserably poor you really are."

I have met that man. It is thus out of my recognized poverty I write this about a very wealthy friend! Not wealthy in the eyes of men but in the eyes of God. A man whose life has been characterized by "leaving all" and "giving all" in following Jesus.

When God called Buck Run Church to go to Romania and plant seven churches in the summer of 1994, we needed another preacher to help us pull off this feat. Larry, of course, was the man. He caught the heavenly vision and has not been disobedient to it from that day to this present moment. He became a founding member of the Romanian-American Board and has participated in sacrificial giving as well as in going to share every year since.

I wish everyone could have witnessed what I have over the 17 years that Larry and I have worked together in Romania. I have seen how the Holy Spirit in a cross-borne life draws others to the Savior and, at times, without a word being spoken verbally! I have seen Larry simply walk down a dusty road in an impoverished Romanian – especially Gypsy – village and the people he would pass would inexplicably turn away from what they were doing and start following him like the proverbial Pied Piper. I once saw a dirt farmer, high on a hill plowing his mule, stop and make his way down the hillside to join a caravan of Spirit-drawn persons who soon would be told of Jesus and His love. Many would come to "know" the Christ who had become resurrected in the cross-bearer's life.

Norman Vincent Peale saw the historic but dead Marble Collegiate Church in New York City come alive and grow again when they adopted that profound scriptural passage as their model for doing the will of God. Larry Baldridge adopted it and embodied it. John 12:32 (NKJV) reads:

"And I, if I am lifted up from the earth, will draw all peoples to myself."

Where in the world is God? He is where the Cross of Christ is. Where men, women, young people, as well as churches put self to death with its desires, preferences, and agendas. He is where those are who are sacrificing everything for the sake of doing God's will on earth as revealed in Christ Jesus. When this happens the holy presence of the Lord fills the life of the Christ-follower and begins to draw others to Jesus.

Ronnie Blanton, a Man Who Found God in the Life of a Sacrificial Cross-Bearer. Ronnie Blanton is also a long-time friend. When I arrived in Monroeville as pastor of FBC in 1974 he was a young man who had messed things up badly in his life. He was a church member but never darkened the doors of the church building. Sin, as he says rather bluntly in his recent testimony, dominated and controlled his life.

Ronnie is the middle of three sons and a daughter of the late L.J. and Nell Blanton, two of the godliest parents any child could ever hope to have. He was raised in a Christian home and brought to church every time the doors were opened. His dad witnessed to him often, hoping that he would own up to his need of a Savior and commit his life to Christ. That was the furthest thing from his mind. He confesses that he was a rebellious child as far back as he remembers. One day, however, there was a special service at church and a bunch of kids walked down the aisle to get baptized. Ronnie thought he might as well join them and get his dad off his back. So he said a prayer and got dunked along with the rest of them.

Ronnie's parents were overjoyed. They felt good that their son had at last had a "once saved, always saved" experience. His testimony reveals that he attended church with his folks until he was old enough to get some wheels. Once he had a car, he consistently skipped church activities and would even lie to say he was going to another church function on a Sunday night. He became acquainted with alcohol around this time and since this was in the 60s this was the only drug around our small town. hese were the days of the Vietnam War, of protests and rebellion, of the hippy movement on the West Coast. The drug of choice was marijuana.

Admittedly, he was a rebel who followed the music of the Beatles, the Who, Jimi Hendrix, and all things wild and evil. He finally found some marijuana in Houston, Texas in 1968 and was off to the races. Ronnie stated, "At that time I knew of no one in my home town who smoked pot, so I may have been the first, at least one of the first. Not a good thing to look back on, but facts are facts. Can't go back and fix a lot of things. As we say in Celebrate Recovery, 'Ain't any future in the past'."

Ronnie's drug problem led to his arrest and probation. He had to be more careful. He wasn't. He married and had a child but continued in sin and in a life of immorality and drunkenness.

Nell and L.J. Blanton ran a successful café for over 40 years in Monroeville and wanted to retire. So they turned the business over to Ronnie and his younger brother, Darrell. Ronnie was 22 years old and had a better house than his parents, two Harleys, cars, and money. It seemed like everything was going his way. Eventually, however, the carousing and immorality caught up with him and he lost it all: wife, child, and business. He was left alone to live in a 16X16 shack he had built for himself out of town. Alone with his booze and dope when he could get it. Alone with no money, no job, and only "good time friends." Only problem was, the good times were gone!

When I came to First Baptist Monroeville as pastor, the first thing I did was to lead the debt-free congregation to cash in some CDs in the bank, purchase three 15-passenger vans (Faith, Hope, and Love) to help implement the church's ministry and prepare to take a mission team to Pippa Passes, Kentucky to work with Larry and the people of Appalachia.

The church bought into this venture enthusiastically. A large number volunteered to be on either the evangelistic team, the children's team, or on the construction team.

We had a major problem. While we had a number of carpenter's helpers and go-fers, we did not have anyone with the ability of a skilled carpenter to supervise our crew. Couldn't find one. Ronnie fit the bill. But he kept stubbornly refusing all invitations. Even all pleadings. Didn't want to be tied up with those hypocrites in the church. You've heard that line before, haven't you?

Early on the Friday morning that our team met at church to leave on mission. we had resigned to the fact that we were going without someone to lead our construction crew. Just before leaving the parking lot a guy pulls up in a pickup. It was Ronnie Blanton who gets out and, with hippie hair five-years uncut flowing down his back to his waist, loads his tools and duffle bag in our trailer, without saying a word to any on our team. What an angel he was. Really. I thought it must have been some miraculous activity of God in his heart that had changed his mind. I later learned, however, that his dad promised to pay him if he would go and help! Well, so much for my lofty thoughts!

Ronnie worked like a Trojan at Pippa Passes. Did a great job. But was a man of few words. We had mid-day devotionals following lunch which, for the most part, he attended but sat by himself on the back row. We likewise had evangelistic services each evening. Some nights he came. Some he didn't. When he did attend, he slipped in after the service began and slipped out while the invitation hymn was being sung.

It was a most successful mission for Christ there in the mountains. It was wonderful working with Larry and Martha. How moved our group was over the selfless living and giving of the Baldridges, who do so much, with so little, for so many. Indeed, when we arrived some needs in the community had drained their resources. Gail and I discovered that there was no food in their cupboard or in their fridge. They had given it all away!

When we got back to Monroeville a fascinating thing began to take place. Several weeks after our return, one Sunday as I sat in the pulpit chair on the chancel I saw Ronnie come into the sanctuary just after the service began and sit on a back pew. He made his way out before the congregation was dismissed. This took place for a number of Sundays. Then one Sunday I did a double take when he came in. His hair had been cut!

I visited with this newly-trimmed young man soon thereafter. He gave me the incredible news that an amazing change had come into his heart and life. He had met Christ and Christ had become real to him. Moreover, he said that he had taken his bottles of whiskey, emptied them and smashed them into smithereens. He had taken his pot and burned it in the little stove in his shack that he used to heat with and cook on. He had emptied his life of the things of the world, let the Father bury his past, and surrendered his all to the Lord. That was when he experienced the change of life. In his words, he had been born again!

I marveled and said, "Man, this is tremendous. Tell me what happened." He said that it all began to happen back in Pippa Passes. His words as I recall them were these, "Brother Bob, I wish I could tell you that it took place because of something you said. It didn't. Neither was it the results of any of the testimonies that were given by members of the mission team. But Brother Bob," he appeared to choke a little as he continued, "When I saw Larry and Martha give their lives away to help folks who couldn't help themselves, it was like seeing Jesus for the very first time! Now, I have decided to follow Him and let Him lead me like I saw Him lead them."

Ronnie immediately became a force for Christ. He became the key speaker on an outstanding lay witness team my dear friend Sonny Feaster put together in our church. A team God blessed unbelievably in bringing many souls into the Kingdom in churches throughout Alabama and other southern states.

Along the way Ronnie married a precious young Christian lady in FBC Monroeville, Melinda Ward, who became a decided asset to his ministry. He began to work hard to make money, not only to support his family, but to fund mission ventures of his own so he could tell others what Christ had done for him. In their forays into Mexico and throughout the U.S., Ronnie and Melinda have seen untold numbers of people come to the Lord.

Ronnie and Melinda are now active members of the Grace Church in Monroeville. He is an elder and teaches on Wednesday nights. What a marvelous work God has done and is still doing in this man's life. It all began when he first saw Jesus in the life of Larry Baldridge, missionary in Appalachia, a man who himself one day heard the invitation of a life changer from Galilee, who then left all to follow Him and gave all to make Him known.

Where in the world is God? In a world that is falling apart at the seams because of sin and selfishness, this is a crucial question. In a world of despair and hopelessness, it is a question that demands an answer. The stories related above reinforce the biblical answer: God is where the Cross of Christ is. He makes Himself known when serious disciples empty life of self and embrace a cross to follow Him. It is a cross of sacrifice. And what is true for the individual is also true of the Church, Christ's body on earth!

Have you embraced your cross of sacrifice for Him? Do others see Jesus in you? Are there persons in your congregation that have walked through the baptismal waters into church membership who were drawn to the Savior because they discovered Him in your life? It is absolutely necessary for your church's outreach and the advance of God's Kingdom that others see the living Christ in your life. In addition, it is imperative for your assurance of salvation that real discipleship is taking place in your life. That you, too, are the embodiment of unquestioned evidence of having left all so as to give all for Him to those who will never meet Him unless in your life!

Let us forever keep uppermost in our minds what Jesus taught: If you and I would be His disciples we must put self to death (empty life of self), take up our cross on a daily basis, and follow Him.

The cross we must bear is a cross of sacrifice. God dwells therein! Is your faith commitment to Christ such that you can accept this? Are you now ready to do so? It is the hope of Glory! It is the hope of your church and mine. It is the hope of our communities, our nation, and our world!

Found in the Uplift of the Cross of Suffering

"I once thought these things were valuable, but now I consider them worthless because of what Christ has done. Yes, everything else is worthless when compared with the infinite value of knowing Christ Jesus my Lord. For his sake I have discarded everything else, counting it all as garbage, so that I could gain Christ and become one with him. I no longer count on my own righteousness through obeying the law; rather, I become righteous through faith in Christ. For God's way of making us right with himself depends on faith. I want to know Christ and experience the mighty power that raised him from the dead. I want to suffer with him, sharing in his death, so that one way or another I will experience the resurrection from the dead!" Philippians 3:7-11 (NLT)

Where in the world is God?

God is where the cross of Christ is. "God was in Christ, reconciling the world to Himself." Christ's cross is a cross of sacrifice. It is also a cross of suffering. Those of us who willingly "take up" this cross daily in significant faith and obedience discover the Living God unlike He is found and known perhaps in any other way.

The lesson of Philippians 3 is that we can come to know Christ by giving up and giving way all claims to His favor by our works of the Law, while faithfully and obediently embracing His cross of suffering. When this cross becomes "taken up" we then experience the mighty power that raised Him from the dead. And discover His matchless presence in our lives. This is true for each of us who are His disciples as well as for the pilgrim congregation we are traveling with through this alien world.

God is where the cross of Christ is! While God was in Christ reconciling the world to Himself, Christ was choosing to presence Himself in those who would become willing to lift up His cross for His sake, engaging His task of reconciliation.

When will you and I discover the God who is in the world? When will we encounter His cross?

When We Lift Up Under Our Own Suffering

The Apostle Peter reminds us that "Jesus suffered, leaving us an example that we should follow in His steps." Oftentimes we in the clergy, seeking to identify for the members in our congregations just where the footsteps of our Savior lead, invariably point out every possible Christian responsibility that can be thought of. Except one. It just happens to be the one assignment the New Testament suggests is the most important. It is the responsibility of bearing a cross of suffering for our Lord! Paul said, in Philippians 1:29 (NLT): "For you have been given not only the privilege of trusting in Christ but also the privilege of suffering for him."

Let the word go forth throughout the churches in America. And throughout the world. Those who are not bearing a cross of suffering for Christ are not truly following Him! And consequently are not truly His! Paul was clear on this matter. He writes in Romans 8:17 (RSV) that "If we are children of God . . . we are fellow heirs with Christ, providing we suffer with him in order to reign with him."

Suffering for Being Human. All of us suffer at times as we sojourn through life. Many suffer most of the time. It is a result of Adam's fall, and our fall subsequently; of a perfect creation and world order that went awry. The biblical image of thorns and thistles outside the Garden is a reminder of the life of suffering that humankind inherited when the Lord shut *homo sapiens* out of paradise.

Human suffering comes in many forms. There is physical suffering. Emotional suffering. Mental-psychological suffering. Relational-social suffering. Consequential, circumstantial, and situational suffering. Religious persecution such as we see on a broad scale in many parts of the world today may embody most, if not all, of these various kinds of human suffering.

Perhaps you are experiencing excruciating pain just now because of suffering in one or more areas of your life. Know what the Father would have us do when our pain becomes acute, seemingly unbearable, and robs us of energy, vitality, and zest for living out the purposes of God in our journey? The answer is simple but profound. We convert *our* cross into the Cross of Christ! Through radical faith we begin to see our cross as His and we obediently "take it up," or lift it up, so as to glorify Him and allow His holy purposes to work out in our lives!

When we lift our cross as His, something transformational takes place. The resurrected life of the Christ takes charge of our situation of pain and turns it into something blissfully wonderful. Through our suffering we experience the glory of the Lord, the wonder of His resence, the warmth of His love, the comfort of His peace, and the power of His Spirit. As such, it opens the door for the miraculous to operate in and through our lives. It then becomes the means of boldness in our witness and the drawing power of our outreach to others.

A Man Called Peter was a best-selling book when I was in college. It was the true story of the famous Presbyterian minister, Peter Marshall, whose remarkable life and untimely death inspired his wife, Catherine, to preserve his memory in writing. Made into a movie, it played a significant role in my final surrender to the ministry.

While the spiritual force of Peter Marshall's total persona impacted my life and ministry greatly, one scene in the movie has stayed with me through the years and influenced my understanding of the cross. It was not a scene showcasing Peter's eloquent preaching, nor his refreshing prayers, nor his infectious walk with the Lord. Instead, it was the moving scene zeroing in on the turning point in Catherine's life of faith. Ill with tuberculosis that kept her bedridden for almost three years, she had come to a place of utter desperation.

There was no known antibiotic to fight the TB germ in that day. She couldn't understand her plight. Her husband was pastor of the prestigious New York Avenue Presbyterian Church in the nation's capital. She needed to be by his side. She had a three-year-old son who needed his mother. She prayed often for God's healing. It didn't come. She wrote letters to everyone she thought she may have offended through the years and asked forgiveness. It didn't bring healing!

Catherine's pain – emotional, physical, and spiritual – had become more than she could bear. On this particular Sunday morning, listening to her husband preach over the radio about surrendering to the will of God, she got off her bed onto the floor and prayed what she thereafter called her *prayer of relinquishment.* Said she, "Lord, I understand no part of this, but if You want me to be an invalid for the rest of my life – well, it's up to You. I place myself in Your hands for better or for worse. I ask only to serve You."

Catherine Marshall not only put self and her selfish will to death in this prayer, she chose to bear up under her cross. Lifting up her suffering so that Christ might be glorified in whatever the Father chose for her.

A remarkable thing happened to Catherine when she converted her cross into Christ's cross. God became evident in her life far more powerfully than ever before. That night, after surrendering her suffering to the Lord in prayer, she was awakened by a presence in her room. It was Jesus! There they fellowshipped and talked together. She in subsequent writings called it the most wonderful experience in her life. Amazingly, she soon discovered that she had been healed. Totally! God then began to make Himself known through her in her gift of writing. She penned over 30 inspirational books through which God blessed the hearts of millions around the world!

Where in the world is God? He is where Christ's cross is.

Is your pain and suffering holding you down? Or are you holding your pain and suffering up? It matters greatly how you answer this because your answer, evident in your life, is a dead giveaway as to whether or not you have truly denied self, taken up your cross and followed Him.

How powerful will be the impact of your witness and mine during our outreach journey if we choose to accept our own cross of suffering as if it were His own, bearing it up joyfully through audacious faith and obedience to His will. Such commitment would allow Jesus, the risen Savior and Lord, to become incredibly real to you and me and to others whose innermost being longs to encounter this reality!

Human suffering is the lot of all who come and go on planet earth. It becomes the blessed opportunity of those who would follow Christ to accept it as a grace gift from God to be lifted up as our love gift given back to Him. And in so doing to gain the happy privilege of participating in the sufferings of our Lord. For His glory and the salvation of many: "And I, if I am lifted up from the earth, will draw all peoples to myself!"

Suffering for Being Obedient. If you and I are obedient to Christ, truly obedient, we will suffer for it. For Christ never asks us to do something for Him that does not require a cross when the thing is faithfully negotiated. It is true of the mandate to love unconditionally, which is the heart of His Gospel. To practice the stewardship of all things life places in our hands.

To engage in the witnessing task in our daily sojourn. Or in the pursuit of peace and justice for all persons we encounter along the way. If it doesn't cost us something of significance, especially significant faith and sacrifice, it is probably not something our Lord will get too terribly thrilled about. Nor is it doubtless very helpful in enabling you and me and our churches to accomplish much of eternal significance!

Nevertheless when we truly obey Him, watch out! A cross is on its way. It will in time be a cross of suffering! For the church and for the disciple. Charles Spurgeon commented on this cross in his devotional on Luke 23:26, where he pointed out the significance of the cross of Christ they laid upon Simon of Cyrene, "We see in Simon's carrying the cross a picture of the work of the church throughout all generations; she is the cross-bearer for Jesus. Mark, then, Christian: Jesus does not suffer so as to exclude your suffering. He bears a cross, not that you may escape it, but that you may endure it."

Spurgeon continues, "Christ exempts you from sin, but not from sorrow. Remember that, and expect to suffer. But let us comfort ourselves with this thought: that in our case, as in Simon's, it is not *our* cross, but *Christ's* cross that we carry. When you are molested for your piety or when your religion brings the trial of cruel ridicule on you, then remember that it is not *your* cross, but it is *Christ's* cross. How delightful it is to carry the cross of our Lord Jesus!"

Gail and I were at a dinner party at James and Patti Cox's house in Louisville. We were, as far as we knew, the only graduate school couple in a group of Southern Seminary professors and their wives. Dr. James Cox, preaching professor at Southern and his wife, Patti, frequently threw parties like these and on occasions included Gail and me. There were two tables of guests on this night.

We were seated with three other couples in the main dining room. We had just begun to be served when a couple of latecomers rang the doorbell. Dr. Cox greeted the guests and I heard him introduce them to those in the adjoining room. "Folks," he said, "I'd like you to meet Paul Turner and his wife, Jane. Paul is a new graduate student, having moved here just this week from Nashville."

My heart skipped a beat when I heard the name "Paul Turner." "Could it be? Could it possibly be," I thought to myself, "*the* Paul Turner who had become my hero while I was in college?" "Surely not," I reasoned. "That Paul Turner would be much older than an incoming graduate student!"

But it was *the* Paul Turner. Following several pastorates, the last one in Nashville, he came to the place that he felt the need for an updating in his ministry, so he took a step of faith and brought Jane and their three children to Louisville so that he might pursue work on a doctorate.

Paul and I hit it off immediately though he was thirteen years my senior. We became close friends. I could never have dreamed that night at James and Patti Cox's table just how deeply meaningful my relationship with Paul Turner would grow to be.

However, I was so overawed with being in the presence of this great man on this special occasion that the thought of becoming a close friend with him was more than I could at this time imagine.

As I sat there at the dinner party my mind raced back to the first time I was introduced to Paul. Think it was Chet Huntley who did the honors on the NBC Nightly News. The date was December 4, 1956. I was a new student at Samford University (then Howard College), having transferred from the University of Alabama when I surrendered to God's call to the ministry.

Paul, 33 at the time, was the young pastor of the First Baptist Church in Clinton, Tennessee. He and the people of his town were sitting on a powder keg. Clinton was the first school system in Tennessee ordered by the Federal Courts to integrate following *Brown vs. School Board*. It was to take place that year in the fall of 1956. The leadership and most people in that quaint, friendly little southern town, while not necessarily elated over the prospect, were ready to abide by the law of the land. But a terrible thing happened on the way to the schoolhouse door for the black students who were preparing to enter.

Things deteriorated in the community's resolve to abide by the Federal mandate. Several outside racial agitators, led by John Kaster and Asa Carter, came into the community stirring up fears within the white population and organizing groups to foster hate to all who would accept the integration of the local school. The White Citizens Council was organized for adults and a Junior White Citizens Council for students in the school. Crosses were burned, threats of violence were communicated to people of good will, shots were fired, dynamite detonated, and riots broke out. It looked as if the voices of the more level-headed community people would be completely stifled by fear.

Kaster and his well organized group put up a slate of local persons to oppose the incumbent mayor and three city councilmen whom they had branded as soft on the issue of integration and accused as standing against their southern way of life. The election was to be held on December 4, the same day the 12 African American children were scheduled to walk to Clinton High School. The hate mongers promised serious consequences if "the Clinton 12" entered the previously white school that day. Good people became afraid. Good people became silent.

But something happened that morning of December 4, as the 12 African-American children readied themselves to walk down the hill from the all-black Green McAdoo School to Clinton High, that would change the history of Clinton, Tennessee forever. God made provisions so that they might not walk alone. He had prepared the young white pastor of the First Baptist Church, Paul Turner, to "stand in" for Jesus in that historic trek.

Paul told me more than once that he had not been an ardent activist for integration. But he had always sought since answering the call to follow Jesus to do the will of God, whatever it may mean. The Father convinced him several days earlier what he must do. On the day of reckoning, God woke him up early that morning with pictures of those kids making their way through an angry, hate-filled mob of bigots who could possibly get out of hand and do the children harm.

So Paul dressed and went to Green McAdoo School, courageously lifting an invisible cross that everyone in town nevertheless saw. He, accompanied by two other men, walked 10 of the kids down the hill to the school. Paul told me that the venom and hate that spewed out of the mouths of those who lined the street was almost more than he could bear, that it would remain with him the rest of his life.

The walk was without violence, but once the students were safe in the school, Paul made his way to his car where he was quickly surrounded, assaulted, and badly beaten as the mob yelled, "Kill him! Kill him!"

Would-be disciples of Christ need to know that lifting the cross for Jesus always, ultimately, leads to suffering of some kind. But it leads to something far greater. It leads to a resurrection to new life. New hope. New victory. A new sense of God's nearness. When Paul lifted the cross he discovered a dimension of God's Presence, grace, and strength not known before.

Word of Paul's beating spread like wildfire through Clinton as the people prepared to go to the polls and vote. The First Baptist Church membership rallied around their beloved pastor as did Christians in the other churches throughout the community. A new power began to surge through the good people of Clinton, Tennessee. It was the power that raised Jesus from the dead. An all-conquering power. The town turned out and voted, swamping the candidates who stood for hatred and ill-will!

On the following Sunday morning, much to the surprise of everyone, Paul made his way to his pulpit. He then preached a sermon, the title of which is engraved in marble on the walls of the Green McAdoo Cultural Center: "There Are No Lines to the Cross."

No lines to the cross. No shortcuts either! The journey begins and is negotiated as the Christ-follower "denies himself," that is, "puts self to death" in the doing of the Father's will. That's when the cross is embraced. That's when suffering can be expected. That's when God always shows up in the life of His faith-full, obedient servant. That's when people are changed. That's when communities began to evidence a new birth of righteousness (doing the right thing!), as did Clinton. That's when the influence of the cross-borne life touches, with Christ's presence and power, persons too numerous to number, in places too far away to ever be known or counted.

As I sat that night in Patti Cox's dining room and realized that one of the great heroes of the faith of my generation had walked into the house, I recalled the night, December 4, 1956 when he walked into *my* life. And how, through him and his courageous stand, Christ made Himself known. And how that revealed to me – as I know it did to thousands of ministers and laymen across America – what taking up the cross is all about.

I have continued to be impacted to this very day by that which Christ taught me through Paul Turner's sufferings. It has remained a source of great strength each time I have faced a cross and was forced to decide whether or not I would lift it and make it Christ's own.

I also remembered at the dinner table how the images of Paul's Clinton experience served to encourage me to seek and do God's will during a perilous episode a few years earlier in my young ministry.

Suffice it to conclude here that the walk of Christian discipleship necessitates the taking up of a cross. A cross that leads inevitably to suffering. But when this cross is borne for Jesus, God reveals Himself in love, power, and in evangelistic suasion. And the Spirit of God miraculously begins to draw people to Himself.

Could it be that the churches in America, as well as in the Western world, have become as harmless and as impotent as we know her to be spiritually because she has lived too long, and has gotten too comfortable, with the thought that she could make it without the embrace of His Cross? What about your congregation? What about you?

When does Christ make Himself known to us? When does His cross become actualized in our lives? There's this other thought.

When We Lift Up Under the Suffering of Others

"When the Son of Man comes in his glory, and all the angels with him, he will sit on his throne in heavenly glory. All the nations will be gathered before him, and he will separate the people one from another as a shepherd separates the sheep from the goats. He will put the sheep on his right and the goats on his left. The King will say to those on his right, 'Come, you who are blessed by my Father; take your inheritance, the kingdom prepared for you since the creation of the world. For I was hungry and you gave me something to eat; I was thirsty and you gave me something to drink, I was a stranger and you invited me in, I needed clothes and you clothed me, I was sick and in prison and you came to visit me.'

"Then the righteous with answer him, 'Lord, when did we see you hungry and feed you, or thirsty and give you something to drink? When did we see you a stranger and invite you in, or needing clothes and clothe you? When did we see you sick or in prison and go and visit you?' The King will reply, 'I tell you the truth, whatever you did for one of the least of these brothers of mine, you did for me.'" Matthew 25:31-40 (NIV)

This well-known concluding message of Jesus in the so-called Olivet Discourses states the case rather plainly: When we lift up under the sufferings of others, especially the most marginalized among us, we embrace Christ and His cross. And, sooner or later, He makes Himself known to us with His blessing and reward.

This truth may be seen as the actualization in Christ of the ancient message of Proverbs 19:17 (NIV), "He who is kind to the poor lends to the Lord, and he will reward him for what he has done."

As we began this extended section on the Hebrew writer's elucidation of significant faith, we now conclude the section reminding ourselves again of His revealing insight, as seen in 11:6, "Without faith it is impossible to please Him, for he that comes to God must believe that He is and that He is a rewarder of those who diligently seek Him (out)."

True faith as we have seen in Hebrews 11, trusting belief and trusting obedience, seeks God out in every occurrence and detail of life. That includes the search for His reality in the suffering of neighbor, known or unknown to us. Especially in the lives of those who are poor, weak, and enshrouded by life's darkness, who cannot help themselves.

True faith seeks to *understand* the plight of the afflicted and troubled. Not *understand* as in the attempt to grasp the meaning of life's situations of despair philosophically, although the human mind will always grapple with such issues. And while Scripture shares with us certain biblical and theological building blocks with which to erect each his own case concerning human suffering, as we have seen above in dealing with the tragic, such exercises alone can be most counterproductive to the task following Jesus calls us to. If we are not careful, these intellectual games, as natural as they are to thinking persons and to those who are seekers after truth can, and often do, keep us occupied with the scrimmaging of ideas that lead to the choosing up of sides as well as the viewing of those who disagree with us as the "enemy!" Consequently, the suffering neighbor is left struggling and dying by the roadside while the priest and the Levite hurry past on their way to the grandstand. Or, perhaps, the locker room!

True faith seeks to *understand* the plight of the helpless in the sense of "standing under" specific cases presented to the Christ-follower each day. Cases the Father gives him that are but opportunities to make a difference in the lives of others for the sake of the Kingdom. The disciple of Jesus thus is led to those in anguish and pain and faithfully, obediently moves to "stand under" and lift their suffering so as to expose the Christ within the rubble of a storm-ravaged life. There the Christ waits to reveal Himself both to the sufferer and the rescuer as the Light of love, healing, hope, and power. The Light that awaits the moment when the faithful up-lifter gives Him an opening to burst forth and dispel the darkness of soul and situation at odds with the purposes of God on earth.

What need we know about our calling to bear up under the suffering of others and thereby to lift the cross of Christ?

The Life that Requires It

Jesus made it clear in Matthew 25 that lifting the burden and suffering of others, especially those less fortunate, is the basic requirement for entering the Father's kingdom and enjoying His special kind of life. Just as it is basic to the call to discipleship and the discovery of true life now in Christ.

Why is the uplift of another's suffering a non-negotiable imperative for those who would follow Jesus? Because the higher life which Jesus came to reveal and offer – God's eternal life – cannot be obtained without it. Keep in mind a couple of important things about this higher type of life.

First, eternal life is all about relationships. Jesus underscores this when speaking with a lawyer who quizzed him about inheriting eternal life. He told the inquirer that it is a matter of maintaining both a sold-out love relationship with God and a sold-out love relationship with one's neighbor.

He identified who our neighbor really is and what is involved in a sold-out love relationship with him. The neighbor is anyone I discover by the roadside as I travel each day, who has had a cross thrust upon him that he is unable to bear up under. He may be someone known. She may be someone unknown. Regardless, a good neighbor makes it his priority to lift the cross and get the person on his or her feet again, whatever the costs!

Another thing about eternal life is that it cannot be entered into unless a death takes place. And death at any level always involves some degree of trauma or pain. Jesus talked about being born again, or being born from above. Such birth into a higher level of existence – into the wonder and enjoyment of the very life of God – cannot be negotiated unless a death takes place. Death to self on a daily basis so that a person may come alive to God and neighbor, and seek above all else to serve God by serving this neighbor. By lifting his burden, if you will.

We see the principle of dying on one level of existence to enter life on a higher level shod throughout the framework of the created order. For example, plant life enters a higher level of life when it is swallowed up in death by the higher animal level of life. Like so, animal life (and plant life) enter a higher level of life when it is swallowed up in death by a higher level of existence, human life. By the same token, men and women enter the higher level of eternal life when they die to self and surrender all they are and have in total immersion into His life and will. It is then that one is born again into the God-level of existence. But God uses a different process to accommodate the same principle when dealing with humankind, the crown of His creation. It is a spiritual process whereby God, by His Spirit, radically transforms human personality to operate in the realm of the higher life of the Spirit while maintaining the individuality of personhood.

The God-level of existence is the resurrected life of Jesus Christ. It is the life of love, joy, grace, peace, purpose, and power. It was made possible for you and me by our Lord's death on the cross and His gift of the Holy Spirit. This life is only tapped into by those of us who embrace our neighbor's cross, which involves our sacrifice to make Him known to the neighbor, for the Lord's sake.

The Love that Enables It

Lifting the suffering that is weighing down on a neighbor's shoulders takes a special love. It is God's kind of love. The love that is shed abroad in our hearts when we are truly born from above. God's kind of love, the John 3:16 love He revealed in sending His Son Jesus into the world, has as its purpose the rescuing of persons perishing in their sins, lostness, and suffering. It is the kind of love that thinks of the other and his or her needs before thinking of self.

The priest and the minister of music, in Luke 10, were doubtless appealing in their minds to some level of love by not stopping and getting involved in the man dying along the roadside. It may have been self-love which is of course the lowest, basic concern of the person without Christ. It may have been love of family they were thinking of. That is, fearing the risk of stopping by that might jeopardize their responsibility in the future to care for wife and children. But cross-bearing love is on a higher level still.

It is implicitly stated by Jesus that the kind of love of neighbor that brings the approval of God is on a higher plane. And the two religious figures in the story hadn't made it there yet! On the other hand, the Samaritan had. He was operating on this level. Indeed, this God-kind of love – we know it to be *agape* love – had somewhere along the way become a part of his very being. So when he came along and beheld the plight of the victim of that brutal attack, "he had compassion on him" and went and ministered to his needs with the goal of getting his new neighbor back on his feet.

For Christ's love compels us to reach out to others in need of a life-changing touch from God through you and me, Paul tells us in 2 Corinthians 5:14. The resurrected Spirit of our Lord, who dwells within the disciple who has been crucified with Christ, causes the believer to do for others in need what no other form of human motivation can get accomplished.

I'm reminded of a story told about Mother Teresa of Calcutta. Some journalists asked and were granted permission to shadow her one day to get a "feel" of the nature of the work she was doing for the poor. They were not prepared for what they encountered. The wretchedness of life of the people she lovingly reached out to was unbelievable. The squalor and filth in which and with which she chose to work was unimaginable.

The stench and smell of rottenness was unbearable to the writers for any length of time. hey caught themselves often attempting to hold their breath as long as they could before breathing. They frequently had to go outside for fresh air because the threat of fainting was always present. One journalist is alleged to have said to this special lady of God at the end of their time together,"Mother, I wouldn't do what you are doing for all the money in the world!" The reply of this simple little woman was this, "Neither would I!"

Eugene Peterson gives us this helpful paraphrase of Galatians 2:19-20 in *The Message*, "I tried keeping rules and working my head off to please God, and it didn't work. So I quit being a 'law man' so that I could be God's man. Christ's life showed me how, and enabled me to do it. I identified myself completely with him. Indeed, I have been crucified with Christ. My ego is no longer central . . . Christ lives in me. The life you see me living is not "mine," but it is lived by faith in the Son of God, who loved me and gave himself for me."

You and I cannot, will not, do the Lord's neighborly work in making Him known to the suffering other as long as we live on and operate out of the human plane of existence. Self is in total control of things on this level. t is not until we become crucified with Christ, that is, we put self to death and take up Christ's Cross in following Him, does the miracle of new birth transpire. It is then that a new spiritual dynamic of being from a higher plane of life – eternal life – begins to operate within us and enables us to do – even desire to do – what is humanly impossible as a way of life. This new dynamic that moves us along on the journey doing the will of the Father is the Holy Spirit. And a special kind of love – *agape* – is its first fruit.

Paul states in Galatians 5:6 that, in the Christian life, the only thing that really matters is faith expressing itself in love. Moreover, in Philippians 2:13 the Apostle tells us how it operate, "It is God who works in you to will and to act according to his good purpose."

The Lord Who Embodies It

As has already been noted, the teaching of Jesus in Matthew 25:31-46 posits a truth too often overlooked by you and me. That, in some mysterious way, Christ takes up residency *in cognito* in the lives of those who are hurting and suffering. Those who struggle to bear up under a cross that is too heavy for them to lift. So that when you and I are moved by the Spirit of love to reach out and lift the neighbor's heavy burden, and allow that person to see Christ, *we* also discover Him there. And as we minister to the hurting neighbor we also minister to our Lord!

There are those who would limit the scope of persons in whose lives and situations the Christ may be experienced when His cross is lifted, to those only who are marginalized and victimized Christians. They underscore the identification Jesus placed upon "the least of these *brothers of mine.*"

Obviously, there are differing views about just who Jesus had in mind. Nevertheless it appears, at least to me, that to embrace a narrow view of the company of persons our Lord was referring to in Matthew 25, is to disregard altogether the larger context of scriptural teaching relating to the activity of the pre-incarnate Christ in creation, as well as the purpose of His incarnation in human history.

As we have seen, it was He who placed "eternity (a God-hunger) in the hearts of all who came into the world." In the words of the Apostle John, it is He who "enlightens every person coming into the world." The fall of man, and each individual's subsequent participation in this call, curbed humankind's hunger for the eternal God and brought on a craving for the gods of this world: pleasure, position, power, etc.

The fall accomplished something else. It blinded the eyes of all persons so that they no longer fully see or comprehend the light that was implanted in their souls for the fulfillment of the Father's purpose in and through their lives. Consequently, it behooved God, because of His great love for the *entire* world, to send His only Son so that those who had lost it might find it. So that they who are perishing in the human predicament might be saved to enjoy His eternal life – life on the highest level. It is the life that is revealed in Jesus of Nazareth.

A narrow view of those in whose lives Christ may be found when we reach out to lift another's cross would completely contradict, again, the lesson in the story of the good Samaritan. The Samaritan doing the unheard of thing of reaching out in compassion to one of a different religious, social, and cultural orientation was the model Jesus used to express the kind of sold-out love for God and others that characterizes the inheritor of eternal life!

Surely these things must form some kind of bases for our understanding of the missionary task of the Church. It is an important basis for our outreach into our communities and beyond.

But back to our premise. When we reach out in His name to bear the burden and lift the cross of another, we find Christ there. And when we minister to the others we, at the same time, minister to our Lord.

There is an old story William Barclay tells about Martin of Tours, the Roman soldier who was also a Christian. One cold wintery night, as he was preparing to enter the city, he encountered a beggar at the gate. The poor man had already turned blue and was shivering in the cold. He asked Martin for help. The soldier had no money, but his heart of compassion went out to this needy man. He decided to give him all he could. So he took off his old, tattered soldier's coat and cut it in two. Martin gave the man half and he kept half for himself.

That night he had a dream. In it he saw heaven, and angels, with Jesus in the midst wearing half a Roman soldier's coat. When the angels asked Jesus where he got the old worn-out coat, the Lord replied, "My servant Martin gave it to me!"

There is yet another wonderful thing about lifting the burden of a fellow traveler beyond the thrill of knowing that we are ministering to our Lord. It is the experience of having Him minister to us at one and the same time. When we lift a cross as His Cross, the Resurrected Christ comes alive, not only for the sufferer but also for us who would obediently be the rescuer in His stead. And miraculous are the blessings of our Lord's ministry to us. Faith, as always, is the key to this magnificent happening. "Without faith it is impossible to please God. For he that comes to God must believe that he is and that he is a rewarder of those who seek him (out)!"

In concluding this section, I share the following words of testimony in support of the thesis that you and I may encounter God in this world whenever and wherever we seek to lift another's burden in His Name. And, as a result, the Christ we meet there lifts our burdens in return.

You have read herein, doubtless *ad nauseum*, several litanies of aches, pains, and – yes – sufferings I have been privileged to experience in my life and ministry for our Lord. Until this writing I have not sought to dwell on any of these trials as those of you who know me will attest. I have included their mention in this writing because the Father told me to do so! So that He might be glorified in the telling. So that as many persons as possible may know that Jesus Christ is indeed alive and powerfully active in the lives of His disciples and in the believing church. He would have the whole world know that nothing is impossible when one truly trusts and obeys.

Could this be the message the Father would have you receive at this time in your faith pilgrimage?

It has been amazing to have been snatched out of the jaws of death on several occasions. And, at times, to have been allowed to keep on going in His stead when it seemed utterly impossible. It has been an incredible journey to pastor great churches, with great people, watching God do great things in and through them. Especially wonderful has been the seventeen years in Romania and in Europe the Father has given me to see His miraculous hand at work.

I am grateful to the Father that, while encountering many of "the thousand and one shocks our flesh falls heir to," He has allowed me nevertheless to be on mission for Him in this theater of operation overseas at least 35 times. Through these years, as first this part and then that part of the old anatomy has continued to breakdown, it has been special seeing God take care of me in the going and, even more, watching Him strengthen me while I have been there for Him. As I have sought to minister to the dear people of Romania, to lift their burdens, I have witnessed with astonishment the Lord coming alive in unbelievable ways to minister to *me*.

Some folks are aghast that Gail and the children continue to let me go. What these friends do not understand is that God has spared my life more than once just so I *can* go and do His will. It may seem strange to you – surely not to those of you who are believers – that when I get on the plane heading out, I get noticeably better. And, after experiencing His presence in unexpected ways in unexpected persons, I have on many occasions experienced His healing, sometimes permanently.

I haven't mentioned thus far that I had serious knee problems for many years that made it difficult to get up and down and walk without pain. But on two separate forays into Europe in 2009, the pain left me during those visits. Only to reoccur after I returned home. However, a remarkable thing happened in December, 2010. Not only did the pain leave me as I embarked upon a mission to Austria, it left me and has not returned since. Praise the name of the Christ whom I sought there, and found. Who touched this unworthy servant with His amazing grace!

I have legs and ankles injured in the car wreck in 2010 that ache constantly and are at times swollen terribly. Would you believe that when I get on the plane their impairment diminishes? As I begin to minister to hurting people, they do not bother me at all. I have a serious incontinence problem stemming from the prostate procedure eleven years ago. On the US side of the ocean, this condition has become at times downright embarrassing but, across the pond, God always takes care of it. One of the few persons who until this writing knew about this problem asked me the other day how I was doing with my incontinent situation. I replied, "It all *Depends*." It really does all depend on how much I depend on Jesus! And, regrettably, I don't always depend like I should! You know what I'm talking about, don't you?

This is what I have discovered through many years of service to and for my Lord. When I go out in Christ's name, miraculous things take place. The Christ I go to expose to others by lifting up their burdens greets me and mediates healing blessings to my body and soul! Why? Certainly not because of anything I deserve. It is solely because of His amazing grace. But I have come to understand that God usually chooses to flood us with His grace through a special designated channel. It is the channel of significant faith. I have learned, moreover, that when I plug this conduit into His immeasurable sea of grace, what He pours out to me is at times beyond comprehension. I know myself to be quite unworthy, that I am but a weak, too often disobedient, instrument in the Father's hand. Nevertheless, I have come to understand just what the New Testament talks about when it refers to believers as being "fools for Christ's sake." I'm just such a fool. Just fool enough to believe Him when He says in Jeremiah 29:13 that when I seek Him with all my heart I will find Him. And He will find me. I know this to be true. I pray that you do as well.

Here in Alabama, I've discovered Him recently in the forlorn life of a distraught divorced mother whose teenage daughter has left home. In Romania, I continue to seek Him out in the huts of impoverished villagers. I look for Him in the bright-eyed face of a beautiful gypsy child, covered with the dirt of years of oppression and abuse, framed by the lines of anxiety over an uncertain tomorrow. I find Him there! And He finds me!

Know what my problem is? I just don't go on this search enough. Here at home or abroad. I simply do not lift nearly enough. And I'm afraid this is the case of far too many of us in the churches in America. What about you? What about your church?

Larry Baldridge is the unofficial poet-laureate of the Romanian-American Mission fellowship. He – like I – is in the golden years of his ministry. But he keeps going because the love of Christ compels him. He keeps going because he looks for and finds Christ there in the lives of those who suffer pain of body and the hurt of prejudice and injustice. And the Christ who ministers to him as he ministers to others, keeps him going. He penned the following words about a special experience of incredible joy that the Father recently flooded his life:

Gypsy Joy

I went to a gypsy village
To preach the gospel there,
And barefoot gypsy children
Were dancing in the square.
And sweet gypsy madonnas
Were singing gypsy songs
To little gypsy babies
Who tried to sing along.

And gypsy men, mustachioed,
With eyes deep souled and brown
Were full of pride in who they were
And danced their troubles down.

I went to a gypsy village –
Good Lord, what joy was there –
And danced with Christ the Gypsy
In that dirt-village-square.

May I ask you with whom you are you dancing just now? Need I remind you who you and I, your congregation and mine, the churches in America, in Europe, and indeed all over the world, must begin to dance with if we, with them, would meet the

Christ as resurrected Lord and Savior? It is one of the very "least" likely of persons you and I would ever dream of including in our plans. He may be someone robbed and left for dead – physically, financially, morally, and spiritually – along the roadside by the adversarial Foe who is warring against us and God's purpose in our lives. She may be some lost soul who is attempting to bear up under the intolerable weight of loneliness. Struggling with depression. Hooked on prescription drugs, or worse.

Get the picture? Don't be surprised if the person you ask God to send your way fits somehow in this mold!

The cross of Christ, while not heavy once you begin to lift it, is extremely costly. The question you and I and our churches must answer, as we contemplate engaging our communities with the possibility of discovering a real live Lord, is this: "Am I and my church ready to pay the price for it to happen?"

Chapter Nine

Seek Him Out in Fellowship with One Another

"We proclaim to you the one who existed from the beginning, whom we have heard and seen. We saw him with our own eyes and touched him with our own hands. He is the Word of life. This one who is life itself was revealed to us, and we have seen him. And now we testify and proclaim to you that he is the one who is eternal life. He was with the Father, and then he was revealed to us. We proclaim to you what we ourselves have actually seen and heard so that you may have *fellowship* with us. And our *fellowship* is with the Father and with his Son, Jesus Christ. We are writing these things so that you may fully share our joy. This is the message we heard from Jesus and now declare to you: God is light, and there is no darkness in him at all. So we are lying if we say we have *fellowship* with God but go on living in spiritual darkness; we are not practicing the truth. But if we are living in the light, as God is in the light, then we have *fellowship* with each other and the blood of Jesus, his Son, cleanses us from all sin."
1 John 1:1-7 (NLT)

I can't recall exactly when the light went on in my noggin and revealed the provocative nature of our English word *fellowship*. I do know that ever since that time I have wondered just why it had not dawned on me sooner. For it offers some titillating insights into the nature of the Church and its mission in the world that would have helped me along the way be a better crewman as well as, hopefully, a more enlightened instructor to those who through the years got on board with me. And to those I may have sought to reach and help aboard.

Fellowship is the conflation of two familiar words, "fellow" and "ship." What a powerful image they paint when they are joined together in a *koinonia* relationship of love. The thought that is evoked by this marriage is both simple and profound. In a Christian context, *fellows* are those persons who have committed themselves to a life of complementary togetherness, to meet the needs of each other so as to enable each other in concert carry out their common life-purpose of loving God and loving neighbor as oneself.

When *fellows* follow Jesus and step aboard the *ship* designed for them to journey on in their common life, for the fulfillment of their common purpose, it may be truly said that they then become citizens of a new community. More particularly, "those who are all in the same boat together."

Fellow-ship. The only vessel the Father has designed to get you and me safely over life's churning, chaotic sea. A vessel He crafted to allow us to enjoy His Presence 24/7 while joining Him in the holy purpose of rescuing those who are perishing in the frightening dark waters all of us must negotiate in this life *together*, or sink into its dark abyss *alone*.

Christianity, as has often been pointed out, is not a Lone Ranger religion. I read a monograph while in college entitled, *You Can't Be Human Alone*. The tides of many years have washed away from my memory most of the lessons in Margaret E. Kuhn's little booklet. But not its overriding message. It convinced me. It was then that I began to understand that you and I certainly cannot be Christians alone!

Would you believe that when I was a young minister there were those in my tradition who debated whether or not a person could be saved and not be a member of a church? Heavens to Betsy! Jesus' call to discipleship was always a call into fellowship! It was a call into a common life with others, each sharing his or her time, strengths, gifts, and resources with the other, so that the weaknesses of each would be compensated for and, *together*, each one would be made strong and complete in Christ and in His Body, the Church. And enabled to do the Father's will inside as well as outside the boat!

One of the more powerful statements the Apostle Paul makes about the believer's place in the church is found in his Roman letter when he says that we who have been called to "belong to Christ" "all belong to each other" (Romans 1:6; 12:5 NLT). He is referring to an inescapable relationship of loving-togetherness each has with the other, that takes place when you and I are truly brought into a relationship of loving-togetherness with the Father through His Son. As a result of such a relationship the Bible tells us that we are no longer our own.

I, in the totality of my being, belong to Christ and to those who are His. And to those He sends my way to touch and rescue for Him. And be rescued by Him – through them – in return! I must be ready and willing to share whatever it takes of my entrustment from God with my brothers and sisters whenever there is a want or lack in their lives. Just as my sisters and brothers are mandated to stand ready at all times to share their entrustment with me in my needs. I belong to them. They belong to me. Because we all belong to Christ!

Our Lord's model prayer is an example of the corporate nature of our shared life together. Jesus did not teach us to pray, saying "*My* Father who is in Heaven." But "*Our* Father." And subsequently every petition that flows from that address is couched and understood with the consideration of one's fellowship in mind. He did not instruct us to pray "For *my* daily bread." Rather, He taught us to pray "Give *us* this day *our* daily bread." The prayer that moves the heart of God is not one that I lift up for my selfish wants and desires but for all who share with me within His fellowship of love. It is, as it were, praying "Father of all of us who have been brought together with You and with each other, grant our fellowship enough bread today to share so that everyone may be enabled to eat."

Let us remember that if we have answered the call to follow Christ we will have met Him at the water's edge and gotten aboard His fellow-ship. For that reason it must never escape us that "We are all in the same boat together." My needs are *our* needs. Our needs are *my* needs. If we are not all in the same boat together, it's sink or swim in the calamitous waters of life. Without a life preserver! Without hope!

Fellowship is the translation of the Greek word, *koinonia*. Along with other cognate Greek words it is rendered variously in the New Testament as common, community, communion, partner, and participation.

In Acts 2:43-47, as you recall, we are told that real *koinonia* emerged out of Pentecost when those who were being saved were added to their number and they had all things common, as a distinct community of Christ-followers. As was noted, those who comprised such a fellowship did not claim that anything in their possession belonged to themselves. Whatever was in their hands and under their control was seen as an entrustment from God, to be held for Him. Relinquished only under the guidance of the Spirit, whenever a brother or sister, or neighbor by the roadside, had a need! They understood that they were all in the same boat together, in their need and in their plenty, when they were on board together with Jesus.

It is obvious that, for the most part, we in churches today – in the U.S. in particular – have "missed the boat" in our understanding and engagement of Christian fellowship, as set forth in the New Testament. A fellowship that was doubtless patterned closely after the common life Jesus shared with His disciple band! When we accept Christ's invitation to follow Him in *leaving all* and *giving all*, one wonders how we can so easily slough off, as we seem to do today, the radical demand for the shared life of loving-togetherness in the church?

Throughout my ministry I have heard what to me is a flimsy excuse given as to why we do not practice the shared life today in the Church. It is because, I've been told, in the early Church it was an experiment that simply failed. An experiment? For crying out loud, says who? Certainly not the New Testament!

If anything, it did not fail. Not in and of itself. It was simply abandoned due to human selfishness and fear among those who, like those of us today, sought a more comfortable, safe church membership, with little cost and devoid of serious discipleship. Devoid of discipleship that calls for the cross-borne life!

An appeal of this book is to you and me and our churches to rediscover significant Christian fellowship, the cross-borne, shared life of loving-togetherness. Life that glorifies the Father and sets His living Christ free to engage those hurting inside and outside the boat with amazing grace and love. This is where true outreach, real evangelism, begins to take place. That which is genuine, life-changing, and ever-lasting!

What can we know about this fellow-ship that all of us must board and journey together with the Father and the Son?

Life Aboard the Fellow-ship is One of Relationships

This of course has been noted above. It cannot be stated too many times if we are to correct the fallacious, superficial understanding of, and approach to, fellowship in the typical church in America today. That which takes place in our congregations under the guise of fellowship is seriously flawed and dangerous. In most cases it is invalidating the life and ministry of Jesus before a watching world while robbing many congregations of the Father's presence, power, and blessings. And is causing millions of sincere people to altogether miss out on their reason-for being in the world!

For the most part fellowship in the church is seen primarily as something *we do on occasions* for our own enjoyment and personal fulfillment as human beings. Who among us does not enjoy – and need – an occasional after-church social "so that we can get better acquainted?" Or the infrequent Sunday school party at a friend's house? These surely are, at least should be, enriching moments in the life of a disciple and his congregation. But, dear heart, biblical fellowship is more, much more than, say, wassail, Christmas cookies, and conversations under boughs of holly, once a year during Yuletide!

Genuine fellowship is not primarily something *we do occasionally* to meet each our own social needs. It is rather something the *Spirit of God does* when He brings us as individuals into a relationship of shared-togetherness with the Father and the Son, and we are thus enabled to share this mutual togetherness as a *way of life with others,* for *their* wellbeing and His glory!

John reveals why he was writing his little letter, testifying to his own experience of fellowship with the Father and Son, "so that *you* may have fellowship with us . . . and with the Father and the Son . . . so that you may fully share our joy" (1 John 1:3&4 NLT).

Often when new members "join" the church, those of us in the congregation are encouraged to extend to them "the right hand of Christian fellowship." Well and good. Scriptural. But, regrettably, that is about as far as fellowship is taken in the average church. Not very far! At times we say the right words to newcomers, "We're happy to have you in our fellowship!" But what fellowship?

Let's face it, most of our churches at best make only a faint stab at fellowship. This is true because somehow, somewhere in the past, perhaps as far back as the Ananias-Sapphira episode in Acts 5:1-11, when fear came upon the church as a result of the couple's disobedience in the matter of sharing, we totally lost the biblical understanding of what Bonhoeffer calls our "life together." A life of relationships: of love, care, and sharing.

With the Father and the Son. And with each other. And with "the neighbor" we encounter along the way.

What does a relationship of biblical love look like aboard Christ's fellow-ship? John in his writings uses three metaphors to help us get the picture.

The image of arital intimacy is utilized to describe, in particular, the relationship that must exist between the Lord and those of us who choose to come aboard His fellow-ship.

Genuine fellowship cannot take place without entering into a personal relationship with another. True love cannot be experienced between two individuals unless the parties make themselves transparent to each other in all things and commit themselves to meet the needs of the other, as revealed by their transparencies, at the expense of self. Is it not so in your relationship with your husband or wife? Your relationship with the Lord – yours and mine – should reflect this same quality of intimate love and commitment.

The Bible has a word for this shared intimate understanding each has of the other. It is the word "knowledge." Knowledge that is only gained through personal self-revelation and experience. In this light, to "know" someone in biblical days was more than just building up in one's mind accumulated facts that he or she may have read or been taught about another. It was – and still is in our Christian context – a real life encounter with another in the depths of one's being. An encounter that begins the process of data transfer from one to another throughout the relationship, data that no one else outside this intimate relationship could possibly know, tell, or write about. In the surrender of self to another's self, two persons become bonded together in a meaningful relationship, to enable each other more completely to fulfill God's will on earth as it is in heaven. And, as a byproduct, to experience – each the other – his or her own personal fulfillment in life.

John tells us that this kind of intimacy with God is the essence of eternal life! Eternal life is not something we "get" over there when we die if we've been good boys and girls down here. It is, instead, the very life that the Father enjoys in Heaven just now, that has been revealed by His Son. One that you and I can have and experience in our lives just now as well! At any given moment in time. That is, when we by an act of radical faith submit our total beings – all we are and all we have – to Him at the water's edge and enter into a love affair with Him. An affair in which we enjoy Him and all the pleasures and delights of His very life and Kingdom. An affair in which He is pleasured by our fellowship with Him and our obedient response to His love.

The beloved Apostle uses this simple but profound language to express this beautiful truth, conceptualized above, in his gospel, 17:3 (NKJV), "And this is *eternal life*, that they may *know* You, the only true God, and Jesus Christ whom You have sent." (italics mine for emphasis)

Do *you* know the Father? And the Son? I mean *really* know Him. And does He *really* know you? If the answer is yes then you are experiencing eternal life right now! And it grows in splendor as we grow in His grace and knowledge, until we pass over the great divide of death and discover the ecstasy of His glory in all of its fullness!

I have been envious of my friend, R. W. "Twister" Garrison, ever since I met him and his lovely wife, Barkley, when they joined Buck Run Church in the summer of 1973. I discovered that Twister *really* knew Ted Williams, my boyhood baseball idol. And I didn't!

I guess I knew just about everything a person could know *about* "the Splendid Splinter," who led the Boston Red Sox into the World Series in 1946 against the St. Louis Cardinals. I may have known more facts about him than even Twister. I knew, for example, that he not only was the last hitter in the major leagues to bat over .400 for a season and that his lifetime batting average was .341. But much more than this I also knew a thousand and one little tidbits, such as how many doubles, triples, homeruns, and intentional walks he had each year in his illustrious career. I even knew the statistical facts about his minor league playing days as well. I knew, furthermore, that in a strategic game in Yankee Stadium in July of 1950, he hit a homerun in the 8th inning to defeat the Bosox's hated enemy. I knew it to be true. I was there. One of the more thrilling moments in my young life.

I knew a world of facts *about* Ted Williams, whom some contend was the greatest pure hitter the game of baseball ever knew. But I didn't know him. Not really. Twister Garrison did!

During World War II Ted left baseball to volunteer for service to his country. He was stationed at the Pensacola Naval Air Station where he taught young cadets to fly. Twister was his plane captain whose responsibility was to make certain that Ted's plane was ready when he took her up in the air. These two guys had daily interaction. For six months. They developed a relationship. My friend, Twister, got to know the great player rather well. His moods. His likes. His dislikes. When to approach the highly controversial, temperamental fellow. When not to.

A number of years after the war, the Red Sox were playing an exhibition game with the Cleveland Indians at Old Parkway Field in Louisville, Twister went out to see his old buddy play. While the teams were warming up my good friend got the attention of a bat boy, scribbled a note and asked him to hand it to the slugger. He had to know him pretty well to write:

Ted,

You'd better send me an autographed ball if you want your plane to be ready for your next trip in the air!

Twister

In a matter of moments Ted Williams came out of the dugout, spotted Twister in the crowd and, with a smile, doffed his hat toward an old friend. The batboy was on his way with the autographed ball.

What do you think my hero would have said if I had sent a note like this to him during that game:

Ted,

You'd better send me an autographed ball if you want me to say nice things about you to all my friends.

Bobby

He probably would have wadded the note up, thrown it at the bat boy and said, "I don't know this guy!"

Remember the words of Jesus in Matthew 7:21-23 (NIV): "Not everyone who says to me, 'Lord, Lord,' will enter the kingdom of heaven, but only he who does the will of my Father who is in Heaven. Many will say to me on that day, 'Lord, Lord, did we not prophesy in your name, and in your name drive out demons and perform many miracles?' Then I will tell them plainly, 'I never knew you. Away from me, you evildoers!'"

Again the question: Do you *know* the Father? And the Son? I mean really know Him? And does He really know you? In an intimate, personal relationship whereby *you* have entered into a love affair with Him that exceeds all others? And are you discovering His self-revelation to you in loving presence, joyful exuberance, peace beyond understanding, and power for living that is beyond comprehension? And are you giving Him your total devotion, not only on Sunday, but during every moment of every day? Are you, in significant faith, seeking Him and His kingdom out in your life as first priority? Are you obeying Him and seeking to do His will above all else as He has revealed it to you in your personal relationship with Him? Consequently, does He know you? *Really* know you?

These are crucial questions that you and I and our congregations need to answer. Now! Before it is too late! For the lifelessness of churches in America is more and more suggestive of the fact that far too many of us who make up their membership do not *really* know Him! We have not personally experienced Him. The reality of His living, resurrected presence is nowhere to be found in our midst. The Spirit of Christ is absent in our worship, work, and witness. No life. No joy. No expectancy. No recognition of transcendent moments when we are gripped by the Presence of a Holy God! Without the Spirit the body is dead! A congregation comprised of persons who have no personal knowledge and experience of the living, resurrected Lord of the Church is one, as it were, with a hearse parked out front of its building, standing by for the burial of the body as soon as the funeral is over.

A watching, unreached world has no real interest in a lifeless church, filled with lifeless parishioners. They care little for a congregation that is not what it advertises itself to be. "A place where you will find God." The Spirit draws people to congregations in which people can come and see the resurrected power of Christ every single Sunday. Indeed every day of the week!

Those we engage outside the boat at times tell us that when they go to church and hear people talk about Christ, they are interested only if the persons speaking appear to know the One they are talking about on a first-name basis. They are eager to listen to someone who has an up-to-date relationship with God and can relate what He is doing in their lives to their own. Someone who seems to be hanging out with Jesus and has talked with Him that very day!

But the alarming fact seems to be this: our churches in America have a dearth of congregants who seem to *really* know Jesus! I have tried in vain over the past few years to verify a statement allegedly made by Billy Graham. Whether or not it indeed was made by the beloved evangelist, there is mounting evidence to suggest that the statement is closer to the truth than we might realize. The quotation that is batted around from time to time, with variations in the wording, is frightening if anywhere near the truth: "Perhaps as many as 80% of the members of our congregations do not *really* know the Lord!"

There is a big difference between knowing *about* God and *really* knowing Him in an intimate, experiential way. I have been acquainted with persons who knew large portions of the Bible – and didn't mind letting you know how encyclopedic was their grasp of Scripture – but who were as mean as a snake. Quite an anomaly for a person who claims to know Jesus. For when a person truly knows Jesus it changes his life altogether (2 Corinthians 5:17)! And places her in a spiritual process of becoming increasingly like Him (2 Corinthians 3:18)!

Many in our country know *about* God. They know facts from the biblical accounts of Jesus, His teachings, etc. Not all of them, regrettably, know the Man! On one of my return trips from Romania I was seated in an aisle seat preparing a sermon God had laid upon my heart. My Bible was open on the tray before me. After we had gotten airborne, a lovely young attendant walked up the aisle, stopped by my seat, put her index finger momentarily on the Bible and said to me, "I know the Author of this book!" Wow!

Until we determine to get to know Him more than we know anything or anyone, we will miss the mark of the Father's will for each of us. We will be forever like children playing with toys in a bathtub. Never knowing, nor understanding, the indescribable joy of a loving relationship with our Christ aboard His incredible fellow-ship. Nor the seriousness of our responsibility within that fellow-ship. Could it be that the foundation of the house, being slowly but surely eaten away by the pernicious termites of unbelief and lack of commitment, must be totally consumed by these insidious enemies of our Christ, and the house cave in – along with the bathtub – before we wake up to the difference?

We must know Him personally, love Him passionately, and care for Him and His needs unreservedly, if we would travel aboard His fellow-ship!

The image of friendship is the picture John uses in his gospel to describe the relationship Christ expects His followers to enjoy with Him and with each other in the fellow-ship. It describes the life-togetherness of all of us who are truly in the same boat together with Him. We are friends!   Not just acquaintances! True friends. What a profound model this is to define our unique relationship with each other. Yet one that, for whatever reason, has been lost to Christianity since almost its beginning. A serious loss!

Ponder with me the words of John, again in his gospel, 15:9-15 (NIV), "As the Father has loved me, so have I loved you. Now remain in my love. If you obey my commands, you will remain in my love just as I have obeyed my Father's commands and remain in His love . . . My command is this: *Love each other as I have loved you. Greater love has no one than this, that he lay down his life for his friends. You are my friends if you do what I command. I no longer call you servants, because a servant does not know his master's business. Instead, I have called you friends, for everything that I learned from my father I have made known to you.*" (Italicized sentences are mine for emphasis)

True friends are those who share life at a deep level. Who share the secret issues of their lives with each other and demonstrate loving concern for each other's needs. They indeed are those who are willing to put self to death if the situation calls for such so that their friends might experience the love of the Father and the grace of Jesus Christ in a life-changing way. And are thereby enabled to experience His remarkable resurrected presence, power, and victory for themselves in this relationship of love.

Again, I do not know how churches came to lose the friendship model for the relationship of those aboard the fellow-ship. It was a tremendous loss. Should we dare pay the price to recapture it, it would make a profound difference in the life of our congregations and in those outside whom we seek to reach. The concept of genuine friendship should be the cherished norm of Christian fellowship in the church. Ever considered that this kind of fellowship is what those hurting and despairing outside (and inside!) your church are longing for? Have you realized that failure at this point is a major factor contributing to the demise of churches in America?

Billie Hanks tells about being called in by the First Baptist Church of Houston, Texas to help them implement a discipleship strategy to "close the back door" of this great church. Dr. John Bisagno was the outstanding pastor of FBC Houston at the time. He – along with the other leaders of the congregation – had become alarmed that, on a recent year when they had gained approximately 1,200 new members, they had lost about 1,000.

Each of the staff began to question his or her effectiveness. If they were losing it. Dr. Bisagno, marvelous pulpiteer, questioned whether or not he had lost the edge in his preaching. The minister of music second-guessed himself and his leadership in the music program. And so on through the pastoral staff.

Dr. Bisagno instigated an exit survey of those who had left, seeking to ascertain what was going wrong in their congregation. The results were astounding. Frightening. And prophetic for the churches in America today. The survey was answered and returned by a significant number of lost members. It revealed that the respondents loved Bisagno's preaching. They thought the music was right on target. That the church's education programs were top of the line. But – here's the kicker – *93% stated that they left the church because they never established a meaningful friendship with any member of the congregation!*

The sad fact is that this problem that had caused great concern at FBC Houston is paramount among the several issues that are strangling the lifeblood out of our churches today. A problem you and I and our congregations are simply not coming to grips with.

One wonders if many of our churches today have become closed societies that really do not care to reach out (nor reach in!) to those who desperately need a Savior and a friend? A Savior who reveals Himself *through* a friend? Has the Church in America become an institution that seeks to save only *itself* and not the *people* God sends into its care? The question that we must answer immediately is whether or not we are willing to pay the price to develop meaningful relationships of love and care. What about your church? What about your Bible study class? What about you?

Little things are telling. Take, for example, Sunday school or small groups in the average church of today. (Not all Sunday schools to be sure. But far too many!) When guests come and visit these groups, they are not always recognized. When records are taken, classes often fail to get their names. When the names of visitors *are* registered, addresses, phone numbers, and other pertinent information are not asked for. Consequently, in these churches absolutely no follow-up to the guests is done by the class! Sadly, not even by the church! Well, maybe a form letter will make it in the mail!

I am of the opinion that every single person who comes into this world travels through it wearing a t-shirt. This t-shirt bears that person's unconscious life message to others. Persons who read it are either turned on or turned off by the message. The message may be, for example, "I'm kind." Or "I'm mean." "How can I help?" or "Don't bother me!" I am also a firm believer that every church, and group within it, greets those who come into one of its gatherings with an unconscious but unmistakable message. In too many instances I fear our congregations are sending a message to those who take a peek into our fellow-ship that says,

No room in the "In"

One of the basic needs that you and I and all persons have in this world is to be made to feel like "a somebody special to somebody else." Regrettably we in the churchess in America have often forgotten this or, perhaps, never learned it at all. *Or really don't care!* And because we are not genuinely seeking to make everybody a "somebody special" by truly befriending them, we are losing members in alarming numbers. And failing to reach the multitudes of persons who are struggling in the chaotic waters of life whom Christ has commissioned us to rescue.

Through the years I have made contact – not as often as I should – with persons who have slipped through the cracks in congregations I have served. At times I have heard a remark similar to this: "Pastor, I missed four Sundays in a row – going through a tough time in my life – and no one in my class, not even my teacher, cared enough to contact me and show concern!" Reckon this may have happened in your church? Or in your Sunday cchool class? God forbid!

I have even been told by persons who have left a church that I have been a member of – more recently than I care to admit – that they came to worship or to a Bible study, sat alone, and no one spoke to them. Sunday after Sunday. They left. For good. Some sooner than later!

We're all in the same boat together when we come aboard Christ's fellow-ship. Right? Well – yes and no. Yes, if indeed we have met Him at the water's edge and committed ourselves to the joyful pursuit of getting to know Him personally as well as those He has brought aboard with us.

Yes, if we have made it our priority to develop an intimate relationship of love and care with and for these friends He has blessed us with on board. But, no, if it means that what we have joined is not truly a fellow-ship. No, if it is nothing more than a social club in which we have our little groups who care only for themselves. A closed circle that others cannot pry themselves into, not even with the proverbial crowbar!

We in our churches must develop relationships of love and care for each other if we are to fulfill our calling. We must become a fellow-ship of friends.

It may sound elementary to you, but it is extremely important to underscore the fact that, the first step to be taken in developing relationships of friendship is to learn the names of those who come on board with us. Or who pay us a visit. It has been said that the sweetest sound to a person's ear is when another person calls him by his name. In biblical days, to know someone's name was to know that person. There can be no relationship of love and care if one does not soon after meeting him or her get to know the other person's name.

Mary joined the church about eighteen months ago. Now on most Sundays she finds me after our second worship service. What a joy it is to get a hug from this dear lady and give her one in return, as an act of affirmation and love. (Dare we call such a "blessing?" It certainly is one for me!) Several months ago Mary exploded a bombshell right in the midst of our church's fellow-ship. "Brother Bob," she informed me, "Did you know that you and Brother Rob are the only two people in this whole church who know my name?" Thankfully this is being corrected. Had it not happened, Mary might no longer be found in our boat, lost somewhere in a sea of forgetfulness!

The need of everyone for recognition – to feel like a "somebody special to somebody else" – begins to be met when we learn the other person's name. This need is further addressed when we move as quickly as possible to get to know that person, his joys and sorrows, while demonstrating genuine concern for the needs of her life and situation. When it becomes known outside the boat – and sooner or later it will if it is so – that the focus of our church or its groups is upon saving *people* rather than an *institution,* we are well on our way to reaching unbelievable numbers of persons who are waiting anxiously for rescue, whatever that may mean to each one of them. When our congregation, or a class or a group within it, bears an unmistakable t-shirt message to the hurting, lost community, that "We care!" it becomes an unbelievable outreach magnet for those outside the fellow-ship, unplanned and never having to be promoted!

Making everyone feel like "a somebody special" of course has its rewards in every arena of life. Let me tell you about some friends of mine.

Waymon and Bonnie Tigrett are two of God's choicest servants. A dear brother and sister in the Lord, they are active members of the First United Methodist Church in Brandon, Mississippi. Together they – along with their son Steve – operate the Brandon Discount Drug Store, a little mom and pop operation on the corner of College Street and Sunset Drive in old downtown. When I say "a little mom and pop operation" I am being more than a little facetious, even though the floor space of their business is only about 40' X 60', divided between pharmacy and area for general drug store merchandise.

What you need to know is that this little building surely produces about as much capital per square foot as any hometown, family-operated store I have ever seen or heard about. When you frequent its premises. you'll understand why. The place is usually packed with customers. Waymon has seven pharmacists working for him behind the counter filling prescriptions in a timely manner. He also has five or six "up front" people working cash registers and helping folks find cough drops, razor blades, milk of magnesia, Kleenex, hot water bottles and the like. I hope you get the picture. It cannot be over-exposed!

The Brandon Discount Drugs was Gail's and my store of preference both times we lived in this lovely town. On occasions when I would drop by to pick up a prescription or purchase some small item like, say, a pack of chewing gum, an item that could have been more conveniently obtained at another, closer place of business, I would ponder what in the world drew me there with all those people? What also kept *them* coming in such numbers when there were six drug stores in the community, several of them of the big chain variety?

One day while in the store the answer came. Loud and clear. As I prepared to pay the cashier I heard a voice call out over the din of many happy conversations: "Aunt Suzie! Aunt Suzie!"

It was Waymon from behind the counter. At the same time, I saw this little old lady about to shuffle out the door, come to a halt and turn around in apparent delight. She was slightly stooped, doubtless from the hard life she and many grandmas like her had to endure, *back in the days.* Obviously poor, her plain faded dress nevertheless was starched to perfection. Her kind little face, wrinkled by the years, was a picture of sculpted beauty. Her eyes began to sparkle and a smile erupted from ear to ear, exposing her few remaining teeth, when she heard that familiar voice: "Aunt Suzie! Don't you leave this store without giving me a chance to speak to you!

"How's Uncle John? How's his leg? Is he doing what I told him to do? Please tell him I said, 'Hello,' And if he'll stay off his feet about two more weeks, keep that leg elevated, he should be fine!

"Call me, now, if you need me!"

I thought to myself as that precious lady left the store, that million dollar smile still on her face: She'll be back. Soon! And so will the rest of us! And many more will come when they hear about a place where everybody is a somebody special. A place where they know your name, and the names of your family members, and what's going on in their lives. And where you hurt. And how they can help. Because, you see, the Father and Son with whom they fellowship and the friends with whom they hang out, *really* care for you!"

Any thoughts from this story that may give you a hint as to where and how true outreach and evangelism begin in the church? About what kind of fellow-ship people down deep want to board? And journey together in?

But, then, there is another important aspect to true friendship that is to be acknowledged. *Friendship always involves an investment!* An investment of time, energy, resources, or whatever other entrustment the Father may have placed in one's hand. An investment to be made in the life of a special person as he or she may have need.

Such sacrifice in behalf of another – even to giving life itself away in her behalf – is never a duty or a burden. It is simply true love expressing itself in behalf of one dearly treasured. In the case of a Christian, it is the love of Christ within that cannot be held back. Paul reminds us, in 2 Corinthians 5:14 (NIV), "For Christ's love compels us ..."

How is that? Paul explains in Galatians 2:20 (NLT): "My old self has been crucified with Christ. It is no longer I who live, but Christ lives in me."

Or as the Apostle puts it in Philippians 2:13 (NKJV): "For it is God who works in you both to will and to do for His good pleasure."

And so, as a Christian – in whom God in Christ dwells – I make investments in the lives of those aboard Christ's fellow-ship. Actually it is He who makes the investments through me. Because they are His friends. And, consequently, mine. I also make investments in the lives of those "neighbors" along the way when the Spirit gives opportunity. Including them in my life and in my circle of friends so that *they* may become both *my* friends and Christ's. In this way the Father is glorified, the church is edified and strengthened, and outreach "happens" without fanfare or manipulation!

I am reminded of Davis and Lynn Woodruff's investment in the lives of Deloris Hernandez and her family. Davis and Lynn are devoted followers of Christ and long-time active members of Central Baptist who, among many other involvements in CBC, work in the church's Hispanic ministry. Deloris and kids are members of this ministry. Out of this setting the Woodruffs and Hernandez became friends. True friends!

In June 2004, Deloris' husband left her. She began supporting herself and children, David and Karen, by cleaning houses. hings got financially tight for this precious family after they were deserted. Besides this, they were having to live in a house that was less than desirable. How thrilled Deloris became when she learned that she had been accepted for a Habitat for Humanity house.

In October of 2004 David, 7 at the time, landed in Decatur General Hospital and was diagnosed with Leukemia. Upon his discharge, Davis and Lynn moved the Hernandez into their home. Since their own two children were now out of the nest, Katie married and Amy in college, the Woodruff upstairs seemed ideal to house their friends for a couple of weeks. The plans were that friends from CBC and other Christians in the community would, over the two weeks, clean up Deloris' place of residence and make needed repairs until the place was made more livable for this much-loved family. At least until the Habitat house could be constructed which they knew could be, and was, months away on the Decatur schedule.

One afternoon while driving back home from a work session at Deloris' place, Davis – president of Management Methods – spoke up and said to Lynn, "You know, as much as we might do to that place, it will never be suitable for Deloris and the kids to live in. David's immune system, in particular, will not tolerate the hidden dangers still there. Know what I'm thinking?" Davis continued, "I'm thinking we ought to tell Deloris and the kids to stay put right where they are with us!"

Lynn, a special woman of God, replied "I've been praying for days now that God would lead you to that conclusion!"

So Deloris, David, and Karen became members of the Woodruff family. Literally. Although they only lived with Davis and Lynn until their Habitat house was built, approximately six months later, the Heavenly Father knit their hearts and lives together into a true fellowship of loving, shared-togetherness that has only grown more beautiful and richer as time has gone by.

Things like this happen, you know, when we all get in the same boat together. With the Father and the Son. And with those He leads across our path. Those who are "somebody special" *to Him* but who need "somebody special" *from Him* to let them know it. And see it. And experience it!

While Deloris, David, and Karen love and appreciate the house Habitat has provided for them, home is still the Woodruff's address in Decatur! It is not unusual for them to come over to spend a night or so, or a weekend. Maybe longer. They are included in every holiday, major event, and family birthday. At Christmas, Easter, and Thanksgiving, as the old song goes, it is "Over the river and through the woods, to grandmother's house we go."

Davis and Lynn have indeed made these special friends their family. They consider Deloris an older daughter. And, correspondingly, David and Karen their grandchildren. Treating them no differently than they do their own biological grandkids, Jake and Savannah. How incredible it is that the Woodruff children, Katie and Amy, have embraced Deloris and her guys as their family as well.

When we invest in the life of a friend for Jesus' sake it is costly. At times our schedules are interrupted. We are inconvenienced. Some personal agendas have to be temporarily put on the back burner. We must of necessity at times cut down on expenditures for our own personal wants and pleasures. But the blessings, the dividends, that accrue are "ten thousand times" more wonderful than the investments we have made in the life of a friend. "Both now and in the world to come!"

When David was diagnosed with leukemia and moved in with the Woodruffs, Davis and Lynn lovingly assumed responsibility to take him to the University of Alabama Hospital in Birmingham for his treatments. *These treatments were continuous for two years!* One day after returning from Birmingham, Davis and little David were sitting together on the back patio. Out of the blue, David blurted out, "Mr. Davis, this is the best day of my life."

Have you ever experienced the joy of giving to someone the Father has brought across your path "the best day of his or her life?" The thrill is absolutely out of this world. Its ripples continue throughout eternity. For that person. For you. For Christ. For God's purposes.

Fast forward the story seven years. David, now a typical teenager, with leukemia in remission, is with Davis doing a guy thing. Having burgers and fries at "Five Guys." Davis, a cancer survivor himself, is talking with his grandson about their mutual experience. Attempting to draw their discussion to a conclusion with a question to provoke thought, he asks, "David, what did you gain from your bout with cancer?"

Without hesitation the lad looked up, an expression of love covering his face, and said, "I gained a new family!"

Ponder that one a little while, dear heart. Dwell on it, until you understand what church is to be about. What biblical fellowship really is. What it means for all of us to be in the same boat together. As friends.

Now take a step back from the story and view it through the eyes of our Heavenly Father. Contemplate its kingdom ramifications. Analyze it in light of the purposes of God for the advance of the gospel of Jesus Christ which you and I can either impede tragically through selfishness and unconcern, or facilitate miraculously through radical faith and obedience. By putting self to death and taking up Christ's cross of sacrifice to follow Him wherever and to whomever He leads.

Take a look at the Hispanic ministry at Central Church, one that was begun as a bus ministry for children. Several years later CBC made a decision that its impact would be far more significant if the target was changed to reach adult Latinos whose children would then come with them to church.

The new strategy was slow in producing results although many outstanding CBC members invested much time, resources, and prayers into reaching these special people who have shown up on the roadside of our community. A people about whom far too many church folks have made the decision, consciously or unconsciously, to "pass them by on the other side."

When Gail and I came to Decatur four years ago we found Pastor David and Yadira Roesener doing a tremendous job caring for their little flock, along with the Woodruffs, Pam and Harry Vice, Jamie and Frank Boyle. But their numbers remained relatively small for several years. And then, boom! This ministry began to take off and grow.

What is the secret? Obviously God is responding by blessing the faithful sacrifices of the Roeseners and those who are assisting them in this ministry. In my opinion, however, a major factor that cannot be overestimated is the loving decision Davis and Lynn Woodruff made to bring Deloris and kids into their home and into their family.

Word gets around, you know. Especially in minority communities. As the message has spread, and continues to spread, that there are Caucasians in Decatur that truly love Latinos, who sincerely desire that they become their friends, social and racial barriers have come tumbling down. And Latinos have come rumbling in. Today there are two Hispanic congregations meeting at separate times at Central Baptist Church.   An increasing number of Hispanics with English proficiency are joining the CBC congregation itself. The church recently sent four of her members for training to teach English as a Second Language (ESL), to help those who speak no English to learn the native language of their adopted country. Another investment that will pay unbelievable dividends for the Church and the kingdom of God in the days and years ahead.

Two years ago I was introduced to a lovely young lady from Cancun by mutual friends of ours, members of another Christian community in Decatur. Her name is Laurita ("Little Laura"). Gail and I fell in love with this precious teenager immediately. And became intrigued by her remarkable story.

She and her brother had come to our city a year earlier with their parents who had fled their native country under threats of political reprisal. Laurita was in her sophomore year in high school and could not speak English. She nevertheless learned quickly "on the job" and finished her first year at Decatur High School on the honor roll.

I will never forget the day we met. It had been mentioned that she possesses a gorgeous high soprano voice. I asked her if she would honor me by singing. She consented and sang "The Ava Maria," a capella, as beautifully as I have ever heard from one so young.

Gail and I met little Laura's family and fell in love with them as well. Our families became friends. Since then we have shared delightful occasions together, including Christmas meals. Jenna Beth Ward, high school senior at the time, befriended little Laura and drew her into her Sunday school class. In May of this year, 2011, Laurita was graduated with Honors from DHS. Three weeks ago at this writing she entered Birmingham Southern College on scholarship.

One of the special joys of my recent months took place on the Wednesday morning before Laurita left for college. She came to my office and made a commitment to Jesus Christ, one she had contemplated for several months. She returned home on the weekend following her first week at college. On that Sunday – just two weeks ago – it was my blessed privilege to baptize Laurita as she made a confession public that "Jesus is my Lord!" "Praise God from whom all blessings flow!"

That is not the end of the story for Laurita, of course. Just the beginning of a life filled with the wonder and thrill of getting to know the Lord in greater intimacy while ascertaining increasingly His will for her life. In such a negotiation she will without question become a world changer for Him. And an inspiration for life change among the untold multitude of persons who will be touched by her life of faith-full obedience.

But that's not all. On the Sunday morning Laurita was baptized, her mother Laura enrolled in my wife Gail's Bible study class for ladies. That very day, this Sunday School class "adopted" Laurita as one of their own. They pray for her, love her, and even send her needed spending money for her college. Wow! Is it any wonder that this class has grown from a few folks to well over thirty members in less than three years? Guess what these girls call their fellowship? "The Friendship Class!"

Friendship. That's what it's all about guys! That's what significant fellowship is all about. That's what true outreach is all about. That's what Jesus Christ is all about. Those who think that we in the church can be successful in reaching people permanently for our Lord and significantly growing our congregations thereby without developing genuine friendships are simply whistling "Dixie!"

The image of family is another metaphor John uses in his gospel to clarify the kind of relationships that exist in the fellow-ship into which all Christ-followers are called. They are relationships similar to those that are found in life between a father and son, mother and daughter, brothers and sisters, and other family members who, with all their differences, are nevertheless bound together tightly by cords of love. "All in the same boat together!"

In 1 John 3:1-12, the Apostle summons those to whom he is writing to celebrate with him the great honor the Father bestows upon those He calls His children and reminds them of the tremendous responsibility that is theirs because they have been born into His family. Theirs is the responsibility to love the God-way, the self-giving Agape way.

Let's get practical about what the image of the family conveys to us concerning life aboard Christ's fellow-ship. The biblical picture portrays the family as fulfilling two necessary relational roles in God's purpose for human history: that of *procreation* and *partnership*.

The Genesis account of creation reminds us that *procreation* was the first mandate God gave to humankind (1:27-28 NKJV). "So God created man in His own image; in the image of God He created him;male and female He created them. Then God blessed them, and God said to them,'be fruitful and multiply. Fill the earth . . . .'"

The world into which Adam was placed by his Creator to oversee was a big one. A lonely one, too! When God had Eve join Adam in the garden to help him with his oversight of that wondrous place, they came together, began to birth children and ushered the family into existence. The family, a social unit of significant fellowship, with a father, mother and sons and daughters. It immediately became clear that this was the desired medium God had chosen to effect His will on earth!

"Be fruitful and multiply. Fill the earth!" That mandate from God became universal. For all time to come. It was and is a mandate for you and yours. And for me and mine. But let us understand the ramifications.

It is to be noted that this primary mandate antedated the first couple's deadly encounter with the old snake-in-the-grass the Bible calls Satan! Evil had not yet entered into the human domain. Consequently, one may infer that the Creator's intent was that when children began to be procreated they would be "godly" children who would, in turn, spread across the face of the earth and make the world His kingdom. A place of love, joy, and peace. An arena in which the Creator would be worshipped supremely above all else.

If Genesis 3:15 is, as many theologs contend, the first statement of the gospel in the Bible, Genesis 1:28 may be seen as the first issuance of the Great Commission! Given to be carried out by special persons who have been inescapably brought together in fellowship groups we call families.

If you are among those who wish to debate whether or not evangelism and outreach are necessary for the Church in a pluralistic religious world, ponder with me what should be a basic question in Theology 101: "Why did God create humans in the first place, crafting them to live together in a social group called family, while mandating that they multiply and fill the earth?"

The concept of family as suggested in Scripture also points to *partnership*. The family was a partnership from day one of its inception. Carrying out God's Great Commission necessitates a partnership of persons who would together undertake a task vital to the realization of The Commission. The task is revealed in Genesis 1:28, "Subdue and have dominion." The word "subdue" is telling. It suggests that from the beginning there was some kind of adversarial force resident on earth that was impinging upon life on this planet. A contrary spirit that was opposed to the Creator's activity of bringing order out of the primeval chaos. To the task of "subduing" you and I, bound within familial structures, whether biological, social or spiritual, have been called.

Just what does planting little colonies (families) of heaven all across this earth require? It requires subduing whatever forces we encounter that oppose God's ingdom in the lives of persons we in the fellow-ship have been commissioned to rescue for Christ's sake! It is engaging in the task of dispelling the darkness that still encroaches upon the light, casting out adversarial spirits whether found in persons or institutions. Even dark spirits that are found at times in the church! It means putting self to death so that Christ can come alive through His brothers and sisters, and His family, liberating the captive so that the Son may be preeminent and the Father glorified. A fellowship of love and concern, when like a family, is incredibly empowered to perform those tasks aimed at subduing all things that are in opposition to the Creator.

Why is a significant fellowship that is like a family so adequate to plant colonies of heaven all over the earth? Even places of spiritual and physical refuge in the middle of hell itself? Because family is a *partnership*. (*Partnership* is that word again: *koinonia*, fellowship.) It is a household of folks with various personalities, gifts, and interests, who are pulling together as one, combining each other's entrustments to accomplish common tasks necessary for each other's well being, survival, and the success of their collective undertakings.

When I was a boy growing up in the agrarian South, farming families often had a large number of children. The multiple tasks on the farm required a lot of hands to perform the various chores needed to keep the operation going. And food on the table for all. And clothes on each member's back. The family was indeed a *partnership*. Every guy and gal pulling his or her own weight to make it all happen. *Partnership* with responsibility and accountability to the group is still necessary regardless of the size of the family.

So it is with the church. Or groups within the church. The family model dictates that all those whom the Father chooses to bring together to do His will have a purpose and a responsibility within this purpose. It is only when all are pulling together, each performing his or her task in God's grand design for that particular congregation, will the purposes of God be fulfilled in the community in which the family is planted. If the congregation, or the small group, is not a *partnership* little will ever be accomplished of eternal significance by that group, however large or small it may be. When there is no *partnership* – all for one and one for all – there is no real fellowship however often the group may meet together.

This then must be noted. *Unity* is the glue that holds the viable *partnership* together and enables it to fulfill its reason for being. I have observed over the years that a strange, remarkable *unity* holds the fellowship we call family together, whether biological or spiritual. It is a *unity* forged by a unique, one might say, mystical love that flows between individuals that have been birthed by the same parent(s). One may surmise that this incredible kind of love is resident in the loins of the father of the family and is passed on to his children. Children different in so many respects yet bonded together by this unique love that begets love among them.

Consider for a moment your own biological family. And the mystery of that miraculous bond that holds you and your family members together. It is a remarkable unity among, sometimes, an odd assortment of diverse persons. Among folks who are different in looks, likes and dislikes, talents, intellectual capacity, educational aspirations, cultural affinities, ideological and philosophical commitments, dreams, goals, values, motivation, etc. But who nevertheless are bound together by this unexplainable emotive force that causes each one to pull together with the other for the sake of the common family.

Follow me here. Is this not what the Apostle John was saying when he spoke about our fellowship with the Father and the Son? When it has been consummated it brings us together in loving fellowship with all others who have been begotten by Him and who love Him in the same way, regardless of vast differences. When unity in the family is absent it is a dead give-away that something is tragically wrong in the fellowship, if indeed we should call it a fellowship. More than this, it speaks to the fact that something vital is missing in our relationship with the Father and His Son. It questions indeed whether or not we have really been begotten by Him.

Jesus taught that unity within the fellow-ship was the critical factor in successful outreach and evangelism in the Church. In His so-called High Priestly Prayer for the Church, as recorded in John 17, after He had prayed for the disciples who shared with Him in His earthly ministry, He prayed for those of us who would believe because of the message of these first disciples. In verses 20-23 (NIV) we read,"My prayer is not for them alone. I pray also for those who will believe in me through their message, that all of them may be one, Father, just as you are in me and I am in you. May they also be in us so that the world may believe that you have sent me. I have given them the glory that you gave me, that they may be one as we are one: I in them and you in me. May they be brought to complete unity to let the world know that you sent me and have loved them even as you have loved me."

Those of us who would dare meet Christ at the water's edge and follow Him into His fellow-ship, to join Him in fulfilling God's purposes in the world, must understand that unity between all of us fellows aboard His ship is an absolute imperative. Jesus prayed that unity would be the most highly treasured characteristic of the fellow-ship that we are called to board, if we would be the crew who would rescue those outside the boat.

Jesus indicated that unity among all Christ-followers is the *sine qua non* for the fulfillment of the Great Commission by the Church, local as well as universal! Unity is an irreplaceable necessity for congregations, and groups within the congregation, to accomplish their part in the Father's Plan for humanity gone wrong. Without unity Christ's fellow-ship can never fulfill its reason for being as it plies the chaotic waters of life in the world. Why so? Because without unity there is no true fellowship. Without unity there can be no effective *partnership*. Without unity the Body of Christ becomes impotent and dynamic, explosive procreation necessary for the Father's will to be done across the globe becomes impossible. Without unity in the Church, Jesus declares, a watching world will not take His claim seriously and people will fail to believe.

What are the Christ claims in Scripture? Jesus claims to be the One who would bring peace on earth. Peace within the hearts and souls of individuals. Peace between persons who are estranged and are antagonistic to one another. Peace within the Church. "Is Christ divided?" Christ's ministry was one of putting to death hostile, evil forces that war against the soul within the human psyche. The Apostle Paul said that Christ was the One who would unify *all things* in heaven and on earth! Consequently, those adversarial spirits that continue to hold individuals captive, foster prejudices of racial hate and discrimination among peoples, and evoke spiritual pride that divide Christians into various camps, completely invalidate the message of Christ to the world!

Jesus prayed that all who would believe on Him because of the witness of the Apostles *would be one*, just as He and the Father are One. Why? So that the world would believe that He is the One sent by the Father.

He knew that His claims will appear to be but hollow superstitious verbiage to those to whom they are addressed if the people who have said that they follow Him are not all in the same boat together. If they – if we – are not united in Spirit and in loving fellowship, daring to accomplish His purpose together, to "rescue the perishing, care for the dying."

How "perfectly" One is the unity that exists between the Father and the Son? How "perfectly" one is the unity that exists between the members of your congregation. And mine? The question is not how similar are we in educational background, economic attainments, standings in the community, interests, political persuasion, or even in creedal or confessional statements of Christian dogma.

The question the answer to which a lost and hurting world deserves to see as well as hear is this: How one spiritually are all of us with the Father and the Son? Such unity of course dictates how one we are with each other in the Church. How one we really desire to be with the struggling seamen, barely holding his head above water, hoping what we say about Christ's love and care is really true and is what we in the Church are all about!

It's as simple as that! It's as demanding as that!

Conclusion

Seek Him Today!

By Rob Jackson

As I am reflecting upon this book that I am convinced God gave Dad to write, I am amazed at the very beginning where Dad wrote, "This book is being put together by my son, Rob, and me." I would read this section and state, "Dad, I am only giving you feedback on the chapters, why do you state I am helping you put it together?" Dad would always say, "But son, you will help me put it together. The time has not yet come when I will need your help." Not until he unexpectedly passed away did I understand. I was needed to help "put it together." Dad was called home before he could "put it together." Once again, another sign to me that God wants us to *Come and See, Jesus Christ is Alive*!

Naturally, the starting point to *Come and See, Jesus Christ is Alive!* is to know God. According to the Bible, humans have sinned, fallen short of God's glory, and the wages of this sin is death (Romans 3:23; 6:23). God is just and must punish the guilty. However, God sent His Son to die on the cross in the place of fallen humanity. Jesus bore the wrath and punishment that we deserve (Isaiah 53:10; Galatians 3:13; Matthew 27:46).

Through Christ's death, the debt of sin was paid and God's wrath was appeased. Because of this death, God now justifies even the vilest of sinners who repent and believe the Gospel of Jesus Christ. A beautiful verse that I learned as a child clearly states, "For God so loved the world, that He gave His only begotten Son, that whoever believes in Him should not perish, but have eternal life." (John 3:16 NAS) What, then, must you do to know God and be saved? The Scripture clearly states, "repent and believe the Gospel" (Mark 1:15).

Your salvation experience is only the beginning of knowing God. As you daily seek Him, cry out to Him, and ask Him to give you a greater love and passion for Him, He graciously answers. Knowing God empowers Christians. And, in turn, empowered Christians enable a lost world to see God manifest himself through transformed lives. In agreement with J. I. Packer, people who truly know God exhibit a great energy and boldness for God. (J.I.Packer, *Knowing God,* 27-31). Without daily seeking to know God, North American Christians will not be effective in evangelism. Without knowing God, you will never be effective in inviting people to *Come and See, Jesus Christ is Alive.*

Since the invitation to come and see is evangelistic, you must understand there is a correlation between knowing God and evangelism. It is the "surpassing greatness of knowing Christ Jesus" that enables and motivates people to do evangelism (Philippians 3:8). Dan DeHaan, therefore, appears correct when he noted that the desire to witness is in direct proportion to our knowing God: "Many people battle with trying to work up a desire to win lost men and women to Christ. They need to understand that that desire is given to us in direct proportion to the communion we have with God" (Dan DeHaan, *The God You Can Know*, 19).

Conversely, if people do not know God, there cannot be an expected evangelistic thrust. What is needed, then, for God to open your eyes to the "surpassing greatness of knowing Christ

Jesus" (Philippians 3:8). Spend time daily with God. Meditate on His attributes. Read, study, and memorize the Word in order to know God as Father, Son, and Holy Spirit. In sum, seek God daily so that you may know Him better. Then, and only then, will you begin to realize that the resurrected power is evidenced only in the crucified life (Philippians 3:10-11).

I am convinced that the entire world could be changed if only one church, let alone an entire denomination, would begin to seek God with all their heart, mind, soul, and strength. There would be a new boldness and energy for God. Spending time with God would so transform Christians that evangelism would become "a burning compulsion within them purifying their desires and guiding their thoughts" (Robert Coleman, *The Master Plan of Evangelism*, 69). Churches that train their members to seek God daily will see the power of God evidenced in their evangelistic endeavors. People will *Come and See, Jesus Christ is Alive!*

Churches that are committed to invite people to *Come and See, Jesus Christ is Alive!* must have power in the pulpit. And, there can be no power in the pulpit unless the pastor spends time studying and meditating on God's Word. After all, the power is in the Word, not in the eloquent skills of the preacher.

Bryan Chapell correctly notes that biblical preaching "converts, convicts, and conforms the spirits of men and women because it presents the instrument of divine compulsion, not because preachers have any transforming power in themselves . . . [God's Word is powerful because] he chooses to be present in it and to operate through it" (Bryan Chapell, *Christ Centered Preaching*, 19).

Not only is it imperative that the Word is correctly preached, but it is also vital that you frequently read, study and meditate on this Word. The Word is both a means to know God, as mentioned above, and the power for living. There is "no healthy Christian life apart from a diet of the milk and meat of Scripture" (Donald S. Whitney, *Spiritual Disciplines for the Christian Life*, 25). Unfortunately, as Donald Whitney notes, "only 11 percent of Americans read the Bible every day. More than half read it less than once a month or never at all" (Whitney, 27). If the Bible is ignored, people will not see that Jesus Christ is alive. Thus, a key for you is to consistently delve into God's Scripture.

Throughout this book, you have seen the importance of prayer. For people to *Come and See, Jesus Christ is Alive!*, you and I must exhibit a heightened expectancy of God, especially in the aspect of answered prayers.The importance of prayer is seen in the life of Jesus.More than twenty times the Gospels call attention to Jesus' prayer life (Coleman, 73). Jesus' life and ministry was contingent upon seeking the Father's will through prayer.Thus, Jesus modeled for his disciples a lifestyle of prayer.

Christ was a perfect example of Paul's admonition to pray without ceasing in 1 Thessalonians 5:17.Jesus' continual communion with the Father is evidenced in Christ's words, "My Father is always at his work to this very day, and I, too am working. . . . I tell you the truth, the Son can do nothing by himself; he can do only what he sees his Father doing, because whatever the Father does the Son also does" (John 5:17-19).

If Jesus was dependent upon prayer to the Father, then we should be even more dependent on seeking God in prayer!

If we truly want to impact North America, and the world, for Christ, we must be driven to our knees before the Father. Prayer is not a brief addendum to the Christian life, but is a crucial part of living for Christ. It is through prayer and repentance that one continually turns self over to God. And, in the process, the Holy Spirit possesses more and more of the individual. The source of the power from on high that Jesus promised is the Holy Spirit (Luke 24:49).

Moreover, when we take prayer seriously, we begin to realize our insufficiency. Prayer takes us to the very throne of God, and in so doing breaks us by His Holiness. It is this intimate exposure to God that enables you and me to see ourselves as we truly are: sinful creatures saved by God's grace. Thus, "when God's people take prayer seriously and enter the presence of Holy God, they will recognize their sin and fall with broken and contrite hearts before His majesty" (Henry T. Blackaby and Claude V. King, *Fresh Encounter*, 209).

If we truly want people to *Come and See, Jesus Christ Is Alive!*, then we must turn to God in prayer.In fact, Thom S. Rainer notes that prayer is a "powerful and pervasive influence" on the most evangelistic churches in the Southern Baptist Convention (Thom S. Rainer, *Effective Evangelistic Churches*, 196). He also asserts that church futurists often omit the "immeasurable impact that prayer has upon churches." (Thom S. Rainer, *Giant Awakenings*, 17). When the church truly turns to God and seriously focuses on prayer, perhaps "Pentecost will visit every day." (Calvin Miller, *Praying Without Ceasing*, 48).

A key to effective prayer is consistency. Start with a few minutes of prayer and then add to this time as one grows in his or her prayer life. Consistency, however, is impossible without planning; to have an effective prayer life, there must first be a plan for it (Whitney, 76). An important aspect of this plan involves setting aside a specific time and place for daily prayer.

George Mueller is a case in point of power through prayer.George Mueller did not see miraculous answers to prayer because he was a "special person." But, instead, he witnessed the power of God because he made prayer an uttermost priority in his life. Do you long for people to *Come and See Jesus Is Alive!*? If so, you, too, must make prayer a priority in your life. Prayer has an awesome role of helping further the kingdom of God: "that purpose won't happen without prayer" (John Piper, *Let the Nations be Glad*, 66).

E. M. Bounds is correct in his assessment that the church needs "men of prayer, men mighty in prayer. The Holy Ghost does not flow through methods, but through men. . . . He does not anoint plans, but men--men of prayer" (E. M. Bounds, *Power Through Prayer*, 14). May all who seek after Christ be driven to their knees, then, and only then, will there be true power so that people might come and see that Jesus is alive!

Finally, Scripture states that faith without deeds is useless: "What good is it, my brothers, if a man claims to have faith but has not deeds? Can such faith save him? . . . Faith, by itself, if it is not accompanied by action, is dead" (James 2:14-17). A major problem with the professing churches in North America is that we never act upon what God tells us.

The Great Commission clearly demands that Christians go into the world sharing the Gospel (Matthew 28:18-20). Without obedience to this command people will not hear that Jesus is alive. Has this book moved you? Then act upon what God has said to you through it!

Again, repeating the words spoken earlier by Dad,

"*Come and See, Jesus Christ is Alive!* calls for radical faith that enables the Christ-follower to put self to death and walk the way of the cross. When this takes place, we are told in Scripture and know from experience, the risen Lord of the Church always comes alive in the life of His disciples and in His congregation, revealing Himself in miraculous ways! Such prepares the way for an expectant Church to "storm the gates of hell" with the reality of our Lord's living presence. This is what a watching, unchurched world will respond to. In curiosity perhaps at first. But then in trusting belief and trusting obedience, after coming under the influence of the loving, powerful, Spirit of the Christ, found within His body and the members thereof."

It is such a crucial time for the churches to mobilize in the power of the Holy Spirit. Many will die – physically, emotionally, and spiritually – unless we go quickly and share the good news of our risen Lord. The Scripture screams with such urgency, "Now is the acceptable time; behold, today is the day of salvation." Tomorrow will be too late for hundreds of thousands of persons who are perishing all around us.

Today is the day! *Come and see, Jesus Christ is alive!*